Endorsements and Praise
for *Lilian Silburn: A Mystical Life*

The reader has in their hands an exceptional spiritual document describing the mystical experience of a contemporary woman, Lilian Silburn, who, having met and merged with a master in India, then returned to Europe to share the experience of "transmission" from heart to heart.

– Exceptional because it is a direct testimony: extracts from Lilian Silburn's diary, and correspondence between her and her guru, which sheds light on their deep relationship, and many photographs.

– Exceptional because this book tells us about the experience of deep silence, an ineffable experience, beyond words, but loaded with meaning. –
– L.M.

In contrast to the ocean of "spiritual" literature that surrounds us, we finally have the biography of an exceptional contemporary mystic: Lilian Silburn. It is written by a close friend, Jacqueline Chambron, who relied on Lilian's personal archives and the testimonies of those close to her.

Jacqueline Chambron tells us how this intrepid woman traveled alone to India after WWII to seek a Master capable of fulfilling her demanding spiritual quest. Through the Sanskrit texts that she had read as an Indianist philosopher, she knew that it was possible for some masters to transmit grace directly from heart to heart, without resorting to any technique.

This unlikely meeting of two destinies took place in Kanpur, India. The Master was neither Hindu nor Muslim ... this universal path not caring about religions. He immersed Lilian Silburn in the pure mystical experience, without asceticism or technique, as she had wished.

He knew how to go beyond all prejudice to give initiation to a woman, a foreigner moreover. He gave Lilian Silburn a complete mystical training and the charge of transmitting to France what she had received. She dedicated her life to it. Her life is extraordinary. This rare book will fascinate seekers of the absolute. — M.T.

In the vast heritage of different spiritual paths, there is an essential aspect that is rarely discussed, that of "transmission." The present work bears witness in an extremely vivid way to this very special experience lived by Lilian Silburn (1908-1993) with her Indian Sufi master and transmitted in turn continuously in France.

Beyond a simple testimony, this work evokes the efficiency of Grace transmitted silently from master to master within the uninterrupted lineage of her Guru. The transmission, free from any form – teachings, rituals, practices – is carried out directly from the master who fills one with Grace to melt the heart and make it suitable "to seize divine impulses on the fly." — C.D.

Lilian Silburn was a great French scholar concerned with many facets of Indian religion and philosophy. She worked with others in French academic circles such as Louis Renou; Andre Padoux, a fine Tantric scholar himself, was a student of hers. She was also among the circle of Indian and European students of Swami Lakshman Joo, the last guru in the direct line of descent of the non-dual Kashmir Shaivite philosophers. She was thus a Tantric yogini in her own right, and wrote on and translated many of the essential Shaiva texts into French. It is a fine thing to have this biography. — T.C.

This book plunges us into the heart of the most beautiful and deepest adventure there is, through the life and personal writings of Lilian Silburn. Animated since adolescence by a strong aspiration towards the absolute, she first became, at a young age, a brilliant Sanskritist whose qualities aroused the admiration of her masters and her peers. Her work in translating treatises on Kashmir Shaivism, led her to India where she traveled in an adventurous and precarious way in search of living traces of this tradition. The anecdotes, extracts from personal notes, and the personal descriptions offered by the author helps us discover the incredible depth of Lilian's leap into a life devoted to mysticism.—E.D.

A magnificent book on Lilian Silburn ... so little known, even forgotten. Very little information exists on this exceptional person (this Master!!). This book is a real gift for anyone interested in Indian mysticism. An easy to read book, with many extracts from correspondence with her guru ... a fundamental testimony. Those who are English speakers will complete this reading with the book of Irina Tweedie (*Daughter of Fire*) who was the other great Western disciple of Radha Mohan Lal. — L.O.

LILIAN SILBURN
A MYSTICAL LIFE

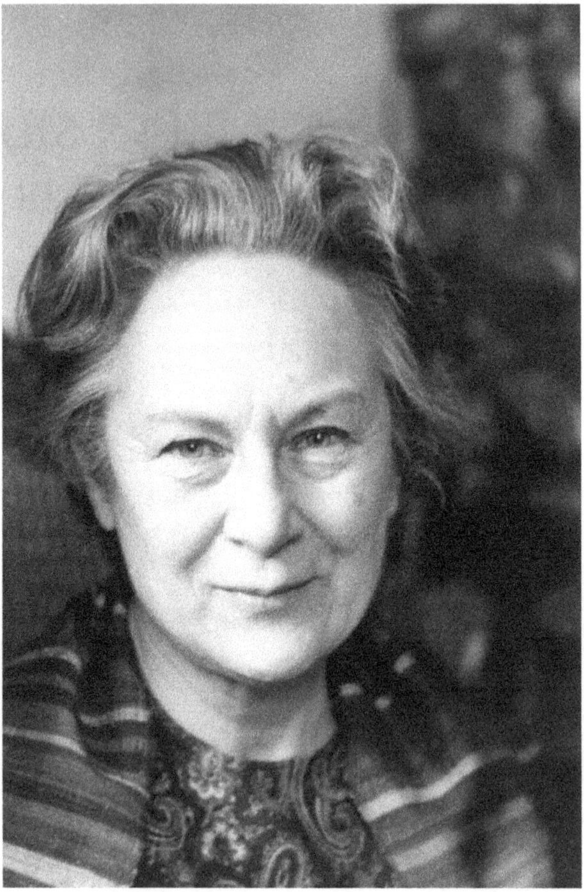

LILIAN SILBURN
A MYSTICAL LIFE
(1908–1993)

Letters, documents, testimonials

A BIOGRAPHY BY
Jacqueline Chambron

English translation by Martine and Stuart Attewell

PELICAN POND

Copyright © 2021 Pelican Pond Publishing

All rights reserved.

Published by Pelican Pond Publishing
P. O. Box 1255, Nevada City, CA 95959

ISBN: 978-0-942444-20-9   paperback
ISBN: 978-0-942444-21-6   e-book

To access the photos in this book that are in color,
please visit www.pelicanpondpublishing.com/LilianSilburn.html

Library of Congress Control Number: 2021948875

First printing: January, 2022
Printed simultaneously in the USA and UK

Translated from the French by
Martine and Stuart Attewell

Original Title
LILIAN SILBURN, UNE VIE MYSTIQUE
Initially published in France by
© Editions Almora, Septembre 2015
ISBN: 978-2-35118-271-0
43 avenue Gambetta 75020 Paris www.almora.fr

v   iv   iii   ii

Table of Contents

Acknowledgments	xiii
Forewords	xv
Introduction	**xvii**
Childhood and Youth	**23**
Her father's death	29
Lilian's studies	32
Lilian in society	34
Love life	36
Note on the "Holes"	38
1949: Departure for India	**40**
Clarifications by Lilian on the nature of her "notes"	40
To Kaśmīr and Swami Lakshman Joo	41
Meeting with the Guru	**46**
Bathing in the Ganges	48
Letters to friends	49
I came to India...	55
The Masters of the Lineage	**67**
Huzur Maharaj (1857-1907)	68
Anecdote: Huzur Maharaj and the prostitute	69
The Sufi (1867-1952)	71

Chachaji, the Guru's father (1875-1947)	74
The Guru (1900-1966)	79
Lilian and the Guru 1950-1966	**81**
1950	**83**
Passages from the Guru's letters	84
Passages from Lilian's letters to the Guru	88
Passages from Lilian's diary	90
Blows or divine touch	93
Personal thoughts	95
Lilian meets the Sufi	99
1951	**103**
Passages from the Guru's letters	104
Other letters from the Guru	106
Passages from Lilian's diary	109
A poem sung by the Guru	109
Lilian's personal thoughts	110
1952	**112**
Passages from the Guru's letters	114
Passages from Lilian's diary	117
Passages of letters to Serge Bogroff	119
Death of the Sufi	119
After the announcement of the Sufi's death	121
1953	**124**
Passages from the Guru's letters	125
Passages from Lilian's diary	127
Passages from various letters	128
1954	**130**
Passages from a letter to a lady friend:	131
Passages from the Guru's letters	134

1955	**137**
Passages from the Guru's letters	140
Passages from Lilian's diary	142
Passages from Lilian's letters	143
1956	**146**
Passage from one of Lilian's letters	147
Passages from the Guru's letters	148
Passages from Lilian's letters	153
Personal notes	154
1957	**156**
Letters from Raghunath Prasad	157
Passages from the Guru's letters	158
1958	**161**
Passages from the Guru's letters	162
A letter from Lilian to a lady friend	166
1959	**170**
Passages from the Guru's letters	171
Another letter by the Guru	174
1960	**176**
Passages from the Guru's letters	177
1961	**182**
Passages from the Guru's letters	184
1962	**188**
Passages from the Guru's letters	189
1963	**192**

Passages from the Guru's letters	193
1964	**195**
Passages from the Guru's letters	198
Passages from Lilian's notes	202
1965	**203**
Passages from the Guru's letters	206
Lilian's notes	208
1966	**211**
Passages from the Guru's letters	212
Death of the Guru	216
Glimpse of the Stays in Kashmir	**219**
Lakshman Joo	224
The difficulties	228
Amarnath Pilgrimage	231
Life in Le Vesinet	**234**
Testimonial	236
Death of Louis Renou	238
Work	240
The new friends	241
Passages from letters	242
Avenue Maurice Berteaux	245
Testimonial	248
A scientific experiment	249
Tea	251
Bhandhara in Le Vésinet	253
Ayguatebia	256
Testimonial	262
1975 – Last trip to India	264
Letter addressed to Le Vésinet	268

Alongside the work on Shaivism	271
Walk to Ibis Park	272
Testimonial – by R.C.	272
Other things said over the years...	274
Impulse, fervor	276
Lilian gets impatient sometimes	277
Prayer	278
Collapse of the ego	278
Love of art	278
Painting	278
Music	280
The Marseilles wave, 1980-1981	282
Testimonials	283
Puech Redon	287
A passing visitor: Minouche	292
Testimonials	293
Time is passing...	296
Testimonials	297
The last days	303
Testimonial: In the continuity	305
The Mystical Dimension	**307**
The Guru	309
Necessity of the Guru	310
The help of a guide is essential	312
Difference between a saint and a Satguru	316
Dreams	317
Some mystical dreams	319
The non-way	**325**
A living path	325
Path of transmission from heart to heart	327
Path of silence	328
Path of surrender	330

Path of love, path of non-doing	330
Path with no proselytism	332
Path of humility	332
Universal Path	333
Way without limits	333
Lilian Silburn's Publications	**335**
Books (in French)	337
Review Articles or Contributions to Collective Works	339
Directory of Collective Works	340
Glossary	**342**
Footnotes	**344**
About the Author	**348**

Acknowledgments

I would like to thank all the friends who helped me,
particularly Robert Bogroff for his invaluable collaboration
in the realization of this book, as well as
Martine and Stuart Attewell for the English translation,
and all those who contributed testimonials
of their personal experience with Lilian Silburn.

Forewords

Colette Poggi
Indianist-Sanskritist, specializing in Abhinavagupta and Kashmir Shaivism

THERE ARE BOOKS THAT COME TO US, we don't know how, and will never leave us. They suddenly open windows that let in the long-awaited light, and then we are free to move forward into this unknown yet familiar space.

Such is the vocation of this book, which is as disconcerting as it is fascinating for those who are attracted to mystical life. It is not an account of a distant exploration of the far reaches of the universe, and yet it takes us on a journey to that original dimension of life where all is one. The mystical adventure, devoid of all artifice, lived in the highest vibration of the heart, as Lilian Silburn confides to us, is nothing ordinary; it is, very rarely, of the order of a fully accomplished realisation.

For this eminent Indian scholar, philosopher and pioneer in the research of Kashmir Shaivism, the meeting with the great Indian Sufi master of Kanpur was decisive. Striking epistolary exchanges bear witness to this path of transformation, both trying and luminous. They have been collected in this book by Jacqueline Chambron, a very close friend who, in her wake, followed the same path; she also recalls Lilian Silburn's childhood and youth, as well as moments in everyday life when the currents of grace flowed. The most wonderful thing about these pages is that it is no longer the person alone who appears, but, through her, an invisible light shines and fills the heart.

Audrey Fella
French historian, essayist and journalist

BORN IN 1908 IN PARIS, Lilian Silburn is a French philosopher, Indianist and Sanskritist. Animated by a deep spiritual quest from childhood, she was nourished by the wisdom of Western and Eastern philosophers and mystics. A CNRS (French National Center for Scientific Research) researcher since 1942, and appointed research director in 1970, she is the author of essential works on Buddhism and Kashmir Shaivism, which speak of ultimate reality as consciousness and cosmic vibration.

During a trip to India, she meets Radha Mohan Lalji Adhauliya, a Sufi master from a long line, who will transform her being and her life. Touched by his presence, she lives in intense mystical states and has the overwhelming experience of the Self. She returned to France with the desire to continue this inner adventure and to pass it on to others through an "inhabited silence," beyond all speech.

In this book, Jacqueline Chambron, who knew her well, traces the path of this remarkable woman and the evolution of her spirituality, which can inspire everyone in their quest for freedom.

Introduction

CONCERNING LILIAN SILBURN, there can be no question of a biography stricly speaking, let alone a hagiography.

So much regarding the essence of Lilian will never be known, said or written. Words stumble, and vanish under the pen of whoever pretends to combine in sentences the subtlety of her presence or the mystery of her destiny.

Thanks to the many writings left by Lilian – her diaries, letters, and correspondence with her master, combined with the various testimonials collected – we have tried to shed light on the depth and originality of her contemporary mystical experience.

I WAS FORTUNATE to live in Lilian's presence for many years, and yet will never be able to find the right words to describe the constantly renewed miracle of her subtle and generous presence.

After meeting the Guru, Radha Mohan, in Kanpur, India in 1950, Lilian continued her research work at the CNRS (French National Center for Scientific Research) whilst also receiving visitors, who came to ring at her garden gate with the hope of finding an "inner opening." On November 1st, 1965, it was my turn to meet her.

I came from the south of France to Le Vésinet, in the west of Paris, just for this encounter. Not yet forty years old, mother of four children between sixteen and three years of age, I was teaching in a high school in Toulouse. I didn't know a thing about Indian culture and the existence of Gurus.

But I was, especially, despairing of finding a wide opening toward the Absolute Truth which I had been seeking since I was fifteen. So I rang the bell and saw a person, seemingly in her fifties, walking briskly towards the closed gate. I felt rather intimidated, dumbstruck. Lilian showed me inside, to a little room that served as an office and a bedroom. She told me about her Guru, and I told her about my children. Then came a crucial moment: she proposed a time of silence, facing each other. Apparently, the sky remained silent, the earth did not open beneath our feet, but curiously, during that half hour, I didn't feel bored at all. Once the silence was broken, I was offered a cup of tea. It was the first one, and wouldn't be the last!

I took leave and as Lilian walked me to the door, it seemed as if nothing had happened. But once I was out of there and on my way to the train station, against all odds, I suddenly felt light and alive: I had reached the port of departure, virtually of course, as the whole journey remained to be undertaken, with its storms and its pitfalls, but the quest was over. Later, I noticed that I had written in my diary that day, totally unknowingly: "wonderment."

It was three years before I could get myself appointed to teach in the high school in Le Vésinet. During those three years, I came to Le Vésinet during the school holidays. And once I was finally settled in the area, my meetings with Lilian became more and more frequent. I attended all the satsangs, with but a few people in those days. I would also meet her between classes for a walk in the Ibis Park, near her house, a park where she would go and walk to relax between two working sessions.

Then there were the many travels during which I was the official driver. Lilian wanted to revisit all the beaches of her youth: from Le Crotoy, in the north of France, to Galicia, in Spain. Then, there was the pilgrimage following in the footsteps of Saint John of the Cross, which took us across Spain from north to south.

I am still nostalgic for those long drives, when I was holding the steering wheel, eyes on the road while the heart was totally impregnated with the softness and depth of Lilian's silent state. Unfortunately, in her great courtesy, from time to time she would oblige herself to regain consciousness and entertain the driver ... who, by the same token, was suddenly startled! Nonetheless, at each stop-over, I was drawn out of this state of bliss, as we had to worry about finding an accommodation for the night.

But the most important trip of all was certainly the one to India in 1975, which was also the year when my son died. Lilian had been assigned by the CNRS to conduct a mission in Kashmir, working with Lakshman Joo. She invited me to accompany her. For me, it was an opportunity to discover India, meet the late Guru's family, his wife and sons. But above all, I had the privilege of spending two and a half months alone with her on a houseboat, by the marvelous Lake Dahl. After such an experience, it was obvious that I was no longer the same.

During all these years, Lilian was leading a brilliant career at the CNRS, translating and commenting on texts of Kashmir Shaivism which she introduced in France. She also published an important book, Buddhism and, in 1982, became director of the *Hermes* publication. For this venture, she liked to invite some of her young friends, whom she found up to it, to participate in her different projects.

This is how I discovered, under duress, that I had a talent for writing; without her, I would never have known: she was always looking for ways to bring the best out in all of us. But under the guise of her various undertakings, Lilian knew how, without seeming, to be unfailingly rigorous with the most ardent of us.

Until the end of her life, she thus pursued the multiple aspects of her activity which I had the great fortune to witness on a daily basis. As she bequeathed to me all of her papers, and much more beyond words, my highest wish is that her Work, and that of her Master, will, by Grace, carry on.

Jacqueline Chambron

Le Vésinet, May, 2021

LILIAN SILBURN
A MYSTICAL LIFE

Childhood and Youth

Lilian Silburn was born on February 19, 1908 in Paris. Her father was English and her mother French, born to an English mother. She had a brother, Oswald, who was born two years after her and a little sister, Aliette, thirteen years younger.

Her mother belonged to a wealthy family, but her brothers and sisters squandered their wealth in games and festivities. Many of them died young, sometimes of tuberculosis, a condition that Lilian will suffer twice later in life.

Lilian often mentioned her very childlike, maternal English grandmother who liked to play all kinds of jokes and games with her grandchildren. Whereas, aunt Marguerite, her mother's sister, weighed heavily on family life by imposing her daily presence. To escape this situation, which became intolerable over time, Lilian had to go away several times.

Her father held a position in the "Messageries Maritimes" which enabled Lilian, from her childhood, to take little cruises with her father and her brother, while her mother was very apprehensive about sea trips. Lilian kept a very fond memory of these days and of this early initiation to a comfortable life on board under paternal vigilance.

Lilian's first months were difficult; she cried a lot, her fontanel was not closing normally. Her mother did not dare move around with her. Did Lilian have a hard time resigning to an earthly stay?

Her mother told her, however, that as a young child, while

sleeping at night, she emitted a fine vibrating sound that resembled the harmonics of overtone singing.

Her parents left Paris very abruptly, but Lilian nevertheless remembered the walks she took as a very young child in the Bois de Boulogne with her grandfather. Her parents settled in Le Vésinet where they would live successively in three houses: the first near the bridge of Croissy, then one on avenue du Belloy, and the last one at 29 avenue des Pages where Lilian will live from the age of fifteen until the end of her life, with her sister Aliette.

These houses were generally small. The last one, however, had a little park designed in the Japanese fashion of the time, a charming park with an old kiosk on rocks where the water cascaded down to a large pool. Large trees dominated the scene, and the abundance of fallen leaves in autumn gave rise to a seasonal rite of their gathering, an occasion for multiple fires, whose surveillance did not go without a certain solemnity. Lilian alone performed this "sporting" task for many years.

Lilian recalled few memories from her childhood, but when she spoke of them, one felt how the vigilant affection of her father, who watched over her education with the greatest care, permeated her whole being. Her father was particularly anxious to enable her to avoid unnecessary constraints and annoyances, not to make her a pampered child, but to teach her not to be intimidated by things without real importance, and thus gave her the taste of a certain freedom of mind.

Lilian did not go to school until about the age of eight. As she tormented herself when her young neighbor, who accompanied her, was late, her father would quietly calm her, stressing the relative lack of importance of the matter. He wanted her to avoid worrying about such irrelevant things, which are dictated only by social prejudice or moral conformism in a society focused on appearance and preoccupied with propriety. She acknowledged that she was totally fulfilled by "her father's so complete and intense love."

She spoke, but rarely, of playing at the far end of the garden with her brother, and engaging with young neighbors through the reeds that separated the properties. She had a particularly strong recollection of the shock she had at the sight of a spring-driven, walking doll. The unusual and disproportionate emotion that she felt at the time later appeared to her as the unconscious premonition of the role that the vibration would play in her destiny or in her profound experience.

Full of veneration for her father, the little girl that she was enjoyed keeping him company while he was gardening, but if he ever happened to cut a worm with his spade, her filial devotion vanished. "You killed him! You killed him!" she protested, and under the virulence of her reproaches, her father was silent, piteous. She had an innate respect for life; the cruelty of nature's law, by which species devour each other, always remained an enigma for her. She never accepted that the cat would eat the mouse after playing with it.

She even told her Guru[*1] who smiled about her indignation. Later it would be mandatory to respect even highly destructive families of dormice nestled on the terrace of Ayguatebia[2] and to witness the wild races of Puech-Redon's[3] little mice. Only fleas would not benefit from this universal sympathy!

Mrs. Silburn did not enjoy the same serenity as her husband; she was totally absorbed by the housekeeping and caring for her children's health, bustling around to fulfill the requirements of her "duty." Lilian often talked about the harshness of Sunday mornings when, as of six o'clock, her mother would be rushing around to go to a morning Mass and jostling everyone in the fear of not being able to meet all of the obligations that she imposed on herself and, by the same token, on others.

Lilian would then join her father who took refuge at the far end of the garden, sorry for all this agitation that he deemed useless, and upset to see his wife exhaust herself in tasks that diverted her from the sweetness of life. Kindness and breadth of vision emanated from this paternal figure as he appeared through her memories. Lilian will be the heiress to her father, just as Aliette, her sister, would be faithful to the sense of duty personified by their mother. Her sister Aliette was born when she was thirteen. She was very weak at birth and would have a retiring nature, whereas Lilian was more outgoing.

Around the age of eight or nine, Lilian contracted broncho-pneumonia, to the great despair of Mrs. Silburn, who incriminated the doctor; he may have transmitted the germ to her due to his negligence, during an auscultation. As a result of this illness, Lilian was sent to the Arès Aerium on the Arcachon basin near Andernos where one of her aunts was staying. She stayed there twice; the first stay lasted eight months. It was an important period. The establishment was run by nuns in a rather wild place near the basin and in the pines. Lilian remembered this period as a time of opening favored by the change of environment. One day, among other things, she was struck by a conversation she heard on the beach, a conversation between two "older girls" of eighteen on the role of Divine grace:

I was on the beach, I heard it, they were talking about the part of the human's effort and the part of God's grace. I understood that that was it, the only thing necessary, the only problem.

And that was, indeed, her only problem until she met her Guru. She often repeated in jest that she was lazy, that she did not want to make any effort; it was her way of expressing her desire for a total surrender to Divine grace, there being nothing else that could ever satisfy her.

During this same stay, an illustration or engraving representing Saint Francis and Saint Claire absorbed in the same ecstasy, fascinated Lilian, dazzled by this simultaneous sharing of the same inner state, a premonition of what she would so often live, first with her Guru, and later with the friends who would be following her. Sudden access to unconscious states during religious services, her interest in the life of grace, and her enlightened perception of others, earned her the reputation of being a "saint." Much later, she will write:

At school, at the convent, they said that I was a saint because I had unconscious ecstasies, and I knew the character of people, and I could also force whoever I wanted to love me.

She was only ten years old then! Later, much later, in 1969 she will return to these places:

A few words to tell you that we have arrived in Saint-Palais via the Arès Aerium – absolutely unchanged except for the new children – Arès however is unrecognizable. This return to the past has left me cold; although it is there that my first mystical experiences took place.

In Le Vésinet, Lilian studied in a private school, with few pupils, and with whimsical teachers. She often spoke of the old priest who taught her Latin and only had her translate Titus Livius, whereas she had a text of Tacitus at her baccalaureate exam.

During her childhood and adolescence, the holiday period was spent at the seaside, a sacred rite for Mrs. Silburn, who judged these stays essential to the health of her children at a time when it was far from being the norm. So for a long time the family rented a house in Le Crotoy, because at the end of the week, on Saturday evening, there was a special train for fathers and husbands who came to join their families for twenty-four hours.

When she was older, Lilian had to mind her little sister on the beach while her mother did the housekeeping with painstaking care, which made her daughter desperate. But in the afternoon, she could engage in sports performances with her brother and friends: swimming, tennis, bicycle races and, from the age of fourteen, metaphysical and mystical discussions with a boy a year older than her, Jean R. The discussions were intense and their hearts very close to each other. They liked to meet in a charming chapel nearby, all in white serrated stucco, which was also a rallying point or a goal of bicycle races. And at the age of eighteen, the two young people, by mutual agreement, renounced their love to devote themselves uniquely to the Absolute Truth. Lilian, at the time, was contemplating a religious vocation.

Later, she will comment: *"...the love of J. R., so perfect, when I was between fourteen and seventeen, and who, like me, chose to renounce human love for the love of God."*

All her life she kept up the habit of such extended stays during holidays, preferably by the sea, dreading the return to Le Vesinet. *"Le Vésinet is a hole,"* she repeated at the end of each summer.

After the death of her father, she made a point of taking her little sister with her, and so stayed in almost all the islands of Brittany: Ile d'Yeu, Noirmoutier.... She would leave for three months, with a huge trunk, finding on the spot modest rental accommodation. She told many anecdotes about these different stays. Among other things, she met Karl Marx's grandson, and she used to describe with a sense of humor his awe-inspiring and unusual silhouette that stood out, with his umbrella, on one of the piers she visited. She was quickly the center of attraction, especially since at the time, these places were not invaded by tourists. But she had to reconcile her older-sister's duties and her taste for swimming and social life. Her great swimming endurance, which she practiced day or night, her many eccentricities, and her knowledge of scriptures and characters, earned her a certain degree of success. But one year, in Spain, her great freedom created a scandal, some people even pursued her with stones, calling her a witch. She had to leave the place.

Her father's death

Her father's death was foreseen and yet brutal, being the consequence of an old leg injury. When her father was twelve, he was hit by a bicycle pedal and the wound was badly treated at the time. Lilian was about nineteen when her father told her about his health difficulties and the worrisome medical diagnosis. Together they searched through medical dictionaries and deciphered the articles only to discover that the outcome was bound to be fatal if not imminent. They kept this painful secret because they thought it unnecessary to worry Mrs. Silburn prematurely.

While her father had gone to the hospital for some simple tests, Lilian and her mother learned that the worst had happened when going to visit him in the evening! The brutality of the shock annihilated Lilian and her mother, while Aliette was still very small. Lilian recalled the horror of returning home, walking under the trees of the Ave. des Pages, in an unreal light.

Despite her deep pain and her young age, she faced the various formalities and some particularly delicate inheritance issues, wisely and responsibly. But the days that followed were most painful. The self-portrait she drew at that time expresses the power of her despair. A dark frowning look, an abundance of hair whose invading darkness underlines the whiteness of a forehead that is as high as broad, and the features of a thin face forcefully express the dark world of mourning and its fatality that leads to questioning oneself about "the enigma of life." At the bottom of the painting: a question mark, made of naked bodies drawn towards a smiling skull. Lilian sank into a feeling of revolt and deep suffering, as she will reveal later (1964) when reporting a dream to her Guru:

At night, I dreamt of my father, a sort of nightmare: I was crying, I was complaining ... and I was telling him how miserable I had felt because of his absence, probably a dream that delivers me from the painful complex of his death and of the revolt that followed.

Once the formalities were settled, Lilian went away by herself for a few months in Italy to learn how to live again, in another setting, in another environment. Original and varied encounters attracted her attention: an old English lady with some odd ideas, a hypnotist, and many others ... an inexhaustible source of anecdotes that she would tell tirelessly with humor and vividness.

When she was about twenty-six or twenty-eight, she spent a year alone in Corsica, and lived in a cave in Porto.

At that time, she was showing courage and a great spirit of independence as well as a fierce love of the sea, nature and solitude. There, she experienced a strong emotion, inexplicable at the time; the sight of a rock in the Gulf of Porto curiously plunged her into a strong state of interiority that made her lament: *"that rock moved me so much,"* she wrote, *"evoking a woman, kneeling and bent down, with a very heavy veil."*

She interpreted it much later as a premonition when she saw her Guru absorbed in that same position, with a blanket over his head. Lilian recounted this emotion as one of the most important ones that she experienced before meeting the Guru, for its special quality and inner resonance. She made a drawing of the rock, which she kept.

In September 1964, in her notebook, she will list this moment among the ten "holes" that, here and there, pulled her out of the deep despair that marked her whole life:[4]

I realized how much despair faithfully accompanied me all my life. It was like a high wall that I kept on following, refusing to step away from it to enjoy life.

A little further and behind the wall, was the only light and life that really interested me: there were about ten holes in this wall that enabled me, from time to time, to perceive the dazzling light.

Mr. Silburn's resources were sufficient but, always worried, Mrs. Silburn forced her family into drastic savings. The house was rented during the summer, and they all took refuge in the little house at the far end of the garden, which left everyone with a very limited space. Lilian was giving lessons at a private school in Saint-Germain where she was going on her bicycle, but she was struggling to climb the stairs while lifting the machine. It was a big effort that strained her heart. With her students, however, she had no trouble at all. Her constant humor and imagination ensured her of their full attention and interest. She even went to the rescue of her colleagues when it was necessary. She often told with obvious pleasure the episode of the burial of the bird. One of her older colleagues had been horrified by the discovery of a dead bird, maliciously placed on his desk by some boisterous pupils. To restore the situation, Lilian decided to organize a solemn funeral ceremony to which everyone participated with a lot of good humor.

Happy times!

Lilian's studies

From 1928 to 1949, Lilian studied philosophy at the Sorbonne, learned Sanskrit, Pali, and Avestan, and wrote her thesis: *Instant and Cause.*[5]

Passing exams was not a problem for her; the fairy of Self-Confidence had touched her with a magic wand when she was born, which she liked to confirm by pointing out the unusual length of one of her fingers. She was, nonetheless, helped exceptionally by a cup of coffee in these very special circumstances, which was most noticeable to those who knew her unconditional taste for tea, and her dislike of coffee.

She recounted how one day, after an unfortunate candidate was accused of not knowing anything, she had answered the examiner, who was turning towards her: *"Oh, I know everything!"* provoking the higher demands of the teacher; but she faced up to it, and at the end of the interrogation the examiner gave in.

She liked to play on situations to suggest their relative lack of importance, if not their derisory nature.

She followed her studies of philosophy without any difficulty, and finished in June 1930. Ignoring at the time that she, in fact, had dual nationality, she thought of herself as being only English, and did not take the course for the French "Agregation" diploma. She decided to study ancient languages. She thought of Hebrew, but finally chose Sanskrit, that she studied, as well as Pali, with Sylvain Levi and Alfred Foucher.

She worked on Vedaism with Louis Renou, who succeeded Foucher in 1936-37, Indian philosophy with Paul Masson-Oursel, and regularly followed his lectures at the Ecole des Hautes Etudes until the war. She discovered the Avesta (sacred texts of the ancient Zoroastrian Persians) with Emile Benveniste. She also attended classes given by Gaston Bachelard with whom she developed a friendly relationship and was, at times, his confidant.

During the war she attended Louis Renou's class on Śankara and became interested in the use of silence in Vedic hymns. In 1947, she obtained the diploma of "Hautes Etudes" with the presentation of the "*Śivasūtravimarśinī by Ksemarāja*" as part of her "Study on Kaśmīr Śivaism."

Introduced to the CNRS (French National Center for Scientific Research) by Louis Renou as a grant-funded Scholar and then full-time Researcher in 1942, she was promoted to Senior Researcher in 1953, Master in 1962, and Director in 1970.[6]

Lilian in society

Despite her deep love of solitude and her passion for study and research, Lilian did not live in seclusion but was surrounded by good friends of quality as evidenced by the following text written by one of them:

"In 1933, at the National School of Oriental Languages where I was studying Tamil, I met two remarkable personalities, friends of Lilian Silburn, Jean Margot Duclos who was a resident of the Thiers Foundation and who attended the ethnology and anthropology classes of Professor Mauss at the College de France, and Śiva Deb, geologist, future Director of the Alliance Française in Calcutta. Jean Margot Duclos, Śiva Deb and Lilian Silburn would get together in the house at Le Vésinet.

"I remember going there and still recall quite well her brother and, of course, her little sister Aliette who, like me, would be a student of Professor Filliozat's Tibetan classes at the Hautes Etudes at theSorbonne in 1944-45.

"In 1935, I remember a remarkable afternoon with the Silburns and their friends in the forest of Saint-Germain where we were all gathered as shown in the group photo. To me, Lilian Silburn is essentially a trail of light, a luminescence that would pave the way for an increased attraction to the Indian and Tibetan world with that of the Far East." – H. de D.

What she loved above all were the deep intellectual exchanges, the original if not eccentric personalities, but she remained welcoming to all. Cheerful and lively, regardless of her inner state, she drew people by her enthusiasm, her vivacity, her great originality, and especially her knowledge of others.

Fearing useless chatter and idle conversations, she had multiple resources. Starting from the premise that people are primarily interested in themselves, she organized different palm reading sessions, proposing a general questionnaire in the manner of Proust, concerning aptitudes, tastes, and philosophical convictions. She suggested that everyone find their own corresponding myth. For herself it was Ulysses. When young, she had asked her mother to make sure that she never married. Her mother was to protect her from the siren's song!

She also did perspicacious and subtle handwriting analyses, which owed as much to her great intuition as to her knowledge of the subject. She focused on capturing a global vision of the personality, rebelling against overly analytic graphological analyses that add or juxtapose clues or details one on top of the other.

Later, she and her friend Anne-Marie Esnoul[7] developed a study of "types" based on morphological observations and their relation to elements of personality. They gathered observations in all circumstances and practiced particularly on the beaches of Brittany during their summer stays. Lilian liked to introduce her friends to the conclusions of their studies, always seeking to clarify and complete them. The selected types bore mythological names but she, nonetheless, refrained from attaching herself to traditional classifications.

She also greatly enjoyed playing jokes and having fun with her friends and neighbors Ida, Philibert, and his wife Gretty. They organized evenings with fancy dress, walks in the forest of Marly animated around scenarios full of surprises, especially in an old tower of Marly woods ... always looking to surprise one or the other by the unexpected. Philibert surprised her in the spring of '42 as she was bathing in the Seine river quarries.

In the winter she skated on Ibis Park's lake in Le Vesinet. One day, she loved to tell, in the course of her arabesques on the ice, she found herself face to face with a bear that had escaped from a circus nearby, but she was unable to entice him into a fervent spin on the ice.

Love life

Lilian's beauty, the intensity of her intelligence, and her imagination fascinated everyone who met her. And her admirers were numerous and of high quality, academics and artists; however, each time a relationship arrived at a serious juncture, some sort of instinct would make her renounce.

Just before the war, she even let the banns be published for a marriage with a philosopher whose intelligence, complementary to hers, made her envision a fruitful intellectual collaboration, but at the last minute, she ran away to Brittany, taking refuge in the house of her friend Anne-Marie Esnoul who had to dismiss the unfortunate suitor.

After the war, however, she had an intense encounter with a prestigious academic. They were two ardent and modest beings, and they hid their love for one another for a long time. They got on profoundly well together. At the discovery of their mutual love, Lilian experienced very special moments, filled with wonder: for a few hours, at the Ibis Park's lake, she was plunged into an unknown state that she would later recognize as that of Dhyāna.*[8]

But Lilian wanted to go to India, in search of a deep opening she glimpsed when reading Shaivism texts, and B. was too intensely demanding. For him, it was *"all or nothing."* So it would be *"nothing"*; it was out of the question for her to give up her quest:

In the end, B. had the brilliant word that relieved me: "all or nothing." There was no answer; it was nothing because it could not be everything.

And Lilian left broken-hearted by renouncing such a deep love. Lilian considered this "no," that inevitably prevailed at each serious encounter, as her personal drama. She will speak of a "flaming sword" that intervenes each time.

Strangely enough, this "no" is like making a clean sweep that clears off desire, inclination, dream: as long as the thing, the immediate and ardent possibility of realization is not offered to me, I continue to dream vaguely, while repressing other thoughts; when it is magnificently offered to me, in a surprising wonder, and in such a simple, easy form, all obstacles being overthrown at once (and each time it was like a miracle because I was loved unknowingly, as much and even more than I loved) then I know, without any doubt, that it is "no": there is no fear of it happening, not afraid of the action and its consequences....

Oh! no, I want the absolute and don't accept any compromise, even though a human love could become an effective, powerful help since it would involve self sacrifice. I instinctively know thatt I must not, and I'm talking about "no" even before having decided, and I, usually so indecisive for this thing that I want so much, and that was good each time, by nature, I made up my mind in a second!

Each being has a drama that repeats itself; it is caused by profound tendencies, so deeply rooted that they plunge into the objective reality and shape one's external life, the events that will recur. And my personal drama is the one I just mentioned. Three times and very strongly, the drama repeated itself and everything was identical, even though the characters were different and each time it was better and better.

At the age of eighteen, thirty-two, and forty, more than three times because I had to say "no" on several other occasions, but I could explain this "no" to myself quite well as I wanted to remain independent; although once I did not understand and was broken hearted, but I continued to say "no" in an agony of despair.

But there isn't any "no" to say because there was never a possible "yes," so I have fun, talk about marriage, accept the engagements, but everything dies by itself and there is no drama because there was neither desire nor will but only imagination, play, amusement. (Extracts from the diary)

Note on the "Holes"

In a notebook, Lilian makes a list:

From time to time about ten holes in the wall enable me to perceive the dazzling light; they should be noted:

- The book read when I was about twelve, insignificant, lent by a

class-mate, in which a passage from the Bible was quoted about the high waters and the hart, an incomprehensible emotion, unforgettable to this day (the Guru promised me these high waters).

- Before the age of ten, conversation between two older girls (18 years old) about the "grace."

- Around twenty, a dream where I was trying to catch a glittering comet through the night, through the infinite space, knowing that the comet was the absolute. I remember it well but no special emotion.

- Dream on the occasion of the predictions of Madame Turc[9] around the age of twenty-two: Everything was grey and dark; I had been condemned, and could not see very well the savages that surrounded me: without any pain other than moral, an infinite despair rather than pain. They cut off my four limbs and I was only a trunk, unable to move; then my eyes and ears were punctured, very slowly each time; I realized that I was blind and deaf; then they cut off my tongue and I was mute, so I realized intensely that I was completely cut off from the outside world and yet I was not entirely dead [...]. I meditated deeply within myself and felt a wonderful bliss; it was the first time that I felt it, that of Dhyāna ... a grey but perfect dream that struck me in every way.

- In Corsica, the sight of a rock.

- At about the same time, I saw in a dream a great handwriting of which I noted the extraordinary movement, the greatness, and that I rediscovered so many years later: it was the handwriting of the Sufi.[10]

- Benveniste's lecture: he explains the meaning of the word Sufi: wool, and I have an intense, inexplicable emotion.

1949: Departure for India

Clarifications by Lilian on the nature of her "notes"

IN THE FOLLOWING SECTIONS, for the sake of authenticity, we have relied as much as possible on Lilian's often hasty notes. But it's important to keep in mind what she specified about them:

If these notes have any value, it is uniquely because of their nature as raw material, as raw as possible, avoiding any interpretation, reflecting as exactly as possible the immediate impression. In addition, I have no thesis to demonstrate: let others give the interpretation they wish. There are already too many works of mystics who adapt their impressions to a rigid religious framework with which they must harmonize. I don't have any answer to the questions I ask myself, I don't want to convince or prove anything. So, I'm simply reporting the events in their order of appearance. The goal in writing is not to draw these things from oblivion, they are unforgettable, but to place them in full, objective light and draw the general direction. If I am incapable of doing this, perhaps others will do it for me. [...]

These things must be noted because of their extreme importance. On the other hand, the rest of my past was of no interest to me, except for those things that it foreshadowed on some rare occasions. My guru wants me to regularly note my impressions, but I have no desire to keep a diary. Why write? I don't wish to be read, these notes are dull, insipid. I also have no desire to write a structured, interesting work that would recreate the events by shaping them, adding, simplifying as it would be easy for me to do and as I should do if I wrote for the public. No, if these notes have any value, it is to relate all the truth about the extraordinary things that happened to me [...].

I write these little things as if they were of some importance: but in fact, they are only a line surrounding a content that, in itself, would be the only thing worth describing ... but I am not conscious enough to do so. It is easier to describe the frame: but the essential content, the painting with all its richness of colors, its warm intimacy is there.... All these pages are devoid of the description of this essential content, although its plenitude is in my heart. And it is silence and peace (September 1950).

To Kaśmīr and Swami Lakshman Joo

After defending her thesis[11] on December 28, 1948, Lilian leaves for India at the beginning of the year 1949. She is going to meet the Swami Lakshman Joo in Kaśmīr,[12] keeper of the Śivaïte tradition that she has begun to study. She wants to consult him about the texts she is translating. But she also hopes to find a master who will transmit from heart to heart:

Mistrustful of autodidacts of mysticism, I only accepted masters of a known tradition and yet who are beyond the rites and beliefs of religions and sects. (Diary)

Everything had to be given to her directly according to what she knew about the Non-Path of Kaśmīr Śivaism. At the end of 1950, when the one who became her Guru will ask her: "What do you really want?" She will answer: *"The absolute, nothing less."*

I came to India for this reason alone, to find a guru, a path, as wide as possible, which is in conformity with the mystics of all countries, of all times, although not belonging to any religion, any sect, above Christianity, Mohammedanism, Hinduism and even Śivaism and Buddhism, and even above all philosophical systems, Neo-Platonism, above all thought, all imagination, all ritual, and all emotion.

What is offered by religions and philosophies is only mental construction or worthless feelings. But here I make an exception for the revelation of the Buddha, but a Buddhism without stupa, without a temple, or a statue of the Buddha. (Diary)

After a long voyage by sea, Lilian arrives in Bombay and travels on to Delhi three weeks later. There, she meets Serge Bogroff, a friend she knew in 1947 through Anne-Marie Esnoul with whom he was studying Sanskrit. Lilian had found in Serge an exceptional intelligence, an original personality and their various exchanges were intense, full of humor, and bursting with inventiveness. In June 1949, Serge writes to his family from New Delhi:

"Lilian Silburn left for Kaśmīr, unfortunately taking her thesis with her. While Miss Silburn was here, we spent all our time invoking the *asuras* [demigods]. At the end, there were so many of them that there was hardly any space left for us in the bedroom. There was the serpent of the depths, the Aśvin always busy pulling the sun out of a hole where he had fallen, Varuna the god of secrets, the one who listens while people think they are alone. I only had time to read four to five pages of her thesis which really seems to be very interesting and which is dedicated to the 'Venerable Biped' (the Buddha). [...] She is in Kaśmīr where she discovered some aesthetics philosophers of which, of course, there remains only one tradition."

These few lines quickly suggest the whimsical atmosphere of their exchanges.

Arriving in Kaśmīr mid-June, Lilian notes:

An unforgettable journey through the high mountains by bus, then the arrival in Srinagar....

Immediately, she is dazzled by the surrounding beauty of this valley of so called "wonders," by the mixture of rock, water, fruit trees and paddy fields:

Everything here is beautiful and fresh. When I entered the Kashmir Valley, it was such a wonder, with its velvety mountains, its silks, its thousands of silvery mirrors, its rice fields.

And it will always be the same amazement until the end of her travels:

Currently, they are filling up the rice fields in Srinagar, she writes in 1967, *the hard and parched earth absorbs.... Everything is so beautiful here ... I am constantly in samadhi* ... nature is softly dreaming in a penetrating, enveloping charm. Everything is blurred and yet a wonderful explosion of plants, flowers, acacias in blossom....* (Letter)

For two months, Lilian is happy to explore the surroundings and discovers with delight the life on houseboats and shikara rides on lakes lined with lotus trees. She learns to sing the *Bhagavad Gita*[13] with a pundit, makes many friends, and visits the Swami Lakshman Joo:

Often, I would go a few kilometers away from my boat, either on my bicycle or with a shikara, to see Lakshman Joo, a yogin who lived on a mountain overlooking the lake. I was working on Kashmirian philosophy.

Lilian is happy to work with Swami Lakshman Joo, "the last to possess the key to the so mysterious doctrine of Kaśmīr Śivaism." It is the beginning of a long collaboration for which she will endlessly express her gratitude.

Lilian then spends a few months on her own, in a mud hut ruin in the heart of the Kashmirian landscape:

That year, I was living near him [Lakshman Joo], in an abandoned mud hut on deserted heights overlooking Lake Dal, toward which the terraces of the Nishat Garden gradually sloped. I spent several months alone, in the heart of this exceptional site where the nakedness of the rocky mountain, the subtle softness of the light and the sometimes vaporous stillness of the lake combine and blend in a harmony and a deep peace, still impregnated, it seems, with the presence of the great Shaivite spiritual masters who probably frequented this place.[14]

In a letter, written in the first months of her stay in Kaśmīr, Lilian evokes with humor her first exercises:

My progress in yoga is not very brilliant. Weary of inferior means, I asked for superior means. Half an hour would suffice to be delivered: in every movement we must find the infinitesimal point where disjunction is possible (Lakshman teaches the junction along the line of his masters, thus continuing the tradition of rishis and buddhist kṣanas); an easy junction is the one between dream and waking, it is there where one has the first impression of samadhi, provided that one remains conscious of the junction.

I tried to practice this means by moving my finger from one point to another, until I realized the oddity of the thing. Only a madman can be careful enough to grasp the critical moment between these two movements of the index; try to make the gesture and you will understand that I burst out laughing, passing it on to Lakshman who claims that no yoga is possible for whoever enjoys a "sense of humor." He does not understand that one can be "eager" without being serious, but he laughs so heartily that the temptation is very great.

During her first meetings, Lilian asked the Swami if he could practice for her the heart-to-heart transmission which the texts mention. He answered honestly that no, but he could, on the other hand, teach her to bring up the kundalini.

For a while, Lilian went on a hill above Lake Dal, where there is a small temple dedicated to Śiva, and did a few exercises at sunrise to permit a raising of kundalini; but she was not convinced, and suddenly remembered the prediction made by a great clairvoyant of the time, Madame Turc, whom she had consulted at twenty- two, and who had advised her to "beware of the snake"; so she put an end to her efforts. The clairvoyant had also seen a splendid luminous R presiding over her destiny: "A luminous R will illuminate your life. His name will begin with an R," she predicted.[15]

Meeting with the Guru

AFTER TWO MONTHS SPENT IN Kaśmīr, Lilian, to her amazement, stayed in Kanpur. Before leaving France, she had vowed that she would never go to Kanpur, such city being of no interest in her research. But in the course of her various meetings in Srinagar, she got to meet the Dewanini* of Kaśmīr who became attached to her. Lilian will then observe a chain of seemingly insignificant events, all against her will, which will inexorably lead her to Kanpur, where the Dewanini insistently invites her to come.

And it is precisely in Kanpur, in April 1950, where the meeting that will turn her life upside down, and transform her whole being, takes place. She finally understands to what luminous "R" the clairvoyant was referring. It was for Radha Mohan, to whom she was guided by an Indian, a college teacher, "who had strongly moved her" for always being in samadhi.

Lilian let herself be dragged to her friend's Guru, who had died two years earlier and was the father of Radha Mohan. She went there, determined to observe the entourage. But, conquered by the peace of the place, she saw nothing, heard nothing, "not even the son of the guru, surrounded by his disciples, all in samadhi."

The son of the Guru became my Guru without even being aware of it, almost without a word, because he speaks little English and I had nothing to say to him. (Letter)

Later, when evoking this meeting, upon Serge Bogroff's visit, Radha Mohan will specify that it was he who had sent for Lilian.

To Serge Bogroff, in front of me, the guru tells of our first encounter. He remembers the smallest details. Already, twelve years ago, he had had a dream or a dhyanic vision; he saw very beautiful beings who would be his true disciples and told his father about it: they would come from distant lands. Then he prepared the ground for this purpose. As soon as I entered the room, he recognized me as being one of them, as he would, in the same way, for Serge Bogroff. I did not come back for two days and the guru sent someone to fetch me.... He also described how I understood everything without a private session; and then, when I left for Mussoorie, how he cut off the current to test me.

It is interesting to report the terms that Lilian used to announce this meeting to Lakshman Joo:

It starts like a fairy tale, and it may also end this way ... and you can be a gnome in this tale if you so wish.... Once upon a time, there was a great Sufi who never died. He now lives somewhere in India, at the junction of the waves of Akaśa*, of the immenseness of its rhythm, which is what his handwriting has revealed to me. When you see it, you will feel a part of its greatness, its generosity, its simplicity, and that immense thing in which all this is bathed and for which there is no name in the science of graphology. And the Sufi had, as disciples, two Indian brothers who became as great as himself. One of them had a son. Now this son is my Guru....

Bathing in the Ganges

Lilian spends a few days in Kanpur with the Guru. She discovers the handwritings of her masters that fill her with wonder for being *"beyond genius and greatness."* She is astonished by the personality of the Guru's father, a personality that she has "*never seen before*"; as for the handwriting of the Sufi, the master of the Guru, she declares that she simply did not imagine that humans could write this way: it is *"of the order of goodness and simplicity."*

The Guru plunges her into a state of peace, silence and emptiness that she had never known before. But due to previous commitments with her friends, she leaves Kanpur, despite the guru's reservations, to go to Hardwar, near Rishikesh, at the great pilgrimage [Kumbh Mela] that takes place every twelve years. On the Ganges, the Sadhu and Sannyasin from the whole of India were gathering in beautiful forests full of flowers.

The first days I enjoyed siddhi*: I had a car make a trip that *lasted two days and one night, instead of just a few hours, to travel three hundred kilometers, in order to avenge the faithful servants who, out of pure selfishness on the part of their masters, had to do a similar journey by train. I spoke Vedic with a blind pundit whom I saluted as Dirghatamas, son of Mamata. [...]*

The pilgrimage was promising to be magnificent and picturesque. But of the pilgrimage I did not see anything. For the third day, when bathing in the Gangā, I saw for the first time a river flowing. Afterwards I knew that I was no longer flowing. On the river banks, I tried to comb my hair and it took hours, as my arm was continuously falling back down. I spent three weeks, wandering in the forests, pursued by devotees, defenseless, unableto drink, eat, or sleep, in what is called ecstasy in the West and here samadhi. (Letter excerpt)

Letters to friends

Of her encounter with the guru and her experience, Lilian left several stories in letters or accounts. In an impulse of generosity, she immediately wants to propose to her closest friends to discover the extraordinary experience that she is going through, and she writes long letters according to the personality of each correspondent. She has left some duplicates. We reproduce below her letter to Serge Bogroff. The reader will appreciate the beauty of Lilian's handwriting, "handwriting that evokes the music of Bach," an amazed friend keeps on repeating.

Never will I manage to write to you. I did it once, at the very beginning, and so many pages about the first seconds of my new life. This life is not a continuation of what I have known and experienced until now. It's a new dimension of being. We would need to make all of the levers vibrate together: physiology, Atman, Kundalini and the extraordinary spheres of the unconscious; to come down, awake, while in deep sleep; the task

being of course impossible, I ask you to please come as soon as possible to attempt the same adventure of the depths.
Lilian Silburn

But it is with a very close friend that she first shares her "*extra-ordinary happiness*" with the hope that she, too, will experience it one day:

It's as if before we were always shivering, hungry, jostled, horrified, exasperated, trembling with misery and suddenly we bathe in peace, we've found a warm bed forever and the calm of tenderness ... we are satiated. From the outside nothing reaches you except voices that penetrate you with joy when they are good and hurt you when the people are hard.... One overflows with love for the crowd and the poor instinctively feel it....

This samadhi is a perpetual sleep of the body and the mind, but where the consciousness is always vigilant, as one is in full possession of oneself without respite: joy only comes rarely when one becomes aware that there is only one thing happening to you. No need to tell you the feelings of gratitude and love that we have for the Guru who gives us such a peace.... I spend my time listening to my new silence and that of my Guru, which is much greater than mine.

> Jamais je n'arriverai à vous écrire. Je l'ai fait une fois, tout au début, et tant de pages au sujet des premières secondes de ma nouvelle vie.
>
> Cette vie n'est pas dans le prolongement de ce que j'ai jusqu'ici connu et éprouvé — c'est une nouvelle dimension de l'être. Il faudrait faire vibrer à la fois tous les claviers : physiologie, āt̄man, kundalini et les extraordinaires sphères de l'inconscient ; des cadres, éveillé, en plein sommeil ; — La tâche étant impossible je vous prie de venir aussitôt que possible tenter la même aventure des abîmes. Lilian Silburn

Letter to Serge Bogroff

Later Lilian will think of J. R. with whom she shared her first inner emotions at fifteen:

Don't think that it is by negligence that I have not written to you in the last two years that I have been in India, but the first year I could only have described to you the beauty of Kaśmīr, my love for India, which was already too much.

Then the second year, it became impossible because last April I met here in Kanpur, by a miraculous combination of circumstances, what is called here a Guru, a spiritual guide, and what I have so much desired since Le Crotoy and even before ... I am realizing it ... and far beyond my wildest hopes.

Never had I hoped to find such a mystic and saint, and not one, but several: his father was a saint, his Guru, a Sufi nearly a hundred years old is still alive, his uncle, wonderful too has died, his older brother is also great, and there are others....

From the bottom of my heart, it was Saint John of the Cross that I wanted to find, Christian humility, inner destitution beyond all vision, etc.

Last April I came to visit the guru for the first time, my critical mind on the alert, and, like the others, I tested him in many ways; needless to say that the photos and handwritings of his family and his masters amazed me.

[...] I was at a famous pilgrimage in the north, in Hardwar. I was swimming in the Ganges when, suddenly, I was plunged into shanti*, a peace that isn't at all in line with what we can normally experience: an incredible sweetness of contact with

one's Self, stopping any worry, a yogic slumber of the body and of thought, but which leaves the consciousness in a soothing state of plenitude.

My happiness was such that, for a fortnight, without drinking or eating, I wandered in the forest full of wild animals that I actually never saw, sleeping under the trees, under white thorns in bloom. I remember, I could no longer speak ... nothing can give you an idea of such a state [...]. One is in the present without being torn by the past or worrying about the future. Art is only a morning dew.

Since then I've been living in ecstasy, samadhi ... my meditation is everlasting. We are absorbed in a wonderful presence that can be called God ... it is such that we are unable to think of anything else.... Plunged in a carefree state, infinite plenitude, bliss which lasts for hours, but also the night of the spirit and its torture which is a samadhi of "too much"; the bliss and the divine love become so extreme that one cannot bear them without moaning. I happened to scream with pain at night ... my joy, which is marvelous for the first second, becomes a torture the next second by its very excess.

It is useless to speak of those things which, as long as you haven't experienced them, will remain a dead letter. But all are intense and nothing is a continuation of what we have already experienced: bliss, for example, is of the whole being, body and soul become one; we are only a conscious mass of bliss and this for hours, no more and no less, bliss in every bit of the body....

But this love without desire that doesn't recognize itself is greater still; it is part of the painful path, of the nights, and few are the ones who experience it; all the other disciples only know the bliss. A month ago, it was a great happiness for my Guru when he saw that such was my way, similar to his....

Perfect surrender to the Guru or rather to God is required, but this surrender comes spontaneously as soon as one has tasted the soothing reassurances, and the Guru never asks for anything other than what you want for yourself.

Guru, rather than God, because at first we have not realized God, or if we realize it, it's without knowing it. Otherwise, any word, any teaching is useless. Everything is transmitted in silence. We don't talk a lot, if not for laughing, as my Guru has a great sense of humor.

As I will soon have to return to France (there is a campaign on my behalf for the succession to the chair of Indian philosophy), my Guru makes me skip different steps, but I must carefully note all of my experiences in order to guide others and also to write later on; needless to say that writing doesn't really enchant me. I only want silence and solitude and nothing else interests me, except giving the same thing to friends who I feel are ready, that is to say, aspiring to the absolute, ready to sacrifice everything for him. And you are among the first ones I thought of.

Lilian now knows a "new torture," that of not being able to help those around her benefit from the experience that is definitely turning her whole life upside down.

People are suffering around me: three saints that I know can give them more than they dare to ask, but they don't want to. They confine themselves to their limited desires, their petty worries; they always want less than what can be given to them. This is the human tragedy ... basically men do not aspire to anything much higher, they want too little....

And yet, after her experience in Hardwar, a new hope was born, that of being able to give peace to those she loved.

Before, I could do so little for others despite all my desire. I was ashamed of the lack of efficiency of my love, of the sterility of my sympathy. Now I'm resting on my love; it is no longer just mine anymore ... it's Brahman who is responsible because he has to infuse it with efficacy.

But she had a painful experience on account of a letter that she sent to a friend at the Institute of Indian Civilization who was so indiscrete as to circulate the letter among her colleagues. Her enthusiasm and wonder for the life that was opening up to her aroused narrow-minded reactions and compromised her definitively.

I received letters from France that are unpleasant to me. I would like to have never written this letter about my experiences because many have read it at the Sorbonne and are talking about me. It was such a personal letter, only addressed to the friend who was with me in India. I would be very sad with all this rumpus and I would have been terribly hurt if I weren't so indifferent now. But maybe one among the many people who have read my letter will be really interested. This is my only consolation.... Shall I stop talking and writing about what I am really experiencing?

I came to India...

The year 1950 is in the middle of Lilian's life; she is forty-two and will live forty-three more years. That year is critical: it marks the beginning of a totally different life, abolishing the past:

I now forget everything, she writes, *there is no more past for me, and this effort that I am making towards the past is torture, it is so far away!*

It is at that point that the Guru asks her to give, in public, an update on her life, which surprises her and makes her protest:

I am going to have to talk to many people in February; I hate this idea. I refused and will try to refuse again, but I'm afraid that my guru demands it. In the meantime, I'll try to win God's favor out of respect for silence.

But Lilian was not able to avoid what appeared to be an impossible task, and she left us her original text, in English, of this public statement, reproduced here verbatim:

I came to India to acquire two main things: Silence and forgetfulness, perfect silence of all the faculties: mind, heart and so on – complete forgetfulness of my limited self. And by a hard paradox, the one who is giving me both has asked me today to speak, to speak in public even, and to speak about my own self.

I must say a few words about my past, for I could find only what I was looking for, though I found much more than I ever dreamt of.

From my childhood I was only interested in the absolute. I was not ten years old when I was wondering and discussing about the most important problem for me then: the one of grace. At that time I was reading the Old Testament of the Bible again and again as others read books of adventures. The only adventure I was interested in was how to get to God.

From 15 to 20 years of age I had decided to leave the world and enter a Christian convent where renouncement is the hardest and contemplation the highest, but I had to wait, my family being opposed to it.

Then I studied philosophy, not for the sake of examinations or for mental pleasure, but I tried to live and feel according to most of the philosophical systems: Plato, Plotinus, Spinoza for instance.

Before I was twenty I lost all faith in a personal god and in the Christian religion, though I remained eager to find a way towards the absolute.

After having studied Western philosophers and mystics I turned towards the East when I was 20 and began a thesis on Indian philosophy. For that I had to learn Sanskrit, Pâli and Avestic.

First I was attracted by the vedāntin Śankara, Rāmānuja and the Upaniṣad. After a few years I discovered Buddhism and gave my heart to the Buddha, Nagarjuna, and Asanga in whom I found the best of masters.

I studied also Rig and Atharva Veda and the Brāhmana for many years, and during the war I devoted part of my time to Trika philosophy; it is a Sivaite system based on very old tantras. It is named also Spanda philosophy, the philosophy of vibrations, and is entirely based on the mystical experiences of the yogin.

In the meantime I was also interested in such old Persian books as the Avesta, the gathas of Zarathustra, and had deep love for Taoism which is the best expression of Chinese mysticism. But I never felt attracted towards Arabic culture. It is why I know very little of Sufism.

I translated Pañcadaśī, Aitareya Upaniṣad, wrote two books on Trika philosophy, and achieved my thesis on "Cause and Duration" ... from the Ṛgveda, Brāhmana to Buddhism included.

In that work I wanted to show, after the Buddhists, that everything is momentaneous and that duration is our own creation. The Buddha, as well as other mystics, had taught me that the present moment is the only real thing: in the actual instant we live, we die, we are "efficient." The creation of past and future is the source of our misery: we only waste our life as we turn constantly towards the past, regretting it, or towards the future in an everlasting expectation, and we do not live and work our deliverance in the very present moment.

Time is a structure, a samskāra*; we know how we create it under the impulse of desire, by our mental dynamism. The problem was then to destroy all those structures, to return to childhood, to live in the present.

And so, long before I came here, I knew in the marrow of my bones that to reach the absolute would be to go above all concepts, all samskāra, vikalpa*; that no thought however high it be, no philosophy will help me in the least to reach my goal. Following Nāgārjuna and St. John of the Cross, our best mystic, I knew that only a being who gets rid of all modes could reach a god without modes.

During those years of hard studies I always refused to marry so that I could remain free. I could not tolerate the least obstacle in my path towards the absolute. In the West I met some people with mystical tendencies, but none had direct experiences in spite of their keen desires.

When I came to India two years ago, I had very little hope of finding a Guru, for I not only expected perfection and greatness, but I asked for someone who was above all religions and creeds, who was not a philosopher, not a vedāntin – who admired Buddha and Jesus Christ as I did because of their universal love. I wanted that my guide had renounced everything though he would be living in the world. He must have no prejudices concerning purifications, food, be above all kind of rituals and idol worship. But how to find such a man in India! I wanted also what Trika philosophy named Samādhi in the world: unmīlana samādhi, ecstasies with opened eyes and that from the very beginning. Now if I admired the Rāja yoga of Patañjali, I was unwilling to try any āsana, prānāyāma, japa, for I put spiritual life at too high a level.

In my heart also I had a mad desire: to realize the absolute by what the Sivaism of Kashmir calls "anupāya*" which is above all the means of liberation (mokṣa). It comes without any effort, spontaneously, through the grace of God and the Guru – for if I came to India, it was in the hope of finding such a Guru. I did not require any instruction through words, for then I would find in *the books, tantra and others, much more and better said than by any living man. You see I knew exactly what I wanted and I was not going to make any concession: either I was to meet, by a marvellous Providence, such a man or woman or I shall have no Guru.*

Something was to help me in my choice: since my childhood I was very deeply interested in studying people: I did much experimental psychology, with the help of graphology, morphology. By voice, walking, handwriting, I could judge a man in a short while and see for instance by a single movement of the hand how deeply he surrendered to god, and so I was not afraid to take an ordinary man for a saint whatever be his fame or spiritual beauty.

During my travel in India and Kashmir I had the good luck of meeting many of their most famous men. But I was so disappointed by them. The best were kind, peaceful, but they had nothing to give to their sisya except good advice. Others were only keen to teach me asana, pranayama ... a few were highly intellectual but had very little mystical experience. Others would try to tempt me by offering me siddhi. Pāni Mahārāja showed me a difficult āsana, where he said that you realize God in half an hour by it.... Then acrobats in a circus won't fail. Most of them were so vain, so proud. I used to test them in many ways and at once they showed their pettiness, their lack of perfection.

In Kashmīr, Laksman Brahmacārin helped me explain some difficult problems of Trika philosophy. He is a good scholar and also a yogin. I tried prāṇāyāma under his guidance and succeeded in originating heat and high lights which never disappeared since then. But he was not a Guru, because he was lacking the power of giving śānti and Samādhi. I tried hard to concentrate during six hours a day but never for three minutes could I stop the work of my mind. During those five months when I lived alone high on the mountain, I achieved nothing. Before coming to Kanpur, the problem was for me to realize the mystical state called Brahman through a perfect concentration of the whole being such as is found in sneezing – the northern tantras say, not I – or in a desperate flight when you are pursued by a mad elephant, or in a fit of anger, and also in the paroxysm of love. The tantras say that the one who is always eager to find Brahman might realise it when under such a violent emotion if he, at once, forgets the cause of it. I could try only sneezing and the encounter with a wild beast, as there were plenty near my hut during the night, but I did not succeed.

How I came to Kanpur is through a miraculous concourse of circumstances and all of them were against my will – Kanpur being without a university offers no interest for my studies – and so I came there for a few days via Lucknow. Then I met a man whom I loved dearly at first sight, Gandhiji, and he promised me to take me to the house where a great saint had lived. I was not eager to come as he mentioned a school of Sufi.

The first time I came here with him, it was only for half an hour. Two things happened. I forgot entirely to study, even to glance at the Guru who was sitting silently here, and I felt somehow that concentration was easier, though I thought that it was an illusion of mine. But I liked the quality of the silence.

A few days after, I came back to see the handwritings and photography of the saint and of his Guru. I was sceptical, acutely critical, as French people usually are. But such was my wonder when I saw the face of Chachaji [father of Radha Mohan]. He had what I shall call the divine touch. I mean that a mysterious hand had moulded, malaxed his flesh from inside so that not a parcel of it remained unshaped by the thumb of the sculptor. I found also the same thing in the face of my Guru, his elder brother, and afterwards in the great Sufi.

That very day also was shown to me the extraordinary handwriting of Chachaji, the striking one of his brother, and the marvellous one of the Sufi, and there were also others I admired much.

I had studied in the British Museum and in books the handwritings of most of the illustrious men of the world, but I never saw one of the greatness of Chachaji. It shows such an immensity and generosity of heart, a humility, simplicity and silence I had never dreamt of. In him all structures were gone. He had left all limits, and such dynamism associated with the depth of peace! But the moment you are grasping how great, how exceptional his personality is, you realize that he had lost it, that very loss being his greatness.

Those things you know better than I do for you lived with him, but I have one advantage on you, I can judge him in all objectivity – and though I never saw him, I can merge in him, as the whole being of a man is in the movement of his hand, as it is in his words, his silence, his smile.

That day I had full confidence and faith in the family of my Guru and the Guru of my Guru. But I had first to test one who is now my Guru. I teased him, making fun of his God.... I tried so many things, but he had a deep sense of humour – an important condition, for it means that such a person lives on more than one plane of reality.

During a fortnight I came every day with my devilish tricks. Not much then seemed to happen, maybe some peace.... Then I had to go, not too willingly to the great Mela of Hardwār. During the first two days I enjoyed the Mela and I thought that I was going to write about it, but on this third day I was lost in the forest. I saw nothing of the Mela, for a new life began for me. I shall never forget that day, the real day of my birth.

In the morning I was swimming in the middle of the Ganga. Then all desire of swimming left me and I was drifting away in the strong current. Then I became aware for the first time of my life that the water was flowing and it seemed strange to me. Only afterwards I understood that from that moment I was myself flowing no more. I could reach the wood on the bank of the Ganga but was unable to dress. I tried to comb my hair and broke the comb in a desperate effort. Afterwards I remained for hours without moving, with a piece of comb in my hand, half-naked, and wondering, wondering, in that new śānti, and the sweetness of the contact with my own self was such that I lost consciousness of everything else.

During a fortnight, days and nights I roamed about in the forests of Hardwār, my sari all torn, sleeping under the trees, eating what a naked sannyāsin gave me, forgetting everything. I was never tired, neither hungry, nor thirsty. I tried to hide myself in the white thorns, but always I was disturbed by sādhu* or pilgrims. I shall not forget also the kindness of the very poor ones. They used to find me during the night when I was so far away, when it rained, and bring me to their tent. When sleeping under a tree I felt, there, in the night for the first time and only for a few seconds, that marvellous bliss that you call ānanda*. Back to Kanpur, during a few weeks my Guru made me experience some mystical states as Dhyāna, Samādhi, but in a bird-flight way.

Here I would like to stop for my task is becoming impossible. For those who went through similar experiences, a few hints would be enough. For those who did not, no word of mine will give them an idea of it. I am leaving aside the essential for it is beyond words and shall only play with small details or symptoms, unable as I am to put the finger on the very life of it.

I have only one desire left: silence. But I am forced to speak and to write. So I go on talking: during the first weeks, I used to remain still for hours, without moving an eyelash, perfectly *satisfied ... I who before could not remain five minutes without working. Sweetness, delight, peace or śānti are the characteristics of that state. But śānti is not worldly peace; it is a new state of being, difficult to imagine, difficult to describe. It is not only the absence of worries but something quite positive. You are perfectlysatiated with the very void you feel in you ... void or fullness, śūnyatā or pūrnatā, it comes to the same. As compared to that, nothing matters; you renounce spontaneously the joys of the world and there is no merit in it ... you can't do otherwise. Then also, prāṇayāma* will come in a natural way. You are bathing in spiritual life without the least effort, even sometimes in spite of yourself!*

Two striking things happened during those first weeks: firstly, blows at the heart, as if the hṛdguhā*, the caverns of the heart, were dug out and an immense presence filled them afterwards, but too immense to be grasped. Then secondly, the waves of bliss, but so excessive that I could not bear it more than one second, and the waves would come in succession for two hours. I had to move, jump, to get rid of it at all cost, for if the first second was marvellous, the next one was wounding.

In June, I left for Mussoorie, but I lost there the śānti I had since April from Hardwar. Again I was in an ordinary state of mind, my śānti gone. All the misery of life came back to me in spite of the affection of my friends. I could not concentrate. During the night I had once more dreams and nightmares, whereas I had none during the three preceding months.

Once in the cinema I felt again in the state of śānti and I saw nothing of the beautiful film. But that state disappeared. Had I no hope that again I should feel that peace, I would no doubt have committed suicide. If you taste it once, you cannot live afterwards without it.

In July I went to Delhi, and, though far from my Guru, he put me back into śānti and new wonderful experiences began. I felt something which I called vibration, or spanda in Sanskrit, according to Sivaism of Kashmir. It is as the scraping of ants, or a slight electric current, and since then I am most of the time half asleep, drunk, diving deep at times, with those vibrations permeating the whole body. Their rhythm varies; in the presence of my Guru they are extremely intense. When I am far from him, they usually fill me with bliss. That bliss or ānanda comes also no matter where and when – during a tea-party, when shopping, on the chair of the dentist – so unexpectedly, and I have no power, no desire to prevent it. I am absorbed in it, unable to speak, unconscious of what people say, think, do. It hurts when they shake me.

But for a few days I noticed an important change: even when speaking, laughing, running, I feel that bliss, not for a long time perhaps, but it is there in spite of worldly activities and as strong as when I lie down quietly.

I know well that I am only on the threshold of mystical life, and what I felt in ten months is probably nothing compared to what I shall experience. The most striking thing is that no effort of mine was required; my Guru or his god did everything. When I asked him in the beginning: "What shall I do?" he always answered: "Do nothing, everything will be done to you." And the miracle happened.

Two great obstacles are found in the life of the mystic who struggles alone for perfection: he cannot concentrate on God all the time, I mean every second (kṣana) of his life as he desires, because his mind is in constant fluctuation during the day and unconscious in his sleep during the night. In agitation and sleep you feel most acutely the depths of human misery and deficiency, and no effort can bring a remedy to it.

But in Kanpur (this very house), here which is the nābhi (navel) of the world, no need for concentration is required: you get so absorbed in yourself that if an effort is required, it is to become aware of the external world, for instance how to coordinate the most simple thoughts, as to buy bread, not forget to pay for it.... The new task before me is to remain conscious at times, and my Guru is not going to help me, he told me.

As for the other human curse, sleep, I perceive a time when ordinary sleep might be excluded, for it happened to me, though exceptionally, to remain a day and night in a special sleep, the nidrā of yoga; it means, always conscious and never tired.

As time remains, shall I mention a few queer states? For instance the one I call ākāśānanta, the infinity of ether: it is no stage at all says my Guru, but as the Buddha mentioned it as the first samāpatti*, I will say a few words about it.

For hours you are floating in space and it is as if the ākaśa of the heart loses itself perpetually within the great ākaśa. Those who believe in levitation simply went through that state: but I knew I was not roaming in the astral world as a friend of mine thinks he does when he is in that mood, for as I had bricks under the feet of my bed, I would have floated feet higher than head.

At moments also, nature and the external world appear so perfectly still and peaceful, as if it had returned to its primordial quietness. At others, the world would seem as full of ānanda. For when I am myself full of it, I am only one mass of ānanda, ghana; as is written in the Upaniṣad, there is no more outside and inside.

Something also striking is that the gap between body and soul vanishes the moment the activity of the mind stops. The bliss you feel is no less sensual than spiritual: it is undifferentiated and it is very important.

Shall I speak also of that soft whirlpool which comes sometimes before Samādhi? There is immensity in it. I am unable to say more about it. Unable also to say a word about the divings. How to express it? The spell of the great magician. And also many queer things, as telepathic experiences....

In the past, from childhood I had extraordinary emotions which I never forgot, for I could not explain them. For instance, someone years ago gave me the definition of what Sufi means: "wool" and told me about the softness and warmth it implies and I was so extremely moved by it.[16]

My Guru also told me the same thing afterwards and I then understood my feelings. In a dream in my youth, I also saw the marvellous handwriting of the great Sufi. When I saw him, it was as if, beforehand, I had known every expression of him, the least inflexions of his voice. And other things also even more striking: there is not only a transformation in the functions of the body but also on the moral side of the character, and it is not without a meaning as you become patient and love for others increases....

How I make mistakes in English for I am not English, but it does not matter. If I were a nice śiṣya*, I would say how grateful I am to my Guru. But I won't because I hated that speaking business he imposed on me. And also he deserves no thanks, for his God is working through him. That God, I can't thank for I did not realize him.

Where shall I hang my overwhelming gratefulness...on Chachaji?

The Masters of the Lineage

"It is the miracle and the vocation of the great mystical lineages to master and preserve the access to the divine currents throughout the centuries. It is an unfathomable miracle, such a succession of disciples, fading away one after the other, losing themselves one into the other, vanishing in the powerful currents of which they ensure the perpetuation and preserve the purity, tirelessly keeping them within reach for those who recognize the spiritual flow in them."[17]

Huzur Maharaj (1857-1907)

Samādhi* of Huzur Maharaj, Raipur (U.P., India)

MAULANA FAZAL AHMED KHAN (Huzur Maharaj) belonged to the Naqshbandi Sufi Order[18] and was also attached to two great Sufis: Mujaddidi[19] and Mazhari[20] who lived in Delhi. Both did great pioneering work in the renewal of this path.

Huzur Maharaj's principal disciple and successor in this Order was Hazi Maulana Abdul Ghani Khan Saheb.[21] Huzur Maharaj was one of the rare Sufis, if not the first, who chose to have two brothers as his "deputies," the father and the uncle of the guru, Raghubar Dayal (Chachaji) and Ram Chandra (Lalaji), who belonged to a Hindu family. Huzur Maharaj bestowed his *adhikara* on the oldest one without even asking him to convert to the Islamic faith, although he would have done so willingly.

Huzur Maharaj had a brother who lived until the age of eighty-eight, but he was so absorbed in God that he could not help anybody. Crowds would still go to him, but he gave only a classical Muslim teaching, thus freeing his brother who dedicated himself to a few disciples.

The Sufi's Guru (Huzur Maharaj, Abdul Ghani Khan's Guru) was so strict that if one only disobeyed him once, it was finished. If he said, "Sit down here in front of me," and if one did not do it, out of respect for him, then it was finished, because at the very moment he gave the order there were waves, a flow of love. But the Sufi himself, although strict, wasn't of the same kind. As for the father of the Guru (Chachaji) it didn't really matter; he transformed the person and generated in them obedience, faith and loyalty. (Notes)

Anecdote: Huzur Maharaj and the prostitute[22]

Amongst our co-disciples, there was a young person, who besides attending the satsang* of Huzur Maharaj, used to visit a lady in a brothel. Some friends brought this to the notice of Huzur Maharaj. He told them to inform him next time when this young man visits the lady. Next time when the young man went to visit the lady, Huzur Maharaj took a bath, changed his dress, applied some perfume and proceeded along with others to the brothel. It was a small place and the lady also knew Huzur Maharaj. She was surprised to see Huzur Maharaj, who asked her to sing. She sang some songs, which to her mind could be of interest to Huzur Maharaj. After hearing the songs Huzur Maharaj inquired about her charges for the night and paid her the fees. Huzur Maharaj was then around sixty. The lady and everyone else were astounded that such a saint would stay in the brothel for the night. Huzur Maharaj, however, asked all the others to leave. After everyone else left, Huzur Maharaj told the lady: "For tonight you are in my service and you will have to obey whatever I command. I do not like jewelry, remove them first and then take a bath." Huzur Maharaj had taken with him some of his wife's clothes, which he asked the lady to wear after the bath. The lady complied with it. After that, Huzur Maharaj asked her to offer five prayers with him (five Namaz). The lady thought for a moment what trouble she had invited for herself by accepting the fees and then told Huzur Maharaj that she did not know how to offer prayers. Huzur Maharaj told her: "You are in my service tonight and you'll have to do what I say. It does not matter that you do not know how to offer prayers. Repeat what I do." She started imitating Huzur Maharaj. When Huzur Maharaj put his head on the ground (in Sijda), she did the same.

At that moment Huzur Maharaj prayed, "O Almighty, with Your kind grace I have brought this lady up to this point. Now it is *You* and *she*." Huzur Maharaj then left that place and came back home but the lady was frozen in that posture. Throughout the night she lay in that posture. In the morning her mother woke her. On opening her eyes, she was baffled. She looked around and told her mother: "Whatever I could earn for you, I have already handed it over to you. Your jewelry is lying there. These clothes I am wearing are not yours, and now I am going away."

There was a neem tree in front of Huzur Maharaj's house. At around eleven in the morning she came there and sat under the tree. Huzur Maharaj spotted her and told his wife to bring her inside and to give her some food. After she had finished with the food, Huzur Maharaj enquired with her whether she wanted to come out of that life and spend a life of piety in the future. She immediately agreed to it. Huzur Maharaj then asked her to pray to the Almighty to forgive her for her past and called that young man and asked him if he liked that lady and wished to marry her. Huzur Maharaj then got them married and initiated both of them in the Order.

The Sufi (1867-1952)[23]

Samādhi* of Abdul Ghani Khan, Bhogaon (U.P. India)

THE SUFI, HAZI MAULANA ABDUL GHANI KHAN SAHEB, was the principal disciple and successor of Huzur Maharaj Fazal Ahmad Khan Raipuri. *"He's one of the most extraordinary beings that we could ever meet,"* writes Lilian.

He radiated kindness, his voice was sweet and melodious, with subtle variations, and possessed a strange charm. He was of great beauty in his youth and had retained this great beauty even when he was eighty-six years old:

I had never seen such a prodigiously high and large forehead that, nonetheless, did not create any imbalance with the lower part of his face thanks to his thick white beard; he had very fine and chiseled Arabian features, pale eyes that, I think, were grey, aclear complexion like a Norwegian, a thick white beard, a full face without any marks, although his body was emaciated when I met him for the first time in 1950.

The Guru used to say: "He was so beautiful, that the ugly people who approached him became beautiful." His mystical irradiation was so intense that even when he was old and sick it was difficult for the Guru to bear. His physical weakness did not affect in any way his exceptional mystical power. "Full of powers from head to feet," said the Guru about him.

After being very wealthy during his youth, he had distributed all his belongings to the poor and lived in a white mud house in Bhogaon, an antique city that used to compete with Delhi in past centuries but which is now only a small and rather poor market town. After undertaking brilliant studies, he was a school headmaster for a long time and, afterwards, was promoted to the role of inspector.

His unique mission was to form masters: the uncle and the father of the Guru, the Guru, his brother and his cousin. He would discourage the half-hearted, non-eager people, and talk about business, being as least spiritual as possible, declaring: "I don't know anything about mystical life, but I heard of two brothers (the uncle and the father of the Guru), that you should go and see. They are saints. As for me, I don't know anything, I can only give mantras or explain texts." But then, these persons were most surprised when they saw the two brothers showing such a great respect for the Sufi. People would rarely stay, only those who were really determined or who had confidence ... those who were receptive.

His devotion and consideration were rare. He was blind but could "see" everything, knew everything. In 1950, whilst invited to the Guru's, he refused to take the cup of tea that he was being offered until the other visitors had been served and had to wait a long time for this single daily meal, in spite of others' protests.

Despite many attempts, never did anyone succeed in taking a

photograph of the Sufi. Many people have tried; when he was seated amongst professors and students, his armchair stayed empty on the photo; he was very surprised by this and would say: "What is it that is missing within myself that does not allow me to appear?"

Lilian recalls:

The Guru used to tell me that his Guru, the great Sufi, had an extraordinary peculiarity, that is not found in any of the other great saints: he was never meditating or in an apparent ecstasy, but always active, talkative, exquisitely polite, never thinking of himself but only of others, so immersed in everyday life that most of the people who crowded to see him would leave feeling somewhat disappointed.

My Guru has the same ideal, but one can detect his ecstasy in his eyes and, often, he stops, unable to keep on talking. What I mean is: he is in ecstasy and reciting a poem in Hindi. If I interrupt him and force him into a third activity, he gives a start, does not understand what I'm saying, can only come out of his trance with great difficulty: I'm hurting him. His gaze is fixed.... Only then do I realize that he was in an ecstatic state.

Lalaji, brother to Chachaji
and uncle to the Guru

Chachaji, the Guru's father (1875-1947)[24]

M. Bhitnagar, professor, neighbor of the guru, and disciple of Shri Chachaji, writes to me:

Chachaji

"I worked out the family history of Shri Chachaji but it is not with me now. I only remember that his ancestors were in the service of the Moghul Emperors in Delhi and migrated to Mainpuri, village of Bhogaon, sometime in the 17th century. The family had a large estate which continued to be partitioned in each generation, but it is said that it was still fairly large in the time of Shri Chachaji's father.

"About the time of the Mutiny (1857-1858), Chaudhary Har Baksh Ray, Chachaji's father, migrated to Farrukhabad where he rose to be the Municipal Granting Superintendent. He had two sons: Ram Chandra, known as Lalaji Maharaj (1873-1931), and Rhagubar Dayal, later known to us as Shri Chachaji (1875-1947).

"Chaudhary Har Baksh Ray shared the tastes of the well-to-do people of his age; he had a concubine. The two boys were deeply attached to their mother, who was a very pious lady, fond of the *Ramayana*, and they had their first contact with the religious life through her.

"The boys received their first education in Persian in a *maktab* (or Maulvi's School), and later in the Mission School at Farrukabad. Shri Ram Chandra studied up to the Middle Standard and Shri Chachaji even less in this school. The elder brother was married at the age of 11, and after the retirement of his father, took up service in the local Collectorate on a salary of Rs 10/per month in 1891. After his father's death in 1893, the burden of supporting the family fell upon him, so his younger brother (Shri Chachaji) grew up under his care.

"Shri Ram Chandra came in touch with Maulana Fazal Ahamad Sahab, a Guru of the Sufi Order 'Naqshbandia,' while still a student, and was formally initiated into the Order at the age of 19 (June 1896). He retired from service sometime in August 1928 and died of cancer of the liver at 1:12 am on August 14, 1931.

"Sri Chachaji's spiritual training was carried on under his elder brother's guidance and care from the beginning: it was only after his elder brother's demise that he started to accept disciples.

"This school, in its present form, was therefore founded by Shri Ram Chandra, and Shri Chachaji was his elder brother's successor. Shri Chachaji always spoke of him as his Guru, and during the lifetime of his brother he treated him with the utmost reverence and gave him unquestioning obedience in all matters, big and small, just as a disciple.

"Chachaji breathed his last on June 7, 1947, at 1:50 pm.

"I had the good fortune to meet him in April or May 1937. You have seen his photograph. He was a short, thick-set person, markedly dark-brown complexion, very expressive features, specially his eyes which were ordinarily abstracted in their looks but could express every emotion very intensely. He had a strong constitution, but on 14th September 1937 he had a paralyzing stroke which disabled him in one arm and leg, and caused other disabilities in his brain. Gradually, a persistent cough, angina, severe constipation and high blood pressure undermined his natural strength and, old as he was, should have incapacitated him for his spiritual work. But despite all these, from early morning, say about 5:00 am to about midnight, he was surrounded with disciples, sitting bolt upright on a chair, a sofa or on his bed (without support), and all the time spiritual transmission or "tawajjah"* was going on despite doctor's orders.

"One never saw him angry or impatient or in a mood to rebuke. He never indulged himself in criticism of other people or creeds or schools. In fact he seldom talked of absent people except by way of praise and remembrance. If he heard bad news, he was obviously concerned about it. No difference could be noticed in his treatment of, and dealings with, the humblest and the highest of his disciples.

"Visitors assembled morning and evening (7-10 am and 5-10 pm) at his house. In the mornings, after the usual satsang, general talk about persons and news of the day was indulged in, and occasionally upadesha (teaching), if somebody asked a question. In the evenings such things preceded the satsang, after which most of the regular visitors left for their homes at about 9:00 pm.

"He insisted on:

- Daily attendance at the satsang, at least once a day.
- Daily writing of a personal diary.
- Noting any out-of-the ordinary happenings in the disciple's life or his personal sadhana* (spiritual practice).

(You know the method and the course of the sadhana yourself.)

"The daily satsang and dhyana was of course a unique experience for those who benefited from it, but even beginners experienced a sense of calm, exhilaration and exaltation occasionally after the dhyana was over. Many people experienced astral colors, darshan* and still higher experiences. But Chachaji always said that these things 'are tangents on the side' and should not be cared for. He described the dhyana without color as 'pure Vedanta'.

"He discouraged reading of religious books except as and when prescribed by him, or talk of visions and spiritual experiences or worrying about them. This, undoubtedly, on the well known principle that any intellectual definition of the Ascent of the Spirit limits it, predisposes one to seek verification of pre-conceived or only 'bookish' notions, and thus disturbs genuine individual spiritual progress.

"Often the post-satsang talks were hilarious affairs, and the talk ranged all over the world and almost nothing except obscenity was taboo. Chachaji almost daily asked one or another in the audience to tell 'stories', and often droll and merry stories were narrated by people. He joined in with his own extremely humorous ones. But, quite often, he talked of his own guru, and of his elder brother to illustrate the course of the Sadhana, or of their ways and manners, their generosity, liberalism, tolerance, humility and other noble qualities. Occasionally doctrinal matters would be discussed but rarely. He never talked about himself or his spiritual attainments or deeds.

"The outstanding impression is of a humble lover of God whose sole dependence in all matters was upon Him, and who made no spiritual claims for himself. A great upholder of tradition, he always spoke respectfully of all saints to whatever religion they might belong.

"A second impression is of his tenderness. Any man and every man's sorrow or misfortune, stories of saints, even fictional tales involving accounts of brave deeds, unmerited suffering, or faith in God and similar situations brought profuse tears to his eyes. I remember his weeping profusely when a song by Sur Das was sung in his presence describing Shri Krishna's defense to his mother against the charge that he had stolen butter in neighboring houses.

"He liked listening to music. He was himself an expert tabla player. And during music in his presence, the audience experienced sometimes ravishing spiritual emotions, more intense than at other times.

"Would-be scoffers remained to honor and to praise him once they met him. His obvious simplicity, sincerity of feeling and courtesy of manner bewitched them. He never indulged in discussion of any kind.

"And every one of the habitués felt that Chachaji loved him most. Indeed, he loved every one of them just as much as he loved his sons. All that was his was theirs – his time, his energies, his spiritual gifts, his possessions."

Comment by Lilian:

I need not talk of personal experiences of his fatherly help and guidance since there is no need to reinforce a genuine saint's life with miracles. But everyone has had one or more such experiences. I myself feel that in a book for the modern man, such things had better be avoided.[25]

The Guru (1900-1966)

MAHATMA RADHA MOHAN LAL ADHAULIYA was the son of two saints, and was just about fifteen years old when he was totally captivated in a single day and for the rest of his life by the master of his father, the Sufi, Hazi Maulana Saheb.[26] During his childhood he was surrounded by powerful personalities and was fortunate to spend almost his whole life at the side of his father and to be in very frequent contact with his father's master; he would sleep next to them and his body became accustomed to very strong vibrations, thus enabling him to acquire his extraordinary spiritual strength. His Guru, as well as his father, initiated him into various mystical experiences, developing his siddhi* so as to make a great master out of him. But he didn't seem to use his powers openly very much.

After solid studies of Persian, he passed an exam that conferred on him the title of Munshi,[27] authorizing him to express his ideas in public but, like his masters, he did not give any speeches, except on rare occasions, such as at a Bhandara,* when he was so inspired that he could not do otherwise. His literary Urdu was so rich and subtle that few people could understand it, in its form as much as its substance. From time to time, he recited his own poems, and Lilian was so sorry not to be able to fully appreciate their beauty.

Although he had a sound constitution, he contracted very serious illnesses since his childhood and until his death: a blindness that lasted several years (between the ages of three and six?) which was suddenly cured from afar by the master of the Sufi, and he surprised his mother by starting to talk to her about the color of her sari. At the same time, they received a letter from the Sufi expressing his joy at the good news (that nobody could possibly have told him).

The Guru suffered all kinds of illnesses: malaria and the rheumatisms that go with it, typhoid, cholera, smallpox (twice), septicemia, liver disorder, abscesses, ulcers, heart attacks, pulmonary tuberculosis, sciatica and constant backaches. Although he was often dying, in a coma, all of this did not leave any trace; his spiritual power increased so much at those times, as well as his felicity, that he considered his illnesses a benediction.

When he received the *adhikara*, a special role granted to those who are worthy of it, the Sufi sent him home with a letter giving instructions for his father. Radha Mohan fell unconscious on his bed and remained there for eight days: one could see him but not touch him because the slightest shock would have caused his death. Since then, the Guru gives in small doses, fearing to cause the disciple's death by a prolonged unconsciousness.[28]

In her diary, Lilian evokes several times the guru's relationship with his master, the Sufi:

My Guru talked a lot to me about his attitude towards his own Guru, the Sufi. He evoked his obedience and his full respect since he was fourteen. He would not look him straight in the face. He said that this veneration is a shortcut: the big secret is to always keep the person of the Guru, present, in front of our eyes. This does wonders. (May 7, 1950)

Lilian and the Guru
1950-1966

DURING THESE SIXTEEN YEARS, Lilian shares her time between Le Vésinet and her stays in Kanpur and Kashmir. She must be in Le Vésinet for her work at the CNRS and her life with Aliette. But the Guru requests her presence in Kanpur, and her work requires meetings with Lakshman Joo in Kashmir.

Her research work, of great importance to her, keeps her very busy; at the same time, she is also profoundly absorbed in the inner adventure that she is experiencing, in unison with, and following in, her Guru's wake; furthermore, she pays much attention to her new task, that she sometimes calls her "mission," toward those who come knocking at her door to benefit from her discoveries. Therefore she maintains a regular correspondence with the Guru.

However, all of Lilian's letters to the Guru, which were sent to him in English, have been lost. But we have the initial drafts of her letters that she wrote first in French. These have been translated for the purposes of this book.

A great number of the Guru's letters, written in English, have been preserved. We have extracted the passages concerning mystical life in general, and retained events marking this period and which are referred to in this book. Thus, we can largely trace Lilian's life during these years, which were so rich and so intensely focused.

All the passages from the Guru's letters are reproduced in his original English.

1950

BACK FROM HARDWAR, LILIAN stays with the Guru who makes her experience, strongly and profoundly, the different states of an intense mystical life ... the rigors of a naked faith.

But in June, exhausted by the heat in Kanpur, Lilian goes to join her friends, the Dass family, in Mussoorie at a higher altitude.[29]

During that period, the Guru loses his mother on June 25th and, thereafter, in August a little girl is born. She will die the following year, to Lilian's great despair, and she will bitterly complain about Indian negligence and denounce the total lack of hygiene in child care.

Far away from Kanpur, Lilian goes through difficult moments. She is worried about her health; a heart condition calls for the greatest caution; after consulting two specialists, she can write: "*A normal life is possible for me as long as I am not tired.*"

In Mussoorie, she is desperate because she has fallen back into an ordinary state. In fact, to test her, the Guru has taken her out of the state of santi-dhyana-samadhi in which she was since bathing in the Ganges[30] and, as well, has stopped the blows at the heart that had started in his presence upon her return to Kanpur. Once, at the cinema, she fell fleetingly into that special state again, but it swiftly disappeared.

She must also face tension in the social life of the family who is accommodating her; then, in Delhi, where she meets the sister of the Pandit Nehru and the Pandit himself, she finds herself surprised to be answering him in French, so absorbed, as she is, in a different state; and finally in Benares, where all the young college girls in her residence want to sleep in her bedroom. So it is a great relief for her to return to Kanpur, at the end of October, where the Guru has asked for her presence on the occasion of the visit of the Sufi.

Despite my decision to stay with the Buddhist monks and go to Sarnath, I was acting as if I was returning immediately to Kanpur. [...] I received the letter announcing that the great Sufi was there, and I took the first train.

That year, between June and October, Lilian received six letters from the Guru.

Passages from the Guru's letters

June 13th, 1950

[...] New life succeeds the destruction of the old. The germination of seed takes place with its annihilation. But absence is darkness while presence is light and bliss. Though they are similar in appearance, yet they are categorically different in effect in the path of evolution.

The tingling sensation I have already written to you is "zikar"* or awakening in the body, sometimes accompanied with new energy.

All aspirants are welcome and I am at their service in the spiritual path.

Let us not bother about appearance but go to reality behind it.

There is a wave of spiritualism passing over the world and those who are sanctified to be susceptible catch a glimpse and become interested in its pursuit.

Death of body is no obstacle in spiritual evolution in our path.

The internal peace is often reflected on the face of aspiring practicants. Suffering softens the hardness and melts solidity leading to pliancy.

June 24th, 1950

[...] I am glad you are having a respite: physical, mental and devotional. It is often necessary that incessant strain is relieved in order that the devotee is prepared for further dole. You should not be impatient, everything takes time and comes gradually; development is a slow process and perseverance is the most cardinal virtue. My reverend father used to say that for spiritual progress three factors are essential:

- Inclination and effort of the devotee,

- God's mercy which is ever present for a devotee,

- And kind help of the Guru which also comes as and when desired and deserved.

The start is made by the practicant and the final is also achieved by him with the ever present grace of the Almighty and help of the Guru till the unison takes place, or the finite becomes infinite. You have to go on till that goal is reached. There is no room for hopelessness in spiritualism.

June 29th, 1950

[...] I wish you were less vociferous and discursive and more introspective and intuitive. It is left to the physician what medicine and what intervals he administers to his patients who must not only be patient but more receptive than assertive. You have only to wait and see.

While outwardly carrying on with all the details of life, the devotee never forsakes the ideal inwardly. This is the life prescribed by the seers of ancient times.

In the absolute, there is no diving deep or flying high; profundity is different. It is all the evenness, quietness, peace and bliss. The desired condition comes as a result of long, long practice when nothing disturbs the peace, like the ocean remaining unflooded by the advent of numerous flooded rivers. That is called SAHAJ SAMADHI* ... automatic balance, equanimity. Spontaneity is the highest form of activity. You need not worry about the evils of others. The devotee must observe the merits of others and demerits of one's own self.

July 17th, 1950

[...] Your kind letters, one from Mussoorie and the other from Delhi, indicate internal revolution and evolution. You need not worry at all. The worldly changes do not affect the ever abiding Absolute. The body, mind and intellect are all undergoing metabolic process – integration and disintegration. This is the way of evolution and the devotee, having full faith in the Absolute and the Guide, keeps himself above and unconcerned, watching and enjoying all that happens. This is the play of the Absolute.

I can be of service to you wherever you are; distance is not much of a hindrance in the spiritual world, if the recipient is all right.

July 26th, 1950

[...] Your present condition is a stage of calm in your spiritual evolution. The tingling, or tingling sensation as you call it, is called in our language "zikar." It is a welcome sign.[31]

I welcome all who come to me or are prompted to come, irrespective of rank or position, be it a Commander-in-chief or the President of a country or a poor man of low position.

The Hatha-Yoga exercises are really amusing. But all the same, if your friends are impressed and satisfied, so far so good. Internal peace and bliss are the goal, however they may be obtained.

In the end I must say that there are different phases in one's Sadhana. But one should be all awake in complete awareness and must make all-round progress. There is no room for lethargy or slovenliness in our way of life.

Ever at your service or the service of humanity.

P.S: No doubt distance does not count in spiritual existence, but when the spirit is physically embodied, a physical medium is necessitated, until it is freed from material grosser associations or entanglements. If and when you feel the need of a closer contact, without which you feel uneasy, you are welcome to Kanpur.

September 19th, 1950

[...] By God's grace your progress is satisfactory. I should say that you have approached the threshold now, and in a due course, as soon as this condition settles down and you achieve stability (*sthiti*) in it, you shall have entered unto the first mystic courtyard.[32]

The chakras* of the Kundalini Yoga are realities, but in our path the main emphasis is laid on the activation of the heart (*anāhatacakra**). The rest of the chakras are transcended thereby and become both active and purified automatically.

Your alternate sensations of heat, uneasiness and bliss are the usual accompaniments of the development you are undergoing.

In spiritual evolution there are periods of indifference or rest after which the course is traversed with refreshed vigour. They will disappear and sublimate themselves in due course, leaving you in that condition of spontaneity (*akarta**) that you speak of.

Further intellectualisation of mystic experience is not helpful ...

not because there is no explanation, nor because it is a secret ... but because search for intellectual explanations necessarily involves too much preoccupation with the mental self that the mystic experience seeks to transcend and thus hampers the plenitude of that experience. There are other objections as well to such premature enquiries into these matters. So let things take their own course, and at the proper time all the right explanation will be supplied by your own self for all your experiences.

Emotions (*bhāva*), as we know them, are an expression of separateness. Identity is fathomless and complete quiet, is it not?

Distance, as I have already communicated to you, is no bar, provided the contact between the powerful transmitter and the susceptible receiver is maintained unhampered as is the case with the radio transmitter. Of course occasional closer contacts are essential at periods of profound progress.

You need not go to my Guru alone. He might pay a visit to Kanpur in the coming winter, else I will take you with me there.

In our path concentration is preferred over dispersion.

Passages from Lilian's letters to the Guru

[...] Then, I knew that these waves were coming from you and I was sure that you were sending them to me. I then felt such gratitude like I had no longer experienced since I left Kanpur. I could remember your face and you were alive. Before, I could only see your feet and during all these months, for me, in a certain way, you didn't exist. I must write the truth as it might mean something.

Is it because all of the depth that was discovered within myself is no longer felt? For example, Saint John of the Cross calls Love for God these blows, wounds to the heart.... But I don't call them anything, although the absorption that I feel could be called Love but without any feeling or emotion.

In my heart, there is neither prayer nor gratitude or yearning for God. Maybe it concerns a bhava* that is so deep, so general, permanently underneath any feeling and that cannot find any expression, either in words or even less in feelings.

Just as I am towards God, I am towards you. To me, you are not real, no more than He is. All your śiṣya*, the members of your family and even your older brother that I only met once are real, well established in reality. But yourself, as well as your Guru and your father, are not quite real beings to me. I never saw you when I came for the first time, and since then it hasn't really changed. You see, you belong to the deep zones of the unconscious, whereas our ordinary feelings are only conscious, limited, awakened by people who are the most in touch with our consciousness.

[...] My freedom is as complete as possible ... and I am not attached to anyone; to nothing, although spontaneously filled with love for anybody. Yet I know how to abandon myself to life (the underlying absolute, non-transcendent), and the sea in which I am swimming taught me everything regarding perfect surrender, but towards human beings and in a systematic way, it seems almost impossible for me.

[...] Your second letter was profound. There isn't a single word that did not penetrate my heart. But it's also a difficult letter. Why did Shiva give me the toughest and strictest Guru of India? My pride and my laziness probably need it and your harshness will help me more than all your kindness, because I was too flattered and adored in my life and I have a fiendish English pride.... But it seems that you have guessed everything and I am so amazed by your vidyā*.

Passages from Lilian's diary

May 7th, 1950

[...] I was smiling thinking of the way I have been treating him, teasing him, always making fun of him or his God, insisting on the stupidity or the cruelty of the latter, blessed as He is that I even accept to talk about Him because that's the only way He can existin the human mind. For I don't believe in God – if I pretend otherwise, it is only because I need a pretext to laugh or make people laugh. We never stop quarrelling: Your horrible Jehovah! And I counter with Siva – I talk about the Bible humorously, and Muhammad is my favourite target. He can't help laughing.

June 1950

[...] Does that mean I have no respect? Deep down, I admire him tremendously but what I feel for him is indefinable and doesn't compare with any sort of feeling, expression, emotion – something profound, that is growing, but submerged under a coat of indifference.

June 4th, 1950

[...] In the evening, I knew that my Guru's brother would be there, just for a few hours.... As usual, we were sitting in the garden, in the armchairs, under the trees. My Guru started by leading the sitting, and I was in a very pleasant state of dhyana. Then his brother took over. It was dark and I couldn't make out his features. At that moment, all I knew of him was his voice: it takes you all the way to the verge of silence, again and again. It is soft, faint, and so calm with subtle variations. So I decided to dive into him (but my Guru tells me that this is not possible). I immediately fell into a state of samādhi, or, to be precise, I was in a contemplative state; for about one hour, I wasn't able to come back to consciousness of the outside world. My

consciousness was almost totally annihilated, except for this impression of omnipresent peacefulness and silence (vibhu). As he was talking, I could almost move, but despite all my efforts to come back to the surface, I sank again. His silence was dragging me into the depth of helplessness. It recurred four times. This "four-four time" samadhi contrasted strongly with my previous experience by the subtlety of its softness and peacefulness. A boundless levity. So, depending on the giver, there are different samadhis: the one of my Guru is heavier and more powerful ... which would correspond with my Guru's personality.

It was only afterwards that I was able to see him – but did I really see him? He talked to me with great kindness. He shows an extreme humility and gentleness: all in harmony. The pure type of a well-read person. To get to know someone firstly through the atman, and only thereafter scatter towards the exterior, following his voice, his features.... My childhood's dream! – instead of proceeding from the exterior to the interior. Isn't this the creative path, that of Shiva, the divine path?

June 8th, 1950

[...] What has changed in my Guru during and since his last fever?... I leave aside the expression of his eyes to concentrate uniquely on this mysterious power that transforms from within each particle of flesh. Only an artist painting his portrait would notice it. This is what struck me on his father's photograph and that I was also to find in his brother and his Guru, the Sufi. I call it the divine touch, because it's as if a divine hand would mould, sculpt the face from within, without missing a single inch. In comparison, other people seem only like mere sacks of flesh, a flesh that no spirit has ever ground, worked and thus transfigured. A great sculptor would stop still, filled with admiration at the sight of such beauty.... But this extraordinary transformation only happens on special days of great mystical intensity.

June 13th, 1950

[...] During this week in Mussoorie, I have lost all absorption in God. I can only feel some peace when I close my eyes for a moment – but it is in no way like the peace and absorption that I experienced in my very beginnings, in Hardwar. I am happy, my girl friends are so kind and enjoying my visit. I am not depressed, but I feel terribly deprived of this thing ... wondering what is going to happen to me.

Strangely, I can't remember the features of Radha Mohan. He's in the darkness, whereas I can perfectly recall mentally the features of all his family members and of those coming daily to visit him.

God, the Guru, all is invisible. But I remain confident. I hope that this is just a phase of the cycle. Is God absent to make us aspire more intensely for his presence? Anthropomorphic explanation. But I will not be fooled. I won't cry out to him, calling him in vain. Yet I feel this absence no less than this incredible presence, be it divine or not....

I came here to join my friends, filled with my new joy, my new experiences.... But I am more inclined to remain silent since I have just lost everything.

Nothing was mine. I don't have any power over these special states. Now, my faith is naked, my love naked, totally bare. To be devoid of everything, such is the path.

November 1950

[...] According to the Guru, there is a perpetual three-time cycle: śānti (peace) – sukha (pleasure) – forgetfulness.

Śānti is a fundamental condition, sine qua non. This sort of peacefulness is entirely different from simple tranquillity or peace and quiet, in the mundane sense of the word. It is much more than the absence of worries, the pleasure of enjoying a comfortable life, beautiful scenery or decoration, all desires being satisfied. No, it's a new dimension of the whole being.

This yoga has a dual power: it acts on our sleep and on jāgrat (wakefulness). It seems that the nature of sleep is changing, and that it is becoming progressively infiltrated by the same mystical states that I experience when I'm awake.

Furthermore, jāgrat becomes like sleep during which the divine work is being accomplished in the still dormant depths of the being. We talk and laugh but remain constantly in its sweetness. On the level of thought (manas), we pay attention to one thing at a time, but at the level of our being, there are many other dimensions ... one can smell, act, think, be, etc. all at the same moment.

Sukha: this is how I call this sweetness and penetrating joy that belong inseparably to the body and the soul. It is so great that one loses consciousness of everything else.... It is sweet, stressless, always the same, can last for hours and permeates the whole body. It is also massive as the whole being enjoys it, except for the discursive mind. One can only close one's eyes, not wanting to think any more and even less to talk. One is totally absorbed in it.

Forgetfulness: oblivion is the springboard permitting a new leap and, each time, these states become increasingly deeper until they form a second nature and are no longer felt as such.

Blows or divine touch

These blows at the heart make up the structure, the essential part of mystical life which they control. They are actually the contact between God and the soul. But an intense and violent contact. They create a shock and cause a loss of consciousness. One is stunned, everything collapses and one faints. These blows come either with a sensation of physical discomfort, more or less localized, or such an intense feeling of joy that it cannot be born for more than one second.

To which tradition could they possibly be connected? To "los toques" ["the touches"] of Saint John of the Cross and the spanda of the Trika philosophical system? I need to draw out the specificity of mystical life. It resides in these divine touches, but how to describe them?

First, there's a quiver, this continuous buzzing of the blood throughout the whole body, especially in the fingers, the lips and the legs, and that becomes more intense as soon as one meditates more deeply.

There are these waves of peace, accentuated by the blows at the heart.

There's anguish that ends in a penetrating sweetness of huge waves of bliss. One slightly suffocates and sinks into oneself with successive jolts, losing footing with surges of unconsciousness.

There's the lake of the heart on which we sometimes float lightly, peacefully, for hours, and into which we sink deeply towards an infinite bliss.

There's distress and too strong a shock for our weakness; the bliss melts on the heart but it is so subtle, so intense that I am incapable of bearing it more than two or three seconds; it moves away for a few minutes if I turn over violently when I'm half asleep, but it comes back with the same intensity surrounded with anguish; the hold is too powerful, the embrace so acute that it becomes unbearable although it is essentially pure bliss.

Then, the everlasting foundation of these states is peaceful meditation which is delightful for the body and a deep rest for the mind. The heart often feels very sleepy, an irresistible sleepiness.

If all these states seem divine to me and essential on the path, even despair itself, it is because they induce an immersion within myself, forcing me into a constant state of meditation, and are peace factors.

In these states, there is no opening towards the past or the future; one lives now, enjoys bliss and suffers at the immediate instant; either blocked or desperate or appeased, the modality doesn't really matter, the result being the same.

All the diversity vanishes, losing all of its interest, since I am inattentive to everything other than the strange sensation or impression that overwhelms me and of which I never tire; since a distinctive feature of these states is that they always seem unprecedented and marvelous, one is never satisfied.

I have lived vertically, reaching more and more unconscious spheres, as there are layers in unconsciousness: one dives into one's self and it vibrates just before sinking into the dark, then again one can see just enough to plunge deeper on a new vibration. This is what I call fanā'*(dissolution), as my Guru mentioned such a state one day as I was coming out of it.

One feels good when coming out of samādhi, of dhyāna, but coming out of fanā, one laments for no reason.

Personal thoughts
(In a separate notebook from the diary)

[...] This life, I don't hesitate to call it divine. Straight off, I was plunged into the divine, from the instant the water of the Gangā flowed for me. And now, I don't quite know how to imagine what my previous life was like, that tension and fluctuation that did not permit one second of rest, although I was exceptionally happy, lively, and peaceful by nature.

My certitudes will build up little by little. For the time being I believe in the Peace that I feel, in the divine force that is operating in me, in the prodigious efficiency of the means, the Guru – but whether a God exists, I just don't know. I am surrendering with faith in everything that is developing within myself, but I don't want to be fooled.

I won't create any idol and will, as much as possible, remain cold and devoid of any emotion and enthusiasm. Acute critical mind, "sense of humor," and laughter will be my most powerful weapons. I won't submit to any influence, not even the one of my Guru, except for his great spiritual magic, the one that is beyond, below words, and that is passed on telepathically and at a great distance.

Mussoorie, June 21st, Samādhi and sleep

[...] Now that I have returned to the normal, feverish state of humanity, I am better able to explicate the differences between samādhi and deep sleep – suṣupti*, or more largely, samādhi and ordinary sleep.

Samādhi is both dense and infinitely light. One wakes up immediately and perfectly fit, just as if one hadn't been sleeping.

My sleep is heavy, with a drowsiness that doesn't exist in samādhi sleep; on waking, one feels numb for at least a few seconds, with a clouded mind, and remembers various recesses. I have many dreams, usually bordering on nightmares.

Samādhi is entirely dreamless; it is peaceful, unified. Only, at the beginning and at the end, we go through different zones. When one goes to sleep, one dives into one's self; when one wakes up suddenly, very often one goes through various zones of joy, peace, sweetness, immenseness, but I don't remember in which ascending order anymore because it is too subtle to be noted down. This crossing only lasts two to three seconds. When out of this sleep, one remains in a state of peace of the same nature as during sleep. Very often, one gently floats during this sleep.

For me, at the beginning, this sleep doesn't last all night: about every two hours, it is interrupted by one second of an intense joy, ānanda.

This rather describes a sort of sleep induced by samadhi. It is the unique one that I have experienced during more than two months. I only realized this once my sleep became normal again.

Heavy sleep in the heart, if one resists samādhi for too long, and continues to act, write, talk, and work: after a few minutes one falls in a heap, remaining still in the same position. One sighs to alleviate the weight on the heart. The heart is swollen, heavy with sleep.

Katha Up. IV. 4: the one through whom the Sage observes these two things, the dream-state and awake-state, once he has understood that it is the ātman, the great, the immense, he ceases to suffer.

Finally, all samādhis are only the signs of our weakness. What is important is the state of śanti that goes on deepening from the first day to the last, and in which holes, that are called samādhi, are suddenly dug.

In 1952, Lilian will specify:

[...] This morning, I have attained nirvikalpasāmadhi: not a single thought remained. It isn't the first time, but this occurrence was wonderful, and then I fell unconscious. It's an obscure state, dark, that plunges more and more into darkness while thinking stops. Immobility becomes complete and there is total obscurity, but one is still conscious as one remains, all this time, well aware of being clear-headed and not sleeping.

Sinking into the depths. It must be nirvikalpasāmadhi; it is neither pleasant nor unpleasant ... pure state of lucidity but with a very pale flame like a wick flickering in oil ... it goes out at the end and I was unconscious, but when awakening I had the proof that I was not sleeping; moreover, I have noted more than once the difference between unconsciousness and full sleep.... It is true that my ordinary sleep tends more and more towards this unconsciousness. I would say that it is becoming lighter, its nature is changing, and it is dhyānasing.

Bodily phenomena:

[...] Spanda of the Trika:[33] *Intense and excessively rapid vibration. Spanda is like the intense vibration of the string of a veena. But we need to be two, says Radha Mohan, for the veena to vibrate, and this fills me with wonder.*

The vibration has its centers, along the spine – the chakras of yoga – the most important one being at the level of the heart, but depending on its position, the vibration starts from the chest or the back. There are different rhythms of vibration: one sort is more subtle and with it comes such a delightful feeling, that we are totally vibrating with bliss.

The vibration is still present, but more or less intense; it is at its maximum after a long period of immobility, when slowly starting to move a limb again. Sometimes, it turns into a quiver and a shiver if there is some external interference.

If anyone slightly touches my chair or the wooden bedstead while I'm in śānti or samādhi, or if anyone stirs on the same couch as the one I am sitting on, this movement will penetrate to my bones, shaking me in a most unpleasant way. Whereas in my normal state, I wouldn't even notice.

Example: Mussoorie. I was at the movies: a child was kicking on the back of the iron chair I was sitting on. I did not mind. After half an hour, I fell asleep, absorbed in that wonderful peace: those shocks became a physical torture. They made me feel sick. I have never experienced such an uneasy feeling before; a car trip doesn't produce the same sensation, except when jamming on the brakes or driving on bumpy roads; but it still isn't the same feeling as the slightest contact with my support. But if it is myself that is touched, I don't really mind.

The stages:

According to Radha Mohan, successive revelations:

- *of the Self*
- *of the ātman*
- *of Brahman*

According to my experience (Hardwār, Delhi):

- *I get in contact with my true, intimate Self. Peace, infinite sweetness. Delhi.*
- *Revelation of the ātman – that is to say: this bliss of the Self is spread everywhere, all of nature is imbued with it (=ātmavyāpti).*
- *Revelation of Brahman? Or Śivavyāpti: I am unable to conceive it yet.*

Lilian meets the Sufī

Lilian is in Benares when she receives a letter announcing the Sufī's [Abdul Ghani Khan] visit in Kanpur, and she leaves immediately.

October 31st, 1950

[...] I saw the Sufi who is staying at my Guru's for another eight days. Previously, a doubt kept coming into my mind: if he is so much greater than my Guru, won't he be my guru as well? Now, I know for sure, without any doubt, that I only have one Guru, Radha Mohan. It is true that ever since the first second, and all the time I was in his presence (presence of the Sufi), I recognized his face, his expressions, his most subtle gestures, the slightest intonations of his voice, and this is odd, but I did see him, whilst I have never been able to see Radha Mohan.

The Sufi remains a bit of a stranger. I could watch him, study him, whereas it wasn't the same with my Guru: before even looking at him, I had peace, and afterwards I couldn't see him. I have ordinary, expressible feelings for the Sufi, whereas I don't have any for my Guru. I am also more profoundly grateful to my Guru because I owe everything solely to him.... But he too owes everything to the Sufi! When I saw them together, many things were revealed to me in this respect.

When I was with my paramesthin Guru [the Guru's Guru, the Sufi], *the first time, I didn't feel anything, but the next morning I remained in a state of bliss for several hours.*

The second day I had intense vibrations in my head – it seems that it's the first time – and a restless night. I was dreaming, stirring, turning over, unable to concentrate. In the morning I was less absorbed than usual. In the afternoon, usual state of "ākāśānanta," spacial infinity for hours, and I remained perfectly conscious although my mind was blank; then I fell into a peculiar state (perhaps sleep?) for a few seconds and was awakened by a terrible blow (or explosion) in my brain, violent although subtle, painless.

November 2nd, 1950

[...] After having spent one or two hours with my paramesthin Guru and, in the end, starting to feel somewhat uneasy, I was woken up during the night by an excessive feeling of joy that swept over me, in successive waves; there were about five of them; each one seemed to last about three seconds. The last one caused me such discomfort that I was unable to stand it for more than a second and I suddenly turned over to the side, trying to either forget, or think, or sleep, whatever I could do to avoid it happening again. But during the hours of sleep that followed, I was often conscious of pleasure: a pleasure that continually surfaces while sleeping. No doubt that these few seconds of intense joy were given to me by my Guru's Guru. The vibration is continuous and often of a great intensity; heartbeats are also very strong. Twice, the vibration occurred in a strange way, in certain parts of the body such as the throat or a leg.

November 3rd, 1950

[...] During the night, I woke up around midnight, in a flow of pleasure. The vibration was excessively intense and the pleasure in proportion. It was bearable although, at times, for some obscure reason, I was compelled to move repeatedly, probably to avoid such intensity. And in the morning, it was difficult for me to remember this experience very well as it did not happen at the level of ordinary consciousness. Memory cannot get over that gap (or level). I forgot the essential – actually it isn't really forgetting per se as, if this incredible thing comes back, I will recognize it. But to remember we must be able to form a concept, an impression, in other words structure the thing, and what I feel doesn't have any structure.... Yes, the essential is not a subject of memory.

In fact, such a night is too much for me, and although I bathe wholeheartedly in this great happiness, during the hour or more that it lasts, there are quite a few portions of seconds during which I would like it to stop because it is always on the verge of being too much. Pleasure, joy, bliss, nothing is suitable: pleasure because it isn't intellectual and the body plays its part. Joy, yes, because it is great but without any part of imagination. Bliss? This word might be too much and expresses a higher state than mine. Although, when I experience this bliss, I don't imagine anything more complete, any higher.

November 6th, 1950

[...] It seems that when I'm with the Sufi or with my Guru and they are quiet, I am a veena that needs to be tuned and the tension of the strings is so hard: three or four keys are the chakras along the spine.

After several lightnings, the feeling of sickness begins, like knots that need to be pierced and untied. The chakras spin like whirlwinds and the vibration is intense, but there are tensions, shocks, nervous contractions in the arms and legs. Afterwards, there is peace and the vibrations carry such an extreme pleasure
– but not always: there is often just a malaise. It seems that too intense pleasure turns into a feeling of sickness or that the sickness feeling becomes pleasure.

1951

AT THE BEGINNING OF MAY, LILIAN goes to meet some friends in Poona. After spending seven months in Kanpur, she is physically and morally exhausted. She had to live in wretched conditions, and she writes:

No water, a terrible heat in all the rooms, cat, mice, ants eating and ruining all the food. No comfort at all and this terrible weakness of mine, physical weakness because of my heart condition, and spiritual weakness that makes life a burden.

From Poona she writes to a friend:

I arrived in Poona a few days ago, the extreme heat in Kanpur was making me sick. For the last two months, I have been feeling a sort of pain that makes me moan and roar.... I must have told you this already and that's probably why you are quoting the verses of a Sufi about lamentations that keep the neighbors awake. What used to be ānanda has become its exact opposite and this torture has nothing to do with what I may have experienced so far; it originates from the anāhata* chakra at the level of the heart. My Guru tells me that it will last as long as I live, but it will vary slightly in appearance. It becomes unbearable because of the heat and makes me feel queasy. This is why yogins cannot live in a hot region. This torture also induces listlessness and an overall weariness. Many mystics never experience it because of their different paths. Radha Mohan, his father, and an old disciple are suffering from it or have done so.

I read a book on the kundalinī that perfectly describes everything that I am feeling. Nevertheless I don't have much courage. Saint John of the Cross was right: ānanda* is only a con game, without this blissfulness one would not be able to bear the specific pains inherent in mysticism. It is like an overflow of love that is unbearable for the body, "smooth and exquisite touch of God," says Saint John of the Cross, which, however, is hardly bearable given our own weakness. I notice an extraordinary concordance between Saint John of the Cross and my Guru.

Spiritually, Lilian is exhausted by the strength and the power of all that is being transmitted to her.

It is possible that the contact with immenseness that I have been experiencing these last months has rendered our ordinary, mortal condition unbearable for me.

Between May and September, Lilian receives eight letters from the Guru who supports and encourages her. Despite her difficulties, Lilian still worries about the trials and concerns of those around her, particularly a Sikh friend deeply affected by a cruel bereavement.

In October, Lilian returns to Kanpur where Serge Bogroff is expected, "a well versed and excellent aspirant," as the Guru writes to her before even meeting him.

Passages from the Guru's letters

May 17th, 1951

[...] Too much of dhyāna with little diversion becomes monotonous and oppressive. But there is no room for disappointment or uneasiness as the "devotees do not perish." Nothing disturbs my peace through His grace.

Lilian's reply:

[...] I have received your letter and it's so kind of you to write to me. No doubt that, as you are suggesting, my impatience is the cause of my difficulties, but, once again, it is also your fault as there's no taste for anything else. You have shut all the doors and the Absolute is all that remains. If this remaining eagerness ever dies within me, it will then be total death.

So you see, I am hanging between two worlds. It's my sole link between two worlds: I no longer have any interest in the ordinary world, not even for art, nor friends. And as to the new world, I have yet to discover it. I practically knew nothing about it. So here I am between two worlds with my impatience as a living bridge.

You are wrong to say that too much dhyana and little diversion can become monotonous. No, all I long for is dhyana and I cannot stand being distracted from it. I am unable to enjoy any entertainment, not even swimming, wandering in the jungle, going to the club, or even reading a book or drawing. I can just about read the letters from my family and my friends. This state has settled progressively on me over the past year. At the beginning, I lost all interest in my previous life. Now, I can't stand anything that is limited and that seems pointless and unusually dreary to me, as my mind stops functioning, as indifferent as a rock. Just like when you are giving me a sitting, especially around seven or eight o'clock at night, and once with an ailment at the level of the first chakra.

At eight o'clock my friends pulled me out of dhyana to go to a gala evening. I told them that I wasn't feeling up to it, but they were most insistent. The car made me sick. At the swimming gala, I was unable to move and became very pale. My friends were really frightened. In the evening, I couldn't eat and I spent a sleepless night, like when you give me a sitting. Since then, I've been feeling sick. Do you think that these feelings of sickness result from being pulled out of such a deep state? Is there any danger when you give me a sitting and I remain unaware of what my friends are trying to make me do? In fact I am unable to either talk or move, but after a few minutes (with the help of the dogs and the baby) they manage to wake me up, dress me and comb my hair. Pure waste of time.

The only thing that I do is write down my experiences, like homework, and in a certain way I forget myself, but I don't think that it can go very far without any pleasure.

Other letters from the Guru

June 9th, 1951

[...] Hypnotism is play of the will-power and thus is a very initial stage on the road of spiritualism; it is only the fourth stage of mind. It is up to this stage that most of the practitioners reach in the West. The Muslim saints were more practical than philosophical; as were the British philosophers more inclined towards discursive knowledge and hard facts of life than to real flights of metaphysicalthoughts, while Indian saints (Hindus) have soared high in theory as well as practice, from the ancient times to the present day; but it is true that one has to surrender in total.

You need not worry about these rest periods in sadhana. They are often followed by more vigorous reactions.

July 4th, 1951

[...] My Guru is well and ever lively and full of bliss emanating waves of happiness all around.

In fact you, and hence all your friends, associates and

companions, are deeply religious and earnest: the two qualities of spiritual aspirants (*jiggasu*). It is a pleasure to meet such noble persons, at whose service I am ever ready.

But you must take nourishing food to keep your body fit. You know that body is also His gift which you must take care of. Is it not?

July 21st, 1951

[...] The feeling of peace in Samadhi is different from, and much higher than, mere physical sensation or a state arising out of any kind of tiredness and it oversizes the latter as you have experimented yourself. Your present state of dhyana is better than what you had before, and you have congratulations for your realization of "oneness."

August 2nd, 1951

[...] Thus our practice has the support of the experience of others who lived long before us.

Your aspiration to be always absorbed in your own innermost self is most welcome, but you need not feel depressed or disappointed when you are not absorbed. The real aim of all practice is all time conscious realisation of unity in diversity, a feeling of exuberance and bliss in all we do ... Sahaj Samadhi*. This of course comes after long practices of which one should not be impatient. You have to continue your Abhyas (practices) and the stable condition will result in due course. Thus has been described by our forefathers.

Yes it is true that some people become intoxicated with power and behave like senseless brothers and insane persons do, but that should not be taken as a model of men. They are really to be pitied.

Do not worry about M. X. and his wife. In this world there are persons of great variety which only shows His Greatness and Grandeur.

Spiritual evolution is a matter of long course, and perseverance is required most in spiritual practice. You need not worry about your kundalinī, explosions and knots. All will be well in time provided you continue your Abhyas with earnestness and patience.

August 8th, 1951

[...] I am glad you read ancient literature on Sufism and got confirmation of your experiences therein.

You are right when you value experience more than intellectual flights.

The stage of fanā'* is very high but there is baqā'* after it. Intuition is surely higher than any discursive or rational knowledge.

You have detachment from the world (vairāgya*) and you have also knowledge (jnana*), but you still need practice (abhyas) to have stability in your achievements.

You need not despair or feel discouraged. In due course of time you will feel the real bliss of a saint, which will abide even when you are far distant from the source.

Do not worry about Mrs X. You can safely entrust her to the care of the Almighty who knows the best for her. You know discontent leads a person to progress and ultimately to satisfaction only if one has the benefit of the guidance of an experienced guide.

September 5th, 1951

[...] The ways of the Almighty are so mysterious.

You may tell your woman friend to try to submerge her mind in the heart. I am not very much in favour of drug experiences.

In the realm of the spiritual life, there should be no restrictions and prejudices, and we have to rise above words to their meaning, which, bereft of personal factor, is one in all religions. Expression is bound to be diverse while meaning may be one; this is unity in diversity.

He is immanent in all forms and names and yet above them. None is able to describe Him. One is lost on a slight vision of Him and rises above all feeling of grief as soon he reaches His proximity, such is His Grace.

Passages from Lilian's diary

Serge Bogroff brought a book of poems by Al-Hallaj; I asked the Guru if he could recite one of his most beautiful poems for us; he recited readily but told us that he couldn't sing it like he had just done for another of Al-Hallaj's poems, because he was not in the mood; to be able to improvise, he needs to get into the mystical state Al-Hallaj was in when writing the poem....

A poem sung by the Guru

I came to your street, to your door
In my great misery; looking for that joy, I sought you out.
I desire, I beg it of you,
That which you were accorded.
Enough for you to stretch out your arms and hands
To change my destiny, I know that will suffice.
All has been sacrificed unto these arms and hands.
All ambition of beauty is lost
When my Beloved's beauty shone.
All my worldly goods came to nothing,

Then I saw you.
What did you see? I saw nothing
But the Beloved merged in me.
The lover loses himself in the memory of the Beloved,
Then it is the Beloved who pursues the lover.
The Guru is filled with immortality
Whereas this body is full of poison.
Whoever gives his life to the Guru is right,
Truly, it is not much to pay.
I have experienced all the essences of alchemy
But none compare with divine love.
Enough that one drop of this love should fall
For the flesh to become gold.
Here is the disciple's plea to his Guru:
"Please, forget me not,
Should you have a thousand disciples,
For there are many such as I
But I have no one like you."

Lilian's personal thoughts

(About the way the genius and the saint await):

[...] One must know how to wait. Talent, always alert, constantly keeps one busy.... Only the genius knows how to wait quietly ...wait for inspiration while not really knowing what he is waiting for. Yoga could also be talent's technique: it enables us, at will, to prepare for special states, but the saint has another source of inspiration, love, life, because life knows how to wait and love is all about waiting. True love is so utterly attentive.

An organic and vital preparation is necessary for the work of genius as well as for the experience of the saint, and this preparation leads to an unpredictable and totally unknown experience.

It's probable that the abandonments that the mystics complain about are the result of these long periods of waiting, seemingly empty, but which are an essential subconscious preparation.

In fact, during the sitting this evening, the idea suddenly came to me that grace, from our point of view, and if it exists, is only about waiting; it's the chasm that will engulf the gift....

I talked to the Guru about these things and he was so happy that I understood them. He said that only a few are able to approach such topics. (Yes, love is awaiting and from it comes self-forgetfulness, oblivion leading to the whole.)

The other day I was talking to him about the Trinity. He then confessed to me, his profession of faith: "I believe in God," *he said,* "that's all, the rest is only a matter of tradition." *Decisive words.*

1952

Serge Bogroff

SOME IMPORTANT EVENTS TAKE PLACE that year. Serge Bogroff had come to Kanpur, for only six days at the end of December 1951. The encounter with the guru had been decisive. He comes back in May and June with Marie Bogroff, his wife.

During a conversation with the Guru which recalls all the trouble he has been causing Lilian for the last two years, she recognizes:

It's true, more torment than happiness, but an interesting life. What makes it difficult is this constant exhaustion caused by dhyãnã or kundalini. Without that, the momentary torture would really be easy to stand ... but despondency and exhaustion are the basis of my new life, together with the heat and the lack of comfort, and this is what has been making my life difficult during the last two years. The Guru gives me the maximum of everything, the most that I can possibly bear. In small doses it would have taken years but I wouldn't have suffered from it. What would have been ānanda has become torment; nonetheless, I don't protest; I have to move ahead very fast. (Diary, April 1952)

In March, the Guru's master, the Sufi of Bhogaon, Maulvi Abdul Ghani Khan Saheb, leaves this world. Lilian accompanies the Guru to stay beside him in his last moments. Predictions are made about her that the Guru translates, but of which, strangely enough, she has no memory.

Visits of Westerners follow one another: Father Monchanin[34] who only comes for three days; he vowed not to stay more than three days in any one place. Thérèse Brosse[35] who comes accompanied and equipped with scientific instruments that prove to be useless.

But in June, after receiving the dīkṣā* (spiritual initiation) together with Marie Bogroff, Lilian leaves Kanpur and arrives exhausted in Kashmir, where she spends *"some happy days, rejoining friends in the mountains."*

She presents her work to Lakshman Joo and enjoys amusing him during their study sessions. She is enchanted by the beauty of the lake and its surroundings, while residing on a house-boat for some time, on her own, in an isolated part of the lake.

She makes her first attempts to merge in the Guru with three of her friends, her first "sittings," and each time the results are beyond her expectations: *"But I'm not forgetting that I have nothing to do with it,"* she writes.

During her stay, she encounters a Bengali swami with long braids whose intelligence attracts her, but he is deprived of divine love, hard and curt with his disciples; and finally, Lilian regrets having met him.

Between June and October, Lilian will receive eight letters from the Guru. They echo his efforts to organize a trip to Kashmir of which Lilian was dreaming, of his various correspondences with Serge and Marie Bogroff, of his fluctuating health condition, as well as other worries for his family.

Passages from the Guru's letters

June 30th, 1952

[...] How sad indeed to come out of dhyana and be away from such a state of happiness. But the task before us is to make this state of bliss a permanent feature.

Never worry as to how advanced others are. Your own faith and devotion can give you success over everything. There should be no doubt in your mind about your own power to succeed. In fact the degree of your success depends upon the measure of completeness of your diving and merging in your own Guru. One's faith in one's own power to succeed is of greater importance than people ordinarily think. And then you have your sincerity, devotion and uprightness which count much in this path....

July 18th, 1952

[...] It is really noble to aspire for realisation of God or ultimate Reality and be satisfied with nothing short of this. In fact it is this Realisation which is worth the aspiration of man ... man who has been endowed with the best of abilities and is sometimes known as the best of His creation.

Experiences of aspirants may have much in common and there is no harm in mingling with persons who are aspirants like us and have such noble record of their lives. In fact one learns much in this manner and this may even be necessary and also otherwise useful. Always however our main attention has to be on our centre and nothing but our Beloved should have place in our hearts.

A boat has got to float in water; only water has to be kept out of it.

You write that you are afraid of disturbing me by your concentration. No, I never feel disturbed by this. After all there are so many people here who have nothing to say or to speak of except their worldly worries and sufferings, and it is all my duty and joy to have them and do whatever I may to give them peace and love. I would really fail in my duty if I refuse to be so "disturbed" as you call it.

Only work with complete faith in your power to do things. After all, when we merge in Him, is not His own power present there at work?

Body is for doing work and the more we work for others and suffer in service, the better it is used. In fact even this goes to help us in making our hearts and inner self better fitted to experience the joy and bliss attendant on our efforts to realize Him.

August 2nd, 1952

[...] Your aim at attaining more and more progress is really the thing which one should have and this really matters. I am ever sorry to say that majority of people lack this intensity of desire for progress.

August 19th, 1952

[...] And I am glad to note you are going on well in "dhyāna" and peace. This peace and joy inside is the thing that counts and there need be no worry if body is busy doing some work or other in the world, for work and noble work done through this body is what is generally seen of us here. Being in the world we have to behave in a manner which is good to us and to others.

The peace and joy of heart which one gets in "dhyāna" can exist even when one attends to physical realities of the world's calls and disturbances from around us, and I wish you could for all hours make this state your own. The state generally comes of itself without our making efforts for that: "Aye! I will be content only when He remembers me," said the poet....

Only do not worry for trouble to me. In fact I never feel trouble in doing my duty towards you all. Where there is love and faith, nothing is pain or uneasiness.

September 3rd, 1952

[...] Never worry for my part. I do not feel any trouble on doing my duty towards you. As for health, it is a different matter and I am doing as I am directed.... "Love" has greatest part to play in our development in this line.

Passages from Lilian's diary

[...] Most of the time these last days, since we visited the father's grave, I'm experiencing the same state as the one I was in last May: feeling slightly raptured and such an intense love although without any object.

I can compare it with the way I felt a long time ago when the one I had been in love with for many years, without any hope whatsoever, and whom I wasn't seeing and purposely avoiding for this reason, unexpectedly declared how much he loved me upon a chance meeting.... That day, his behavior, his strange invitation proved it to me, and the following days his words confirmed what did not really need any confirmation.

For two days, I was giddy, filled with wonder. Anything that could happen afterwards did not matter much and I knew that nothing could happen because I did not want it to, but the surprise and the certitude brought such a sweet joy upon me, wiping out past and future.[36]

What I'm feeling is similar but without any reason nor object and the rapture is greater and more complete, more regular because the purpose, if it exists, is within me. This is why I think that it is a great love, because it reminds me of the other love ... and it is perfect satiation and fullness. One cannot desire more as it is already a bit too much, and out of time, in an eternal present that stretches out to infinity....

... Yes, my human love was hopeless, without any expectation, worry-free; it had to be experienced hastily as well as peacefully: in haste because days were numbered, but endless peace because it had no end. Here, this new love only has the appearance of peace, and my eagerness and impatience give in when it manifests itself. It drowns all eagerness: eagerness and fullness, two alternating poles which are calling and responding to each other.

Last night, he was suffering a lot: disciples massaged him during the sitting. I asked him if, in his system, the greatest crime wasn't for a disciple to kill his Guru! He agreed entirely, oblivious to the trap.... "But no disciple wants to kill his Guru." Oh, I said, conceitedly, there are different ways of killing, one is slow, unerring.... Then he smiled. But I'm looking for a means to stop him. Every night, it's too much and I'm worried that he becomes paralyzed like his father. But what is there to do? Even if I don't go to the sitting, he will go on nonetheless, as distance is of no importance.

Serge Bogroff complains not to be able to concentrate on the Guru because he has totally forgotten his features. Same thing for me. The Guru says that he too experienced the same kind of phenomenon with his own Guru; one can never recall his features or physical appearance ... isn't that strange? It is an absolute void.

During those days [of the Bandhara, January 30 and 31] *there was a large assembly and I was treated with great affection; I am truly part of the family. One of the important disciples said that I would become a great Guru and the Guru did not deny it.... But I just couldn't care less; it didn't arouse an echo in me ... I am not even riled up. Any shadow of personal behavior within me seems to have disappeared....*

... In the evening, a two-hour walk with the Guru and four disciples; we walked a lot and on the way back the Guru slowed down; he would have liked to lie down on the road, and if the pace is too slow, I start to totter. Neither of us could hardly stand up ... I was feeling completely drunk, as a result of the Guru's continued presence today.

While walking, he told me that in terms of ānanda*, he too was not favored – like for me, it is rare – but that doesn't matter very much, as if ānanda is without obstacles and difficulties; it is *like a one-legged man; consolation, hope, ananda aren't an end in themselves and can become the greatest obstacle for whoever stops and delights in it. Such is truly my opinion.*

Passages of letters to Serge Bogroff

[...] No, you don't have what you call "universal love," but a sort of very soft rapture, like mine, which makes us totter. I only experienced universal love for three seconds, stealing it by chance from the Guru: and it is something so incredible that it seems impossible that you could experience it without giving it greater importance. It is neither love, nor universal ... it is beyond words.

[...] I was watching three disciples for three seconds; they were no longer themselves but something else (maybe Śiva) and I too no longer existed. I had no feelings for them and at the same time, on the emotional plane, it was like the discovery of the child, who, watching some men, says to himself "humanity." I was amazed, filled with wonder ... and then no matter whether one adores me, or another kills me, it had no importance. But I have already forgotten everything.

Death of the Sufi

Then came a telegram announcing that his Guru, the Sufi, was in critical condition.

Lilian accompanies the Guru to Bhogaon:

[...] He has remained totally numb for four days, with cold hands and feet. Which sort of insensitivity is it? He was lying on a dirty bed but he was so beautiful! Although his body is nothing but skin, and bone, the face is replete, appeased; the temples are hollow, no wrinkle, thin nose, delicate mouth, strong chin. He is

blind but his eyes were pale like his son's, which I think were grey, and the complexion was like that of a European; I was very close to him, and dared to look at him. I was shooing away the flies. Then, he started to moan, to make efforts to vomit; he recognized the people, talked a little. He is in terrible pain....

For the first time, the Guru found that he was weak, as previously it had only been a question of physical weakness and his spiritual power was unbearable. But this time?

Hour after hour, he got better, was able to eat a little. He inquired about me, and told me that he was praying for me to reach my goal. He asked for the Guru and my instinct told me to go as well: I arrived at the very moment when a great thing happened: I could guess without really knowing, but the Guru was happy to have me by his side. The Sufi told him things that he never had the opportunity to say before, and along with the words there was something else, perhaps of a mystic nature.

The Sufi gave this last advice to the Guru before dying (for my benefit):

"People won't accept your path as you have been taught; adapt yourself accordingly to time and people."

Indeed people wouldn't put up with remaining unconscious for eight days like the Guru did. There isn't the same courtesy towards the masters any longer, whereas in the past one wouldn't say one word in their presence, or ask any question and there was no reproach: "total self-effacement." But this politeness isn't indispensable. Only love counts, and it is generated according to the capacity of the heart which receives it.

At three o'clock we left for home, and during the journey back the Guru confided much to me, expressing all his love. He told me that if the Sufi dies, it will make a big difference for him and his work because he draws a lot from him. He knew that he would live a while longer. In the rickshaw taking us to the station, he wanted to be on his own in order to meditate and find out whether his trip was necessary, and he knew it.

He also told me how the Sufi and his family's hospitality was so perfect and attentive; they keep offering us meals while noting that he was not partaking. This is true, but he is welcoming and hospitable, only his wife and sister-in-law are less so, and since they are the ones who prepare all the meals, and not him, the result isn't very pleasant. He suffers from it without really understanding the reason for this lack of hospitality, which in fact he largely ignores as people don't complain about it.

After the announcement of the Sufi's death

Thursday evening, March 6th, 1952

[...] I went to visit the Guru earlier than usual and there, I learned that the Sufi had died. The Guru was silent. I sat down beside him and remained silent. We were in a deep state of dhyāna: it was the great waters, infinitely still, without a ripple, but samadhi was more dense and gloomy than usual; this calmness lasted for hours. An hour later in his bedroom, the Guru cried a little. On the train, he said to me that his Guru's death would be dreadful for him and that he would not be able to go to his funeral. His disciples announced the death to me right in front of him. But half an hour later, he wished to tell me himself, with such sadness, he said: "He passed away," *then* "now I am an orphan." *Natural father, spiritual father, both are dead. "Orphan" made me smile a little, at fifty years old. But I can only imagine how hard it is to lose your Guru, as there is no other love like that.*

My state? I am not deeply affected, but the Guru's pain flows automatically through me. There's a trickle in me coming from the Guru, like oil that is imperceptibly dripping and spreading, permeating everything; oil of love, of softness, anointing oil, which also insulates, detaches from everything else, pale oil, iridescent oil, it has various aspects and its flow rate also varies, but it rises little by little.

I'm a boat that is taking in water and sinking slowly, especially if my dhyāna gets deeper. Suffering that only affects the subconscious and flows from the unconscious.

Note the Sufi's last words to me before his death as well as in the garden in Kanpur:

"Follow my boy. Never leave him. He will lead you to the goal."

He prophesied about my future ... but did not clearly say what it would be.

When the Sufi was dying: I was watching him, on the edge of the abyss, lying, so peaceful.... He was neat and refined, and two days before his death he asked for a comb and combed his beard.

April 1952

[...] This morning, I was saying to myself that I was like an exhausted, terrorized woman, who is being carried through the furnace by her Guru. In fact, she is even too tired to be appalled and doesn't worry about either the place where she is being taken or how she is being carried; all the time, she's a bit unconscious and sometimes totally unconscious, in a dead faint because of the excessive danger and the horrors she is going through.

Everything is too much for her and she shuts her eyes, surrendering. She doesn't know if the one who is carrying her knows where he is going, but she doesn't have enough strength to walk by herself and she has faith. So yes, exhaustion, indifference.... It is true that there are delightful moments of rest, but because it's a long and terrible road, she actually refuses to rejoice, to stop. But this isn't out of laziness as I cannot walk on burning firebrands or on water. I must be carried and I don't know anything about the journey: I do all I can to avoid paralyzing my carrier and increasing his burden, but I suffer to be such a weight for him.

1953

Year of trials: bereavements and mystic night

Lilian loses her mother in April, and Serge Bogroff dies in September.

In Kanpur, during the winter, Lilian manages to work, but by springtime she is exhausted by the difficult living conditions, no comfort, no friends to help her and, above all, a succession of mystic states, sometimes terrible, in which the Guru plunges her. Therefore, she is in a hurry to leave for Kashmir, despite the Guru's incitements to delay her trip, as he knows that she is going to have to deal with troubles.

Nonetheless, Lilian sets out ... and everything goes wrong. "A wall" rises in front of Kashmir; she must turn back to complete bureaucratic formalities in Delhi. It is there that she finds a letter sent from Kanpur announcing her mother's death:

It was as if I were morally blind, I just couldn't understand, I was hoping that it was a mistake.

Lilian returns to Kanpur, where she goes through painful days before heading back for Kashmir, where she will prepare her trip back to France. When she sails from Bombay on September 27th, she is in such an internal state that she neither misses India nor desires to return to France. She wanders around the ship like "*a ghost,*" indifferent to ports of call, and arrives in Marseille on October 10th.

She learns of Serge Bogroff's death upon her arrival in Le Vésinet, where she finds a letter from the Guru in her mailbox, and also from Ida, a neighbor and childhood friend.

The eight letters from the Guru of that year are addressed, for one part, to Kashmir, and the other part, to Le Vésinet. The first ones are about some travel plans to Kashmir and France, the second ones cover the beginning of what she calls *"her mission."*

Passages from the Guru's letters

April 18th, 1953

(Announcement to Lilian of her mother's death)

[...] It was on the 16th in the morning that we received a wire about the illness and this morning about her death. Believe me, I am one with you in your bereavement, but it is at this moment that our sādhana* is put to test; you will not be upset at all.

May 16th and June 1st, 1953

(The Guru starts to address administrative requirements for traveling to Kashmir and France, but his health is not good.)

June 3rd, 1953

I am always at your service and would welcome your friends when they call upon me. All through last month, I was remembering you, though physically we were apart, yet I was spiritually with you. I am glad you too felt the touch.

July 4th, 1953

I have a place for all your friends in my heart.

Always try to get yourself absorbed in your Guru. I am

always ready to serve you and your friends in any way you like.

From a worldly point of view there are so many worries with me and around me, but I assure you I am full of peace and bliss.

July 10th, 1953

Apparently we are at a long distance, inwardly it is not so. I am glad that you are feeling so.

October 4th, 1953

(After Serge Bogroff's death)

The day Mr. Bogroff left this world, his pious soul came to me. I found him quite happy.... No doubt his heart was full of love and service.... May his soul rest in everlasting peace in heaven. He is with me. He will always remain alive by his good actions. People whose heart is full of love and service never die.

October 22nd, 1953

[...] You know it is difficult to express what I feel for you and dear late Mr. Bogroff. You are appointed there. You are at liberty to do whatever you like for the benefit of the people....

Please never be disheartened. In this world everybody is to die. Now you prepare the field there, and I can be there at any time you like.

December 8th, 1953

(The Guru expresses a great sadness over the death of Serge Bogroff.)

December 12th, 1953

[...] I am fully satisfied to know that you always remain in contact, though from the worldly point of view you are at such a long distance from this place....

In the night get yourself merged in your Guru. In the day try to serve people spiritually. Never be disheartened. World is full of worries. One has to face whatever comes before. Let the time come when you will know what you are.

December 24th, 1953

[...] It is very good if one can remain in "dhyāna" while working.

I do not consider that it is very necessary for all to reach the highest stage of realisation, though it will be very nice if they can.

Even one or two, may God grant them that stage and power, can be sufficient for spreading this mission.... I will be leaving Bhogoan tonight and hope you will try to catch waves as they pass from here....

It will be good if they can meet you oftener (the persons that you mentioned to me) and I have hinted them to do so.... After all, we have a great service to do for all ... at least as many as we may.

Apparently it is beyond doubt that you are so far away, but in the heart of hearts it is quite the opposite case.

Passages from Lilian's diary

[...] I would have liked to be alone with the Guru so that I could talk to him: during three and a half years we've never been alone, even for ten minutes, except while walking in the crowd of Kanpur or in a rickshaw.

I wish that he could give me some instructions about his path: he speaks so much in Hindustani to the others. But he told me that his father and his Guru never spoke to him but would send him vibes while they were taking care of other people's minds; and whenever he spoke, he automatically expressed their thoughts or rather they spoke through him.

Passages from various letters

[...] A few days after writing this letter to you, interested as I was to take note of various mystic experiences, I received a letter from Jacques Masui[37] asking me, with great insistence, if I could start writing a book about my experiences which he would publish in his Documents. And while I was holding his letter, still unread, in my hands, our Guru was telling me that his great desire would be that I write about my experiences so that his father and his Guru may be known.

On the boat back to France:

[...] I would like to note what this night has sui generis but I am not able to. It's the other side of this extraordinary state of bliss which also cannot be described, and right now I'm constantly alternating from one to the other, as dhyāna is common to both of them.

At the moment, on this ship of mediocrity, the music is horrible, alternating between screeching Indian film music and occidental Casino music, but I'm so indifferent that I just don't move.

Yes, at this stage it would be so nice to be on my own, in the middle of nature, preferably the desert as beauty doesn't really matter.... Not doing anything, never talking, constantly meditating (Fathers of the Desert), that's when we get away from everything, and there is really no merit in it or any asceticism. It is nonetheless a mystical state. In the heart one has a symphony that is too subtle to be heard, and we would have to stop, remain silent, peaceful, perhaps, to be able to enjoy it, figure out some chords or rather echoes, but this is just impossible to do, there being so many disturbances and such excessive noises that prevent us from hearing these internal rhythms, so vague yet so penetrating....

Neurotic state, yes, if it wasn't for this positive subtle counterpart, but it is so subtle, so inexpressible. I exclude from it all the wonderful mystical experiences of the past, the joys, the nearly physical sensation of pleasure, everything that I'm describing which is clearly and fully perceived. No, I've entered another phase where everything went quiet, except for the outside noises that just don't interest me anymore. And new internal chords are being tested, but it is too distant and deeply felt; I can't hear anything, or is it a symphony that only consists of a few keys, as if the musician was only touching the instrument without producing any sound, but we know that something is coming up. We would like to listen.

I really find my example so boring. I'm only writing out of duty.

To be perfectly honest, I should add that this prelude to a symphony, if there really is a symphony, bores me.... Its subtlety eludes me and I am not making any real effort to go deep down into the depths where I might hear something ... thus constantly feeling contemptuous of myself, and that's where there is the most subtle torture: fear of deeper samādhi. (Diary)

1954

Lilian spends the year in le Vesinet but prepares her return to India during its later months. She is recovering painfully from last year's bereavements.

After her stay in India, which lasted nearly four years, she must put her affairs in order and deal with all kinds of formalities, so she complains of not being able to get absorbed in herself, except *"in moments spent waiting, in trains and the metro."*

But the experience of transmission grows, becoming more and more important. Spontaneous transmission to friends around her, while watching a movie, for example:

I was sitting next to Gretty and instantly I fell into dhyāna, that particular state where one can give, and Gretty felt a great deal. She lost her sense of Self; she stopped feeling her body as a searing heat rose up her spine to her nap ... it lasted a long time.

The memory of that film session will remain vivid. Lilian liked to evoke the amazement it caused her, for long years thereafter.

At that moment, it's a consolation *"because those days, I was so miserable that I couldn't absorb myself in my Guru and yet the moment one who is ready sits next to me, I'm automatically transformed into an instrument, without wanting it, without effort."*

Lilian discovers the multiple and inexhaustible aspects of this mysterious life; the states of being vary, depending on the friend who sits next to her ... they are subtle, violent, gentle....

Passages from a letter to a lady friend:

[...] This emptiness is fundamental: It's the framework on which all mystical states are woven; this is what, in my mind, characterizes mystic life, separating it from a pious and religious life: no emptiness for the pious man, but states of amorous and joyous exaltation, while this terrible emptiness marks the mystic.

Śūnya, ever increasing vacuity, is the essence of Buddhism and what makes it a mystique, the rest being rather morality ... the same vacuity to which you refer in your letter concerning Saint John of the Cross. Patanjali in his Yoga Sūtra defines samādhi as "the absence of all mental fluctuation." Yoga too is, therefore, built on this same emptiness. Muslims have fanā', no baqā'* without fanā'*, emptiness. The arid desert of the spiritual Wedding.

Only the Upanishads talk about plenitude and I'll try to show you that it's the same thing (hoping that you will soon feel it). It's as if something very positive was digging holes in you just to better fill them in afterwards [...]. This void of all sensitive and mental operations is essential because you enter a very new domain, like a night, where nothing familiar can guide you. This is why a guide is necessary. At the beginning it feels like emptiness, but in reality, it is fullness, only the mind is not sufficiently refined to be conscious of this too subtle life. Saint John of the Cross talks about the Israelites who, used to rough food, remained insensitive to the delicious taste of celestial manna. Little by little, this emptiness becomes softness, bliss, and takes on all forms of mystical life.

When this emptiness has become fullness, again a new phase of emptiness becomes necessary (dig deeper to better refill?). The plenitude digs ever deeper, one even falls into painful nights so much so that this emptiness is absolute nothingness: ordinary life loses all meaning and mystical life offers none.

Then, again, fullness returns, more intense than in the previous cycle: unless a wondrous love fills this void. It seems to me there is a cycle of regular phases, but I do not know if it's the same for everybody. Try to make sense of yours.

So, it's all the same, calling and answering in mystical life: harmony, gentleness, love, emptiness, plenitude, etc., these phases follow on from one another automatically; the Guru probably has the power to shorten the phases. But these are just passing states; one should not get attached to any one or the other, nor indulge in depression when the period of emptiness and annihilation comes around, because that is what permits the jump forward (one step back for two steps forward).

This darkness, that Saint John compares to a light that dazzles and blinds you, forms the essence of progression, but without a guide, as the study on the Carmelites showed, you could stay there all your life. Personally, there is nothing to be done about these phases: just let them come and go.

As for the "influence," as you call it, it is not necessary that you feel something. The deeper it is, the less we feel. During the first years, I was in a normal state as soon as I was in the presence of the Guru: the rest of the time I was as if drunk, immersed. So I was writing letters and pages of philosophy in his presence. It's better not to feel anything.

What's important about acceptance of the influence (actually, there is no "influence") is our meditative attitude, vigilant, forgetting oneself, without expecting anything in return: this intense fervor, without purpose, supple, is inaction in a sense.

Have I already given you this example? You want to visit a virgin forest, wonderful and dangerous, and you fully trust your guide: so you will have to imitate your guide, watch his every gesture, hide yourself when he hides when there's danger, become silent suddenly in order to watch a bird....

You will be totally absorbed in your guide, always available, even to halt abruptly or run. You will develop an extraordinary instinct permitting you to divine his intentions, and little by little you will function as well as he in the jungle. But he who only listens to himself, his desires, noisily, with panic and irritation, will see nothing of the forest and will displease the guide who won't take him with him. The Saint is he who always watches for the will of God in order to surrender to it fully.

This example shows very clearly what is the inactivity of the disciple, in the Taoist sense, inactivity that is compatible with a series of efforts and an often tremendous efficacy, but this is not ordinary effort. One great secret is to find the right effort, that supple intensity. Some have intensity without fluidity, others have fluidity without intensity.

As for emptiness, you will see that it has an infinite variety of forms [...]. It is for you to discover and tell the Guru without fear about your doubts and surprises.

Try to concentrate without desiring emptiness too much either! Relaxation rather than concentration. Intentional desire (Vedic, kratu), that's the danger. Because what we want is absolutely not the mystical life which is sui generis, which comes of its own accord, so unexpected and unimaginable: the wished-for goal is so much beneath what you will get; so desire without object, and you will always find your way!

The Guru rejoices to see friends gathering around Lilian and that will be at the heart of their exchange of correspondence that year during which Lilian receives about nine letters.

At the end of the year 1954, she meets André Padoux and his family. In this regard, André writes about meeting Lilian:

"It's in New-Delhi, where I was posted, that I made her acquaintance in 1954 and we started a relationship, at first professional (she oriented my research towards the work of Abhinavagupta, then helped me prepare my thesis), and then friendly and caring, extending to our whole family, lasting until her final days. She was to us a loyal friend, a support in difficulties and sorrows: we found in her an assistance that went beyond everyday problems...."

Passages from the Guru's letters

January 20th, 1954

[...] I am glad to know that gents and ladies like to have company with you. This is not a question for a day or two.

Please go on serving, having no idea of compensation in mind, our service is all for Almighty. Everlasting peace is an ornament of a human being.

February 27th, 1954

[...] The annual Basant* Bhandara* is over. This time more people attended the function than was expected ... it was the double of last year's attendance and so were the expenses. All the time during the function there were waves passing and people tried their best to catch them whenever they might. You too appear to have caught them.

I have not seen people coming there unless we are all one ... ever united together in the bigger and more permanent realm of spirits. May they too avail the utmost out of these opportunities.

March 25th, 1954

[...] It is so good that people there are taking so much interest in this path. No doubt this is the greatest service we can to do to humanity.

Dreams are sometimes indicative of our mental condition and good dreams which concern holy saints and prophets show that one is passing rather a holy and healthy mental life. It is all a good sign, though not the best state....

I always take in my fortune to help anybody in the path as much as I may.... It is all due to the lotus feet of my Guru and revered father, as well as by the grace of God. I always remain glad and peaceful.

April 20th, 1954

[...] For progress of those coming to sit with you, you should have concern but no worry. Much depends on one's own keenness.

It is love – selfless love for all that could raise sincere men to the condition of mystic.

I am happy to learn that so many people are taking interest and feeling the joy of His remembrance. I congratulate them all for their sincere efforts and wish them every success.

Physically the distance is great, but when all lovers are linked by force of love, we are nearer to each other than by physical bodies.

May 26th, 1954

[...] I am happy to learn that you are working so hard and the mere fact of having served so many people in this right and noble path should give some satisfaction. These who have intelligence and understand are in some senses better than those who follow and cannot understand.

Pure love and eagerness to learn a thing is of great help, but understanding also assists one in keeping steady on a path and so if Mrs. X and others ask you questions, do not worry. By and by they will be satisfied, their doubt and questions will get their just answers as these people take more and more interest and walk with eagerness and sufficient steadiness in this path. Force of love too may at occasions give them silence. It is good when one feels inner strength and happiness. Much depends on one's own belief in his or her own strength to do a thing successfully....

It is good of you that you pray for me. You must do it often. There is nothing wrong in prayer. God listens to all who approach Him with sincere heart.

July 11th, 1954

[...] Let things take their turn. It is also good if one can use his time in the service of humanity, in meditation or remaining near the Almighty in the midst of so eager people as you have there. It is satisfying to learn that all those coming there take so keen interest and are so anxious to attain progress. They are all welcome here.

We are not all very far off from each other.... It is hearts and love that matter and not physical distance.

August 8th, 1954

[...] When you come here, I shall no doubt be glad to be at your service – all of you – for the utmost period it may be possible.

A lot of credit goes to you for your sincere efforts there, and it is the result of that so many people there have such a keen interest in this path. One has to face a lot of worldly troubles when entering into spiritual life. It requires a long period of life, but I should say, to be devoted the whole life. For the last several months I am under a lot of financial troubles and worries. At the same time I am always glad at heart.

1955

DURING THAT YEAR, LILIAN LIVES IN INDIA, mainly in Kanpur, but she also makes several trips to the Himalayas and Benares.

Her return to India was spoiled by the presence of Mrs. R.: *It's as if Mrs. R. had poisoned my life, her spitefulness perverted everything. May I have as much love as she has hate.*

Lilian is bewildered, disappointed, in a state of uncertainty:

Finally, the best moments are when I merge in the Guru to give to others, but at the moment there aren't any "others."

Mid-January, Brij Mohan Lal, the Guru's eldest brother, dies in Bombay. He dies while in "samādhi," the day before the wedding of the Guru's eldest son.

He too would give samādhi to his disciples. The latter experienced a new, wonderful state, but on coming out of it, they noticed that their Guru looked strange. He said to them: "I'm feeling fine but I'd like to lie down and rest." And he died a bit later, alone, without their knowledge. It's very sad, as a great and very wise master is passing away.

Lilian liked him, found him handsome, with wide eyes shining with love, gentle by nature, refined, subtle and very cultured; but she regretted that he had tried to shake her faith in the Guru and would keep the nicest room of the house padlocked *"while every centimeter was so precious for the guests!"*

Lilian used to tell that one day the brothers had organized a "samādhi contest": the Guru won. She appreciated the particularly fine and subtle resonance when "diving" with the Guru's brother, but it was always the same.

He would compare the state of fanā'* and then the one of bhairava to a diver: at the first dive, one doesn't see or hear anything, and is unconscious of everything; then,

Brij Mohan Lal

little by little one stays longer and more freely in the water. Finally, there are some remarkable divers who stay submerged for hours and are able to see, hear and organize their liquid universe; such is, after turya* and fanā'*, the turyātīta* or state of bhairava; although submerged in the Absolute, they are acutely aware of the phenomenal world; they don't come out of the sea anymore.

In 1952, regarding the two brothers, Lilian wrote:

The elder brother's samādhi is subtle, of an infinite softness, one feels so light, it all happens at the forefront of the mind; it can be compared to the subtle and nuanced singing of Elisabeth Schumann. The Guru's samādhi is more powerful, profound and inwardly stirring, like Marian Anderson's organic singing.

The Guru's son's wedding took place eight days later, but *"cremation or marriage, the Guru is always in the same state."*

During this period, Lilian is discouraged, she doesn't see her Guru regularly but *"He's so beautiful! And what a greatness! I must admit it, even when I'm unhappy. He also has the right word, the profound word, original and unique.*

He has the kind of genius that I admire. He always goes straight to the point, the essential: which is God, he does not forget it. But I do forget.... It's only when I lose myself in the Guru and forget even the Guru, that I move towards the Thing or follow it a bit better."

In the spring, in Kanpur, Lilian finishes the correction of her thesis, "Instant and Cause," published later in the year, but presented four years earlier.

I'm going through a happy period, each morning I go in the forest, near the ponds, to proofread my thesis and it's an enchantment.... A velvety atmosphere, sparkling water, but there are prowlers.

The Guru is multiplying the sittings. She writes: *"I am drunk with so many experiences,"* but her body is exhausted by the strength of the currents and her participation in the Guru's physical states.

In April, Lilian leaves for Kalimpong, district of Darjeeling, meets the Dass family, travels with a friend, Denise Delannoy, and works a lot. She observes that too high altitudes have a negative effect in terms of attaining inner profoundness, which is recovered below two thousand meters. She receives most of the Guru's letters during that period.

At the end of September, as soon as Lilian is back in Kanpur, the Guru pursues his task, and Lilian finds herself submerged by the superabundance of grace:

It's a sea that is engulfing me, with its successive waves.

Later she will write: *"I'm just about drowning, I'm suffocating, the problem with this lineage is not to continuously think of God, but rather to forget him."*

Between November and December, Lilian travels with a friend, Odette V., to Benares, where Lilian meets a Sanskritist Gopinath Kaviraj,[38] and they visit the places where the Buddha had been.

Lilian rediscovers the pleasure, that she thought she lost, of visiting India. At the end of December, once back in Kanpur, she goes with the Guru, his younger brother and a few disciples, to visit the graves of the previous masters.

Passages from the Guru's letters

April 22nd, 1955 (Lilian is in Bengal)

[...] You should never feel aloof from me. I am always with you....Please pray for me.

May 8th, 1955

[...] Of course, everybody has his or her own limitations, but if there is an open mind prepared to receive what is good and right and to modify oneself accordingly, there is nothing to worry about. Many things can be done by right efforts and many more by prayer.... I am praying for you all and you should also do the same for me.

We may just avoid feeling pangs of difficulties if we can have the right attitude towards them. And then difficulties too are transitory!

May 12th, 1955

[...] Really, you are quite right. Your doubts are sound.

I am really sorry to say that my heart could not throw clear reflection upon you. As soon as spiritual love begins, the whole worldly attachment becomes dry.

The experience of the great man is that, in this life, when real progress or advancement begins, the world and worldly things become dry and go away, off from heart and mind. By and by one remains aloof from action in life. It takes time and thus one has to devote his life. Doubts are usually created here because self is going to disappear or is merged somewhere. The mind with all its activities tries to win and defeat bliss (ānanda) or other things of the way. I tried to adopt the same course or system that was done by my Shri Guru Maharaj [the Sufi, Abdul Ghani Khan]. By grace of God you have seen him many times. You also remarked that he never used to speak to me much. He never scolded or showed his anger to anybody except this humble self. He never gave me sittings as given now to the people....

I assure you that I have not seen or found any better man than him. No doubt he possessed extraordinary Godly powers. There is a Hindi couplet of Mirabai who has been a great saint, the translation of that is given here in my words: "I shall adopt the same course or way by which my beloved attracted me."

Please don't fear for your good self or for your fellow brothers; now a quite new system will be adopted for your people (Westerners). I shall try to change the course according to your liking and I am sure of the success.

July 10th, 1955

[...] Our duty here is to keep our brain and desires in the right mood and line and not get perturbed or swayed by storms of difficulties.

He cannot be formed by practice, by learning, by power, etc. but whole-heartedly by devotion. It is always coming from heart to heart. At such stage, doubts do not arise.

August 6th, 1955

[...] Household worries are so much after me that sometimes it becomes difficult to face them.... One can meditate alone. Spiritual improvement depends upon deep devotion. What you have experienced during 4-5 years towards spiritualism, people coming to this place for the last 20 years have not been able to understand.

September 21st, 1955

(Account of his unsuccessful attempts to go and join Lilian in the region of Colonel Dass.)

Passages from Lilian's diary

[...] In the morning, dhyāna full of sweetness with a culmination of successive dives in the unconscious. I stay with the Guru as of seven o'clock in the morning until noon. In the afternoon, I sleep as if I was knocked out. Then I work and at around five o'clock, I go back to the Guru's and stay with him until eight or nine in the evening.

I'm going to give my own distinction of the different samādhis:

Samādhi of stupidity: I am there, open-mouthed, empty mind, with a key in my hand, the lock to be opened, but understanding to put the key in the lock is way beyond my capacities.

Samādhi of emptiness or diving (although I could make some distinctions between the two), it's the one in which the caves are full: there is no thought. Unlike the previous one which is made up of unconsciousness, the samādhi of diving is made of consciousness (but without thoughts).

Samādhi that fulfills, that nourishes, that fills with soothing satisfaction. It's the one that I'm usually experiencing these days. It is so delightful, so sweet, settling in little by little, (slowly) although at the limit of pain.

Samādhi of wholeness. You are satisfied and full of peace.

Samādhi of ananda, bliss, with delightful and steady vibrations. It finishes as it started: and here again, without any new thought.

Samādhi of love: the one I prefer. We're raptured by an aimless love without object. Full samādhi might only be emptiness, but when coming back to consciousness of oneself and the external world, everything you look at becomes marvelous, the bird, the dog, the child, the Guru. You are a mass of sweetness and tenderness, and your whole being is lost in love, outside of which the eyes are closed with a peculiar expression of inner laughter.

Samādhi of atipūrna, the overflow, the fully cruel one, in which the samadhi of plenitude of full love and bliss seems to disappear, sink in, and lose itself. Surely (without any doubt) it's the best one, but you're wailing (bellowing), screaming (yelling), whining constantly. The heart is heavy, burning, but is it samādhi? A spiritual and physical torture, but not mental. It isn't always thoughtless, although you are unable to divert your attention from the pain, even for a second.

Shall I add the samādhi of infinity or ākāśa? You're floating, so light, lost in infinity, not only spatial, the limits disappear. As sometimes it is without any thought, I call it samādhi.

I didn't want to learn Hindi-Urdu so that nothing would disturb my nirguna* meditation – neither a sound or a form should interfere.... I wanted the essence, completely bare.

Passages from Lilian's letters

[...] When I was in France and we were meditating seriously, I was shaken as if by a strong wind, bending forward then straightening up, and so on.... Was it my imagination? Impossible to fight against this force. The Guru told me that's the way it always is: he too receives the divine influx (al-faïdh, grace?) and distributes it among the disciples he has appointed. So each one is shaken in this way. But near him, we never experience that.

These days, an old man from the school, fellow student of my Guru's father although less ardent than him, lawyer in Kanpur and a great mystic poet of India, became quite fond of me and comes every day to meditate with me. He gives me a lot too, but I don't know what it is, as the essence is always indescribable. Like me, he jerks about: it's the waves touching the heart, and a stronger one makes you swoon; fortunately, a jump relieves the tension. This is the divine touch that Saint John of the Cross talks about. The Sufi calls it "touch of love."

The Guru was telling me that if we could touch, only once, this wellspring from which he draws himself, it would be sufficient for life. This very morning, he was explaining to me that we first receive the flows of love from the Guru.... When the disciple has within himself the source of this love and no longer needs to receive it, he then becomes a Guru.

Another letter:

[...] If you haven't felt anything much in Kanpur, don't be surprised, as feeling isn't what is essential. In my case, it's after a few days and far away from my Guru, that I was suddenly immersed in a wonderful state. Maybe it's more durable. I also know another person who had only seen my Guru once, and who, a few years later in France, was immersed in the same peace as the one she had momentarily experienced in Kanpur.

It's likely that my presence has a certain influence, as I just need to merge in my Guru to be like him. As well, I'm at your level so I can give spontaneously, whereas the Guru has to come down to your level and it isn't that easy. What I find marvelous in this system is the possibility that we all have to give to others – at the movies, even my male and female friends become semi-unconscious. I even have an amusing example: a friend of mine, who is not very advanced, gives extraordinary peace (that she doesn't have all the time) to an attractive young woman who, for years, never saw me, and after meditating with me when I was back in France, did not receive more than from my friend.

To her brother:

[...] Life is an inexhaustible flow: we are constantly projected beyond ourselves into the future by a vital instinct of prodigious strength. Our fervor projects us into the future like a springboard without our stopping even for a second; even during sleep the impetus is there, projecting desire and thoughts that accompany it, forming the waves and agitation of the sea of the vital river. But we only become aware of this if it all stops.

Mystical life is a general slowing down of this flow, and from time to time – in samādhi – its complete stoppage, but only for a short period of time. The saint, impassive, is a master of arresting this flow.

As soon as the flow stops, we experience an extraordinary peace, and, once in a while – always? – a bliss that is ordinarily never felt – as if we were sinking into very soft cotton wool.... Again, there is here a variety of different states: sweetness, vibration producing a nearly physical pleasure, bliss of the soul itself – annihilation which is only peace. When again we bathe in this sweetness, we know that this is reality itself, that life is nothing else but this bliss, this infinite peace, but we are spoiling it with our endless desires for anything except this Essential which fully satisfies the desire....

Lilian notes in her diary:

[...] Here is what I wrote to him: I'll note it here because it will be useful again and I am not sure whether it is correct. It's an explanation of a moment: I must keep it. Later on, I'll smile about it.

1956

IN KANPUR, THE YEAR STARTS OFF BADLY, with the birth of a hydrocephalic child at the hospital, the Guru's grandson, who won't survive. On this occasion, Lilian rises up against the status of daughters-in-law in Indian families.

Lilian is in a state of depression linked to that of the Guru's *"because I love my Guru so much, I want to share all of his sufferings even physical, his financial and other worries, but this time, it is just too much for me."*

So she decides to leave for Benares, while, at the same time, deeply regretting it. *"Even when very close to the Guru, one feels so lonely, and he is part of my soul."*

In Benares, Lilian enjoys once more *"the gentleness of Indian crowds"* and meets again the famous Sanskritist Gopinah Kaviraj who greets her with indifference.

Back in Kanpur, she attends the Bhandara; she experiences an acceleration and the Guru explains: he is not depressed but at the "galloping stage." *"At every moment, he jumps forward and it's unbearable for disciples who, like me, are following him step by step."*

Passage from one of Lilian's letters

[...] The other day, I understood what was prakāśa*-vimarśa*, my usual mystical state, but I had never made the connection. Prakāśa is what dominates in dhyāna and shines on its own in the nirvikalpa-samādhi*: Imagine a castle, fully lit, that one would go through without seeing anything, in a constant flow of light. Vimarśa is awareness, I watch this, that, I think, I recognize, I orientate myself.... In ordinary life, vimarśa completely covers up prakāśa, yet the latter is still there, otherwise we wouldn't see anything, but we never perceive this beautiful light for itself; we are only interested in illuminated objects.

In my ordinary state, prakāśa with its peace, its silence, is at the forefront and often absorbs vimarśa: awareness doesn't come easily near the Guru and yet consciousness remains.

Afterwards, she prepares her trip back to France where she arrives on April 7th, after one month on the boat. Difficult trip:

[...] Inner death, inner silence of death, but peace swamps everything.... Nothing can trouble me, neither the thought of the ones I am leaving behind or the ones I am about to see again, but at the same time what a peace, what a break!

In Cairo, encouraged by her cabin mate, she rides a camel all the way to the Sphinx: *"We had a good laugh, as my cheerfulness is still there."* In France, Aliette joins Lilian and they both go and spend two weeks in the south of France before getting back to Le Vésinet.

Lilian will receive about eight letters from the Guru that year. The Guru informs her of the wedding of Durgesh, his eldest daughter, and the joys and worries that it entails. A girl's wedding is very costly in India and the Guru doesn't have much money. As always, he relies on Providence, without ever asking anything of anybody. "But God reacts at the last moment and it's just about enough ... useful but stingy!"

For the Guru, it's a succession of all sorts of worries, illnesses and a fall.

Mentioned are the names of Philibert, whose visit is awaited, and Munir Hafez [Islamic specialist, 1911-1998] whom Lilian was so delighted to meet in 1954.

A message comes back continuously: the impatience with which the Guru's close circle is asking for news and Lilian's return.

At the end of the year, the Guru himself cannot hide his own disappointment when learning that her return trip was delayed.

Passages from the Guru's letters

April 7th, 1956

[...] Now you might have reached France. You know well I never express my feelings. I have been praying for you to be quite happy during the days you were in journey.... Oh! life is very short and one has to do much. May God bless you with every success in life....

I am fully satisfied because my 'God' has always been kind to me. Please pray for me....

May 26th, 1956

[...] The marriage [of Durgesh] was a grand one. Every moment people were feeling the Grace of the Almighty. I was always surrounded by the pious souls of my parents and Shri Guruj Maharaj and other Superiors.

God is so kind to me that nobody has been able to come to know as yet from where such a great expenditure was done. You need not worry. My life is full of struggle. One must face all the worldly things and troubles.

My dear Lilian, the time is not very far when you are expected to be surrounded by a mob all the time. One who can get himself absorbed totally and permanently in the Guru all the time will surely reach the Goal. I am very much impressed by the gents and ladies who come to you. All seem to be in a good mood. Now you may judge very well for yourself. Progress is always with the intense love and affection.

June 17th, 1956

[...] During the last week I am sure you might have felt something more because I remained totally absorbed in you for a long time. Nothing is supposed to check spiritual currents. Such waves can be and are sent from one corner of the world to the other. If the receiver is quite good, a saint can transfer all sorts of things. This is what I have come to know by my Superiors and Gurus. You please go on diverting people towards God or to gain the constant and everlasting peace. The more there are worldly worries, the more one goes higher and higher. You are appointed there to spread spiritual mission.

It is a fact, unless one forgets self, there is no possibility of advancement in this line. Whatever you have written in your letter is quite true. Really there are few people who follow the path according to the system, and it is beyond doubt that it mostly depends on the spiritual guide. Your satsangis* are good. If they really take interest, you please go on giving them sittings and also try to circle their thoughts with your hidden spiritual power. Thus I am certain out of them one or two will be a true follower.

July 24th, 1956

[...] One should always remain prepared to face worldly troubles as well as anxieties. Such things divert the people and take towards the spiritual goal. He who enters the spiritual boundary is welcome and he who crosses all the spiritual worries and troubles is more fortunate. One can pass this stage only by the help of a spiritual guide. Such sorts of things are used to coming again and again. Unless one becomes a master, there is a danger. It is the reason a true follower becomes a devotee of a spiritual guide (in other words, Guru).

You are appointed there. Please go on working without any desire and you will be successful…. Some people have got natural instinct and so they are turned in no time, and some take time.

You may go wherever you are invited, but please try to spread the experiences you have obtained.

September 5th, 1956My dear Lilian,

The reasons of such quietness are quite clear. It is not strange you fell down and got hurt. It was to happen. Thank God you escaped. The system in which we are all ongoing is full of love and it carries us towards the Goal through the worries, troubles as well as dissatisfactions….

There are very few people in this world who really want peace and bliss or pleasure, and among them some follow the path or doctrines. Fortunate are those who get themselves totally surrendered. Really it is a pleasure for me you are improving day by day. If anybody comes to you having faith, no doubt he will be benefitted.

It is a fact that the dead body of a saint does not spoil for a long time. Some say that there is never decay. Only advanced people do realise this. If you did not feel anything on the tomb of Saint John of the Cross, it matters little. There must be some reasons. Sometimes saints are not in a position to come to know anything about the saints or people who have left this world.

I have spoken to you many times on this point. Have regard for him as he is supposed to be a great man of his time in European countries.

Convey my message to them that without personal satsang* it is difficult for one to reach the goal. A spiritual guide must be very strong. He ought to be a master of transferring all the things coming in this path. Without faith, a spiritual guide is always helpless.... The best thing for human being is to realise Self....

You are appointed there. Please try to carry them towards peace and bliss. By their writings they seem to be very noble and kind. May God bless them and others with keen desire.... Only by the Grace of Almighty one can face all the difficulties.

September 24th, 1956

[...] I am astonished to know you are not improving. There is nothing in this world to check spiritual currents. Most of the time you are remembered and you also feel your presence here. Sometimes it so happens that one does not think towards improvement. Society is also a great cause of it. You ought not to be disheartened. I assure you the spiritual things once experienced fully well are never diminished. No doubt constant satsang is very essential....

You are never supposed to destroy the order and likewise you have touched my heart by writing so. If you do not get sufficient time for meditation in the day, please try to get yourself absorbed in the night. For this, night is very important.

One thing we must keep in our minds: all the spiritual progress depends upon the experiences. For this we will have to search and select an experienced and realized person. Only nearness and pure love of such person, take toward the goal. Nothing is important but constant satsang and love.

The real thing, when time comes, is gifted, as it is beyond the power and skill of a human being to obtain....

May God bless you with all your hopes and desires in this world as well as in Heaven.

Please go on praying for me as well as for every soul.

November 5th, 1956

[...] During the time of my illness I thought of you much. I am sure you might have felt it. Here everybody is feeling your absence.

No doubt the worldly worries take us toward the spiritual Goal. Peace should never be disturbed, this is what is obtained or experienced with the spiritual guide. Really it requires constant satsang. You took notes on this particular thing many a time. Sometimes direct currents are used to go from this side. Try to receive them. You may please instruct all the satsangis there to remain in receiving mood. Such things are very important....

December 9th, 1956

[...] I received your affectionate letter. I am very glad to go through the contents. One who tries to merge all the time must receive the currents.

Really you have tried to understand the system. It is all and all love. What is in the heart of heart never can be written in the books, although the learned people have tried their best to explain, even then it remains secret. The Grace of satsang can never be explained. It is to be realised. The people of this age think that reading of books and idol worship is the main thing and there is nothing beyond this.

The sitting is not given to everyone, and it is not for them who are narrow-minded.

It is a fact and one should not doubt that God is very kind to the poor people if they remember Him in heart and never forget. Please go on praying for me.

I remember Miss X. and also your other friends. Those who come to you are mine....

Passages from Lilian's letters

[...] Here, from all points of view, I live in vismaya* and camatkāra* [wondrous awareness and wonder].

However, the first years are the most wonderful, because it is a continuous succession of unprecedented newness. We are all the time in rapture.... It is the same thing for whoever would suddenly discover the Himalayas after the desert heat. The first climbs are magnificent, the view of the mountain tops.... But at high altitude, one feels lost, weary, until one gets used to the mountains.... The wonder is at the same time less frequent but also much deeper. It is no longer a question of amazing discoveries but of life or death. (March 2nd)

I don't want anything else but God and I don't want God at any price....

About the question of a visiting Western friend: "Is your Guru omniscient?":

I had never asked myself such a question, because it is true that he does know many things that we ignore, is able to see the future, the past, read inside us at will, to go for a walk in Paris and come back with such comic and personal impressions that there isn't any doubt that he actually went there (the Concorde bridge: he notes the way people dress, men's and women's overcoats having the same length, etc.); nevertheless, he isn't by any means omniscient.

Just before my friend's departure, the Guru described to him everything he had experienced during these three days, in an even better way than he could have told it himself. Consequently, my friend decided in favor of his omniscience!

Personal notes

Majorca:

[...] Same desolate state, its extraordinary regularity over the past few years should be noted. It is as stable as my peace. This morning, for the first time, ecstasy while snorkeling. As a matter of fact, my meditation is profound all day long and there is a sense of well-being in my body. But all the rest bores me.

In India, when I was submerged by this same desolation and it was very hot, without any comfort or pleasure whatsoever, with no beauty, I would dream of Spain, of the sea, the freshness of the breeze, of skin diving, of the scent of pine trees on the beach.... It seemed to me that if these conditions were fulfilled my happiness would come back....

Being here all together, as a family, in this dream place, carefree, I must admit that my distress is even more complete than it has ever been, since I now know that nothing can ever lighten it: we have seen magnificent cliffs and a purple blue green sea. I slept under the pine trees, in an exquisite softness. I swam among the sparkling fish, the seaweed and the octopuses. But it's like in the Himalayas, facing the snowy peaks ... like in Kashmir, on the lake full of lotuses, and its silky and velvety mountains.... Nothing can offer me the slightest consolation; nothing anymore penetrates my being's superficial external shield. Nothing, other than ecstasy.

Tonight, I was going up a hill to have a higher view on Pollensa-Puerto, but I knew very well that I would hardly look once I reached the top, or if I contemplate a sunset over an infinitely calm sea, the charm won't be able to reach my heart. So I understood what is happening to me, what I don't want to admit to myself, as it would go beyond the premises, take a step forward that my honesty does not permit, but psychologically I must admit the fact, if from another point of view nothing has been proven. I am in the same state as someone who is dying of love for a departed one or an absent beloved. This is the way Spanish saints describe their state. But in my case it isn't latent love of mature age, as I have been fulfilled last year and even the years before, and just recently by a handsome Spanish man who was more than willing. No, I'm not thinking about a man, not even about my Guru, as beside him my pain is the same.

I don't want ecstasy. I don't want this bliss that fills me anymore. I want the Being at its source, and refuse all of its presents; it is He only that I want. But it's the Unknown. And I want him non-stop, and since there is nothing I can do to get him, I'm distressed and longing and not moving forward towards him. He dug caverns just for himself inside me, but he doesn't fill them up. All the rest gets lost there like an atom in an immensity. I'm not trying much anymore to cast atoms around to fill them.... In this world, I know that there is no more joy, as I've had a taste of a Bliss that extinguishes all others. Isn't it one of the most cruel situations that can possibly be, such an absence, full of presence or rather presence which is equivalent to an absence?

1957

LILIAN RECEIVES THIS YEAR'S LETTERS from the Guru in Le Vésinet from where she will be leaving for Kashmir at the end of August.

During the first months of the year, the Guru is very seriously ill. Lilian is informed by Raghunath Prasad, a very close disciple of the Guru, who sends her two letters. His case is considered hopeless; it is a desperate situation: "He was as stiff as a piece of wood and completely unconscious for two months." But his Guru appeared to him and to his wife, as well as to his brother, to let them know that he was going to recover.

In this regard, we can recall that the Guru once told Lilian that he had died twice, but was sent back by his Masters because his task wasn't finished.

In February, the Guru is so weak that he can't even be carried to the location of the Bandhara: "Without him, you can understand that the Bandhara is lifeless, but nonetheless, we had to celebrate it, as Bhai Sahib[39] desired," wrote Raghunath Prasad.

The Guru continues to suffer from several health problems: ulcers, fevers, various inflammations. Doctors are recommending a year's rest; he cannot resume work, which weighs heavily on his financial situation that is going from bad to worse. He is waiting for Lilian.

In September, a letter from Portofino, Italy, arrives in Kanpur; it's from there that Lilian leaves for Kanpur and Kashmir via Bombay.

Later, she will often recall this short stay in Italy together with Philibert and Gretty, as well as Ida and her husband; it's on that occasion that they met Padre Pio:

We didn't feel anything either during the Mass or during the day, even though we were next to the confessional; he seems terribly sad and pretty tough. What a difference with my Guru! But the stigmata are clearly visible during the Mass that he celebrates remarkably well.

In Assisi, it was something else; Lilian and Gretty are overwhelmed at the top of the stairs of the Basilica of Saint Claire, and Philibert, who is mocking "all this is silly nonsense," falls, his heart on fire, with intense emotion above Saint Francis' tomb. He will regret for the rest of his life having been evicted by the caretaker at closing time.

After ten days with the Guru, very weak physically, Lilian takes refuge in the high mountains, to complete some work for Louis Renou, the Guru's presence being so hard to bear.... But, she writes: *"as soon as I saw him again, I was filled with wonder by his kindness, this undefinable spiritual thing that makes us touch something divine."*

Letters from Raghunath Prasad

February 1st, 1957 (The Guru was very ill)

[...] Even in his unconscious state he muttered out your name several times and remembered you. He is too weak even to speak, yet he asked me to write you all about him.

February 27th, 1957

[...] You know, when the physical strength goes down, the spiritual side gains strength. The currents were so strong that it was nearly impossible for me to keep straight in his room. Everyone passed into samādhi.

Only a few were allowed to attend him. The currents were not confined to the room only. They went far off in this world. It is therefore no wonder that you were receiving them....

Passages from the Guru's letters

March 24th,1957

[...] After a long and serious illness I am writing you this letter. My fingers even now are shivering. However, I have made up my mind to finish it.... From a worldly point of view, I was quite unconscious for three weeks. In the end the case was declared altogether hopeless. By the grace of Almighty and due to the lotus feet of Gurus and Superiors, the soul came back in the dead body.... No doubt these are very hard days. God may help us to bear all the troubles....

My illness has proved a boon to me from a spiritual point of view ... you please go on praying for me. There is a great burden upon me. I also wish to retire.... You were and are always with me.

April 21st, 1957

(The Guru is still sick, abscess and fistula.)

[...] I am very thankful for all your satsangis brothers and sisters. It is only God's gift that they are so much inclined to this System; let time come and they all will be benefited. I pray for all. These days, currents are going rapidly. One should receive them. You are by the grace of God appointed there. People who come to you are fortunate; they are sure to get peace and bliss.

May 7th, 1957

[...] My illness has become very long. Doctors say that I must take rest for one year at least. Physically and mentally I have become very weak. By the grace of God and lotus feet of Gurus my heart is very strong. God is so kind that peace is never disturbed, although from the worldly point of view, you can only understand under what circumstances I am going on these days....

It is all due to your good and generous heart that such nice people are coming to you....

I think you care much for me and this is the reason that you remain in sleepy mood. Believe in Him. One day you will be on a highest stage. I am always with you. Always try to get yourself absorbed. Say my B.C. *[bon souvenir]* to all of your spiritual brothers. One day, I shall be there.

May 15th, 1957

[...] It cannot be explained in words how eager I am to see you and all your spiritual brothers....

Life is short and much work is lying there to be done.... You ought not think for any sort of complication. Every thing is for the best ... I am always with you. All the satsangis brothers and sisters must believe that I am always nearer to them and one day I will be there. Must keep in mind that such sort of people are always seen worried from the worldly point of view. This is one of the main reasons that they reach the highest stage. This knowledge is transferred from heart to heart. They are fortunate, those who take part in the life of a saint.

June 5th, 1957

[...] It is a fact that from a worldly point of view I am passing through hard times. I thank God, I am very glad. My heart is free from all these things. Spiritual currents are regularly sent. Please try to receive them.

July 11th, 1957

[...] I am glad to know that you are expected to be here in near future. Your company is very pleasant.... It is over beyond imagination under what circumstances I am going on for the last several months. It cannot be described how He is kind.

We people never trust on Him. We always try to put ourselves in many shapes before the public. This is first and foremost thing; we should forget ourselves and merge in the spiritual Guide. Indeed this requires unchangeable affection or love.

I am very glad to write to you that unknowingly you are found merged. When one comes at this stage, one cannot grasp the ideas. Now you require constant satsang. God is helping and you will be here in near future. He has left me in this world for some work. From the worldly point of view I remained unconscious for more than two months, but at the same time I was as conscious as soul is supposed to be. At that time, many a time you were with me and always with the same spirit as you have always been.

I fully remember your friends and try to send the currents required. They are all nice. I have got also great feelings for them.

September 11th, 1957

[...The Guru received a letter from Lilian, sent from Italy. He is looking forward to her forthcoming visit and informs her of the death of a son of the Sufi.]

1958

AT THE BEGINNING OF THE YEAR, LILIAN lives in Kanpur and also stays in Benares. She arrives in Kashmir early April where she is happy to work with Lakshman Joo. The Guru would like to join her there but encounters insurmountable difficulties: one of them being his medical condition and the need for a traveling companion.

Lilian's greatest concern during this period is the organization of the Guru's trip to Europe. To start with, a travel authorization needs to be obtained for France and Belgium.

However, the Indian government requires exorbitant financial guarantees. Many Indian people, who had left India without any resources of their own, had to be repatriated at the government's expense. *"It has really become difficult to obtain a foreign passport."*

Lilian concentrates all her efforts on resolving this problem: first of all, having to go through required procedures and formalities, and putting up with Indian inertia; there is also the need to find a discreet benefactor who would leave complete freedom of movement to the Guru in Europe; and finally, some worry remains concerning the Guru's capacity to adapt to France and that of France to the Guru.

My Guru is a peasant of the Middle Ages, with rough manners, who blows his nose (albeit ecstatically!) in the tablecloth.... I can't imagine him in a salon.... In addition, he has great contempt for women, and I want him to recognize the value of the Western woman.

Lilian will come back to Paris in September, exhausted and fed up with all the discomforts of India.

"I think that I will only go back to India chained to the bottom of the hold or in the belly of a whale. If I go back of my own accord, it's that I am a great saint – unless it's to have the Guru pull out the harpoon he has embedded in my heart!" she writes to a friend, in the spontaneity of an intimate correspondence.

It will be two years later before she returns there, and not in the belly of a whale, but of her own will in the cabin of an Air France aircraft. What shall we conclude?

There are ten letters from the Guru dating from that year. Six were sent to Lilian in Kashmir and four to Le Vésinet. They are full of his unwavering serenity despite the repeated attacks of the disease and recurring financial problems, and express his full trust in Lilian regarding her mission toward the people who come to see her or will do so in the future.

Passages from the Guru's letters

April 13th, 1958

(Lilian is in Kashmir "for a few months.")

[...] One thing I want to tell you, that you must never feel worried of me. Thank God no trouble with me.... You see life is very short. One must realise Self....

May 6th, 1958

[...] I received your letter when you have left Delhi for Kashmir. I understand that you are well and quite happy there. Under the circumstances you need not to remember me as well as in this place. I think the table is turned.[40] I passed my time with my revered Shri Guru Maharaj for more than 20 years like this. You have also done his Darshan. It is a fact that I have not been able as yet to find any equivalent man like Him....

From worldly point of view I am never happy and from spiritual side I am always cheerful. The grace is always with me. I wish the whole thing be transferred to you.... One is supposed to face, as well as bear, the worries, troubles and difficulties.

May 30th, 1958

(Very hot weather, bad health of the Guru, difficulties for the trip to Kashmir.)

June 14th, 1958

(The Guru has an abscess on his face, suffers from the heat and "There is an unbearable pain in the back on the right side.")

July 1st, 1958

[...] It is quite true, I would have never gone to Belgium or France without taking you with me. My mission is there only through you.... No pay, no other means, even then we are passing our time comfortably. I am sure God will help me. His grace always remains with me. You see worldly worries are only for short time. They do not affect much....

If the grace of God is with us, I shall try to put you in new stage. I always try that my troubles and worries are not transferred to you, since you most of the time remain absorbed, hence everything is transferred.

Please go on praying for me. Really life is short and much work is lying to be done.

July 17th, 1958

[...] I am sorry that this time you are not receiving clear currents. Sometimes I have been in nice mood. The fact was that from worldly point of view I was going under troubles and worries but that was only physically and mentally. It does not affect the heart and soul. Constant satsang is most essential. I think from spiritual point of view you are not happy there. There are so many things which cannot be expressed. They are only transferred from heart to heart.

September 14th, 1958 (Lilian is in France)

[...] A man is supposed and expected to bear all sort of sufferings which come before him. I have been trying to remain with you from the spiritual point of view. You will feel so. I am sure others will feel like us.

October 10th, 1958

[...] It is a fact, the worldly anxieties and worries etc. do not affect my heart. My brain is also not disturbed. There is some effect by and by on my general health….

I am glad to know about Mrs. Gretty's state. She flew in air. She saw her body below; it means she felt that something was quite out of her body. She enjoyed it very much. At the same time she suffered and was eager to come back in her body. It is very nice stage. Her soul went out of the body. She can progress very steadily. How good it would have been if she was here or I would have been there. She has not seen my physical aspect. You may realise well how her heart is for me. For this you have been deputed there. People who are beyond whim will practically realise.

You should never think that you do not know this or that. Everything is within you. You are related with those pious souls who have merged in Almighty. I assure you, I always think of Mrs. Gretty, Philibert.

There are other men and women, brothers and sisters whose face comes before me in Samadhi. I think they will also come to you. Sometimes I think of you all for a long time and, in the good state it is, tried to be merged. This was the reason you felt so many queer things....

November 20th, 1958

[...] I always think of you. I am sure you feel the same. Every satsangi there is charged through you. I assure you and please give assurance to all the satsangis, one day I will be there. God is kind and manages the whole universe. You remain very busy. How good it is if everything is done with meditation. It is not difficult for those who know how to merge in a spiritual guide. This is the first step and one should be accustomed to it. I do not know why there is an idea in my mind that your younger brother and sister would be benefited without the least effort of the currents that go towards them. They do not receive because they do not know the method. You are appointed there. People who will come to you, I assure you, they will be benefited.

December 31st, 1958

(Bhandara of 25th, 26th, 27th December 1958)

[...] The Grace of Bhandara* cannot be explained in words. This time was the best one. Everybody and whoever was present there felt the same thing. Beyond thoughts and whims direct currents were coming there. World and worldly things were far away from mind. The whole atmosphere was full of love and bliss. Everyone was feeling so.

The gathering was more important than the previous one. I wish you were here. Oh this world prevents us from all good things and right actions. I am sure you would have meditated during the Bhandara days. Many people enquired of you during the Bhandara days. Your circle of acquaintance is very large. Everybody wants to be your friend.

As bad ideas from evil people, bad smell from flowers etc. is transferred, just like this, good things from good people are transferred from heart to heart. This is a secret. Only those people who come into contact with a saint can well understand.

Take the mission all over the world.

A letter from Lilian to a lady friend

To A.C., April 1958

[...] But I'll try to explain the complexity of mystical life:

Imagine that all your life you've been going round in circles, thirsty, feverish, in a suffocating heat, jostled by a cantankerous crowd, restless, in a bitter and pointless dispute; there might be a smile here and there, but you can't even stop for a moment and smile back.

All of a sudden, not knowing how, you end up in a magnificent cathedral. It is peace, coolness, all thirst is quenched. Everything is beautiful: but it's dark, you can only guess things, poking around, but you are feeling so well that you have no desire whatsoever to explore this huge place. And there is a very gentle presence that brings you all that you wish, a wonderful voice. All misery is forgotten. Outside noises are muffled.

From the threshold of the cathedral, you try to attract others describing as best as you can the peace and the coolness awaiting them. Little by little, this presence reveals itself to you, but at the same time you feel a bit lost; if the presence doesn't manifest itself, you suffer, you're longing....

It's a whole new life. You confide in others up to a certain point. At first, you only describe the cathedral.... Like a young lady who describes the wonderful ball where she met the one she loves, without ever mentioning him to her friends. But after the engagement, she will talk freely about him, describe the gifts he made, but without mentioning their mutual love. Once married, she will confide even more, describe their trips, etc. But still, she will keep the essential to herself.

Mystical life is richer and more complex than ordinary life; it has its depths and its more superficial zones which aren't those of love: such as the kundalini, the physical impressions coming from peace, everything that is safe to be served up for public consumption. It's like entering into the cathedral, a new world of harmony and extreme subtlety.

But this is only the threshold of mystical life. It's only the entry into oneself and already, it is extraordinary. When bounced around and tortured in the crowd, one couldn't think of anything, or love anybody. In peace, one is entirely available: one can give oneself to love, stop in order to love, and dream of the one we love. It's like good health for someone who would be ill. Then only can we do a lot and in peace. In fever and pain, the effort taxes too much, it becomes feverish, we think we're doing a great deal, we're restless, and confuse delusions with lucid thinking.

Does this give you an idea of what is mystical life? It isn't a religious and pious life that keeps on deepening; no, it's a new register of the being, a totally new realm into which we are precipitated in an instant.... We feel that we must inform everyone, at least all the ones we care for. So they know that there is something very close. Even though, I loathe all propaganda, the missionary spirit.

We don't profane this domain by talking about it due to the very fact that we have nothing to say about it. It's like telling a deaf person that we went to a concert and listened to such and such piece, without dwelling on the acoustic pleasures that were experienced....

Love only is sacred and secret, and here again all mystics have sung it, even the Christians. For a long time, I was shocked by the erotic or secular tone of both Persians and certain Christians, but it isn't easy for them to express themselves differently, if they don't want to be dry and bland.

Another letter to A. C.:

[...] Mystical life? Based on my experience and the very ancient treaty that I am translating, it's as if we could see a beautiful sky through a fine black wire netting which would represent an infinite variety of figures: hen, dog, house-boat, and we would be convinced that the sky is just this infinite variety of images that is very close, when in fact it is only pure undivided consciousness and boundless bliss.[41]

In the same way, because we only want the limited – in love, in knowledge, etc. – we're continually cutting up the wonderful reality – unique – into thousands of things, and we exhaust ourselves going endlessly from one to the other. Any pleasure experienced is nonetheless the infinite bliss underlying the wire netting (like blue is the blue of the sky) but cut out, limited, miserable. The knowledge of each object is really the light of heaven (consciousness), but so fragmented that it has lost its glow.

Same thing for life, for infinite love, as there is no other life, no other love than this Reality. But we see them so split up that they lose their meaning, their greatness, their unity.

However, each time it is Reality that we vaguely see, as without it the wire netting wouldn't stand out against a bright background and would be invisible. The wire netting is arbitrary, whereas

Reality is unadorned.

Certain beings, saints, great artists have a wire netting that is less cut-up, larger; narrow-minded beings only have a tiny corner of wire netting, with an unlimited number of pieces cut out.

There are two possible attitudes: either we are extraverted and are constantly weaving a network, or we are introverted, and it is the entrance into mystic life, but it is so rare. If it only happens for one second, the wire netting disappears and we can see the big sky and its infinite, dazzling light. But we can only have one or the other: either Reality or the wire netting and its artificial cuts, although there is, here and there, a one and only reality that is universally called divine.

The book that I am translating cites one hundred and twelve means of attaining this reality and break the netting. Either we stop the activity generating this grid at its source, which means that we prevent any desire or limited knowledge from appearing –or we concentrate on one desire, one knowledge, any object, or love etc. in such a way that we only look at the sky through a single hole while all the rest of the wire netting disappears, and through this hole we can see the beautiful pure sky, since the grid is no longer perceived, but it is only for a short time. Nonetheless, a breakthrough has occurred ... we understood, we do not forget, we were bedazzled. A bit like the sky, the reality is pure, simple, grandiose, infinite, luminous, unique, peaceful, and sweet. Should add love and bliss, and also that this marvel is captured in us, the netting separates us from ourselves – and also from the universe....

This comparison that I have just contrived for you will serve as a preface to my book, as it explains things quite well.

1959

LILIAN, IN LE VESINET SINCE SEPTEMBER 1958, will spend the whole of 1959 there. She is eagerly awaited in India in the autumn but, finally, she won't be going.

From this year, there remain around ten letters, all permeated by a deep and intense inner closeness which has nothing to do with geographical distance.

The Guru encourages Lilian and incites her to devote herself to her mission. He worries about Aliette.

Lilian works on the *Vijñana Bhairava* and receives friends.

This year, the wedding of Lilian's brother, Oswald, takes place, and there is also the death of an aunt whose estate will cause a lot of embarrassment to Lilian and Aliette. Their aunt had been drawn into dubious schemes by a swindler and the nieces had a difficult time dealing with this. The Guru reassured them.

In June, a son of Ravindra [the eldest son of the Guru] is born.

The Guru and his close circle seem to be living in expectation of Lilian's return to India.

Passages from the Guru's letters

February 17th, 1959

(After the Basant Bhandara*)

[...] The gathering at the time of Bhandara was more than previous years. The villagers were in great number. Arrangements had to be made just in time.... I wish you were here. Nearly 80% of people inquired of you.... I think you must have received the Bhandara Grace, you seemed very near.... I was in no state to lie down on any side before Bhandara. Only, just a day or two before this pious function, I found myself quite in a position to work.... It is wonder there was no trouble of pain as well as tiredness. I was so empowered by Almighty....

March 16th, 1959

[...] Physically you seem so far. Really you are not. I always try to remain in contact with you. In case people come to you, they shall be benefited.

April 5th, 1959

[...] Your long silence was greatly troublesome. Whenever I thought of you, it was quite clear that you were all right. Even then in the physical world everything needs to be quite apparent. Heart is full of feelings. Such things cannot be explained in words. In satsang your presence is highly required. My revered Guru Maharaj [the Sufi Abdul Ghani Khan] whom you saw so many times used to say that by love and courtesy people reach to the highest level. What greatness he had in him. I have not seen such a great man as yet. Really you are very very fortunate. You were before him with me the last time. At that time he delivered most valuable things to me and also spoke very highly of you. He ordered me to translate all those things to you in English. I did that. All that idea always remains in my mind.

You are quite fit for this path. No doubt you will reach the Goal. You are appointed there. Please take the spiritual mission or message round the world. You have been made for this purpose. I often remember X, Y and other satsangis.... There are many gents and ladies who have to come. Let time come and we shall see each other.

May 9th, 1959

[...] I have experienced many a time that you remain with me. You do what is needed. You are quite right.... Really you are very fortunate. You did Darshan of my revered Guru Maharaj. One's heart must melt with love and peace. You know he was very kind to you. It is an admitted fact that he was an extraordinary man.

You please do not forget me and do the work of my respected father and revered Guru Maharaj. You are appointed to spread the real mission of such great men. Please take their names round the world. Most of the time in meditation currents used to go towards you....

Your younger sister is of a very quiet nature. Most of the time she remains busy. Really it is a pleasure for me. She is happy and in good health.

Please, whenever you get time, do meditate.

June 22nd, 1959

[...] Lilian, you can very well understand what you are for me. The fact cannot be explained in words. At the same time my revered Guru Maharaj was very kind and affectionate to you. He of course was very much pleased with you. From the worldly point of view you are really very far away from me, but you are sure of it that you are quite near to me. Your presence is really needed here. Spiritual life requires constant satsang....

In this world, fortunate are those who, in spite of having lots of worries, always remain above and absorbed. Such people are somewhere and rarely found.

You please go on doing your work smoothly. You ought not worry that few people come to you.

June 30th, 1959

[...] People wish to see you earlier, you have won the heart of so many people. The world is full of worries and ambitions. In the satsang of saints, one comes to know that only love of God is essential. In the end nothing remains but love. I pray the Almighty to give His pure love in this world as well as after this world.

July 29th, 1959

[...] Life is very precious and, for life, a good health is needed.

I think of you. Sometimes there remains no difference. You receive the clear and direct currents. My Guru Maharaj was very kind to you and wanted as well to transfer spiritual things to you. Let time come and it will be done accordingly.

September 1st, 1959

[...] It is beyond imagination how anxiously people are waiting your arrival. Really people like your company. It is a fact your behaviour with the human beings has been very nice....

I am quite satisfied to know that you are receiving good and strong currents. Please get yourself absorbed in them. Thus one can understand well how the spiritual training is given. Time and space can never be supposed to be an obstacle on the way ... you are appointed there. I am sure the people or your friends who are in search will be benefited through you. Please give a flash of peace to human beings.

October 20th, 1959

[...] I am really very glad to know that you are feeling better and enjoying there with your friends. You are receiving there strong currents also. The time comes when one comes to know that such things are transferred from heart to heart. You understand well. If heart is full of love, currents go from one corner of the world to the other in no time. Such currents are full of bliss, peace, power and intuition. Love is always formed in the hearts of Saints. Such people are only free in thoughts and ideas. We should always keep in mind that God is only to worship. Saints are the main fountain ... whoever comes to them is directed towards Almighty. Thus people feel bliss and peace. Your spiritual service is praiseworthy there. Satsang is the main thing in this life. You are appointed there. Please create true love in the hearts of people. True love means service.

Life is very short and one has to do a lot of work in spiritual life. May God give you time and bless you with every success in life.

November 16th, 1959

[...] There are many obstacles in this world. Constant satsang for sometime is now very essential to you. Let us pray to Almighty God to give time, life is short, and one has to do much.... Please try to transfer to the others what you have gained.

Another letter by the Guru

We are introducing a parenthesis here to insert a letter sent by the Guru in November 1959 to a lady friend of Lilian's (M.B.), who meditates with her in Le Vésinet:

> [...] The more one surrenders one's lower self to the higher self, and allows the latter to work, the better. In fact it is our smaller self, bound by the body consciousness (which includes all our

worldly selves and possessions), that stands in the way of surrender and renders the working of the higher self infructuous.

One of the best ways of surrender is meditation. In it, as it grows deeper, one not only loses the binding self-consciousness, but opens oneself to the inflow of the higher force from beyond and within, which, imperceptibly, begins to mould the thoughts and actions of the disciple.

After constant practice for some time the change in the outlook and behavior becomes perceptible to ourself and others. The intensity of desire leads to the exclusion of other thoughts. The concentration on the desired object or thought leads one to meditation which again leads to the silent state which is the forerunner of opening to higher influence. Awareness, while awake and doing worldly work, to the inner thoughts and feelings will, step by step, enable one to discern the change in oneself. That this awareness becomes automatic and is never lost should be the aim to cultivate and achieve.

By and by, it will lead to the realization of the subtle and higher all pervading superconscient force, which is the root, the substance and end of all actions and activities.

As one realizes this higher force, one becomes the instrument of the divine will through whom this higher self begins to work for the good and betterment of the universe.

It is the preparatory period which takes time. As soon as one is ready, the grace, the power and the awareness begin to descend.

1960

LILIAN LIVES IN LE VESINET IN 1960. She devotes her time to her friends, her sister Aliette, and above all, to her work, as the publication of *Vijñana Bhairava* is imminent.

During the summer months, she stays in Brittany, in Paramé, at Anne-Marie Esnoul's house with whom she works, and enjoys as much as possible bathing in the ocean and solitary walks along that coast of Brittany that she likes so much.

From this period, eight letters remain in which the Guru mentions the friends, Aliette, household concerns, but especially how eagerly she is awaited in India: "One cannot imagine how impatient everyone is to see you."

Lilian flies to India in October, with a stopover in Greece that she visits on an organized tour; on the plane taking her to India, she doesn't hesitate to give a silent sitting to a Muslim from Pakistan: *"He wanted it so much!"*

At the beginning of November, she is back in Kanpur, with her Guru:

In the excitement of her return to Kanpur, she writes: *"I found him more wonderful than ever.... I am already receiving overflowing spells that take me out of my depth.... Ah! If you could only feel the kindness of my Guru, see his eyes!"*

Eager to send to France the final pages of her publication, she only sees the Guru two hours per day.

At Pushpa's[42] where she is staying, she doesn't have any place to work or retire, and doesn't dare to take refuge in a hotel so as not to offend her hosts. So she complains about the depressing living conditions.

In December, she attends the Bandhara of Bhogoan:

The trip was as much exhausting as wonderful, in appalling material conditions with no possibility to meditate or to be alone, even for a few minutes, both day and night.

Since then, my Guru's eyes are gleaming: he is really beautiful and, what was rare a few years ago has become almost permanent: it isn't beauty or radiance, but kindness, suffused love that flows from everywhere; needless to say I am constantly moaning day and night, and have a sore throat....

Passages from the Guru's letters

January 10th, 1960

[...] The Bhandara was held in the memory of my Sat Guru [the Sufi] at Bhogaon on 25th and 26th December 1959. The Grace of the said Bhandara cannot be explained in words. You understand what happens there. There was a good gathering. Many people would like to see you there....

I am now busy in performing the duties of the coming Bhandara which is going to take place in the memory of my Respected father on the 1st and 2nd February 1960.

I wish you were here on such occasion. You know people come from far and wide and they want to see you. It is a fact, everybody remembers you.... During the Bhandara days the Grace descends, please try to get yourself merged for a long time in day and night.

January 25th, 1960

[...] The annual religious conference, the Bhandara, in the memory of my father and mother is going to take place on the 1st and 2nd February 1960. I wish you were here. People are expected to join this function from far and wide.

February 15th, 1960

[...] There was a great mob at the time of Bhandara. Many people (gents and ladies) remember you and some were very eager to see you. I am really very glad to know that you and your friends and satsangis brothers and sisters realised peace and pleasure there too. Now it is beyond doubt, time and space count for nothing....

Miss Amina [an Indian friend visiting Paris] wants to see me there in near future. She has explained in her letter that she often goes to you. Whenever this happens, she gets there peace as well as pleasure. Such news gives me satisfaction. It means I am there with you all in a different shape.

Only in spiritual life one can know that there is no narrowness and hardness. One's heart should remain full of love and kindness. I have told the people that you are not expected here till the month of October....

March 14th, 1960

[...] The good news in your letter is that you are intending as well as trying to come here during 1960.

The dream of Mrs. X is nice, you were in a deep state and something out of that was transferred to her. At that time her receiver was good. Mr. Y's state is also the same. Let him resist. One day in any case he will go on. I am sure, he will receive more and more.

Everybody cannot be kept in moaning state. One does not moan by mouth or breath. One does not weep by eyes or with tears. It is a fact, heart melts and eyes as well, as other main limbs of body follow the heart. Time comes when heart awakens; one realises every hole in the body from head to foot is awakened. When one becomes a master of such state, there is undisturbed peace and bliss. Realisation of soul begins.

Whatever you have written for M., G., and P. is correct. They really receive peace and bliss through you. At the same time, they ought to understand in the same way. One who realises and keeps that in mind, and after brings that in action, is expected to reach the goal. Constant satsang, service and sacrifices create love which carries us towards the idealism.

You are performing your duty well there. You have been appointed there to work. Now imagine, please, how God is kind to you and his Grace is going from one heart to the other. May God bless us with all these good things.

April 15th, 1960

[...] We are very glad to know that you have determined to come to India during the year 1960....

One cannot understand how eagerly people are waiting for you.... Children and all the members of my family are very glad to know that you are coming here after a few months.

May 1st, 1960

[...] You can understand well under what difficulties people of the time are going through. Such sort of hardship, dearness problem, is prevailing all over the world. I am also in the same condition.

Somehow or other, time is passing. In every respect we are at the feet of our Master.

The world is really full of worries. Faithful, grateful and kind people are somewhere found. It means the number of such people is not much. I always pray to Almighty to give me and to all the satsangis brothers and sisters undisturbed peace, pure love full of pleasure, Parama-Ananda*. May God bless us with all things which He thinks proper. Really it is beyond expression how eagerly you are awaited here.

May 25th, 1960

[...] It is not at all difficult for you to understand under what hardships I am going through. At every step we should pay gracious gratitude to Almighty who gives us power, energy and courage to face difficulties, etc.

Please get me remembered to all the satsangis of that place. They are my brothers and sisters. It is a long time since I received a letter from any of them. I am sure you are quite satisfied with your spiritual stages. Let time come, if God is kind, the deficiency will be made good. May God bless you with every success in life.

September 9th, 1960

[...] It is true, God helps those who help themselves.... It must be kept in mind that life is short and one has much to do. In this life it is necessary for a human being to obtain undisturbed peace. It is beyond one's power, knowledge, intelligence, etc. It can only be gifted by complete spiritual guide. Constant satsang with spiritual commissioned officer is required. It is really a pleasure to all of us that Almighty has again given you chance to remain here. We should pay thanks.

I am sorry to inform you that the old lawyer passed away.... His end from the spiritual point of view was very nice. Indeed all is well if end is well.

October 3rd, 1960

[...] The old lawyer wished to see you once more in this world. He had a very high opinion of you. His end was quite satisfactory. He was free from worldly desires. There was not the least care and anxiety in his mind ten or fifteen days before his death. May God give him everlasting peace and rest in heaven. Indeed time is veryshort for all of us in this world. All superior Gurus have passed away. We should mould ourselves as directed by the great men of the world who died before me....

All satsangis brothers and sisters who come to you and sit in meditation seem to be in good state. Sometimes currents are received and they are returned accordingly. I wish them success in life. Let time come and we will see each other.

1961

LILIAN SPENDS THE FIRST MONTHS OF THE YEAR in Kanpur. She puts the finishing touches to her work, *The Vijñana Bhairava*, that is to be published this year.

She attends the Bandhara during which she undergoes a very powerful experience:

My Guru explained to me what I was feeling, so it is mystical.... If you could only imagine! The heart flutters like a frightened bird held in one's hand, that's trembling and wants to fly away ... and this, non-stop, especially when deeply immersed.... I must get used to this new state.... Such an opening of the heart happens precisely during the Bandhara.

My Guru says that during two days, the sluices are fully open, and I am starting to believe it, as what I have just experienced seems important and doesn't depend at all on my Guru's will.

She writes to a friend:

But my Guru must accept the grace; he is so filled with wonder by what he continues to receive from his Guru and his father, even from those prophets who frequently appear to him: Jesus Christ, preached very well, Muhammad, filled with immense love, Moses, tremendous but tough, Joseph, so beautiful. My Guru never saw the Buddha.... What still needs to be explained are those currents that pass by so fast that we must seize.... Of course, there is no external grace coming from some external God. It's purely an inner matter: in some way, we are the grace....

In March, Lilian leaves Kanpur and goes to Kashmir where she is always happy to work with Lakshman Joo.

During her stay, she receives nine letters from the Guru. They evoke the concordance of her inner states with those of the Guru, the intimate oneness of hearts that is beyond space and time.

In July, Mrs. Tweedie, the "Russian lady," is mentioned for the first time. In August, Lilian will make the famous Amarnath pilgrimage with her.

Afterwards, Lilian goes back to Kanpur where Mrs. Tweedie had already arrived at the end of October. Mrs. Tweedie wanted to meet the Guru before continuing her journey, and the encounter was decisive [see *Daughter of Fire: A Diary of a Spiritual Training with a Sufi Master,* 1986].

From October to December, Lilian resides in Kanpur.

Letter to a lady friend:

Do not worry too much about spiritual life or progress: such a worry can even be a hindrance. It doesn't matter really, as long as there is progress over a long period of time; the daily highs and lows aren't very important, nor is emptiness, as it signifies that something new and subtle is often initiated.

Passages from the Guru's letters

April 5th, 1961

(Lilian is in Srinagar)

[...] Really, I was in a nice mood lately. You are quite right to say so. It is beyond doubt you were with me for a sufficient time during those days. From the worldly point of view you are at a distance of about one thousand miles from this place, but as soon as one merges, there remains no time and space....

You are justified to write that Lakshman Joo is a great man....

Please do not take trouble for me in any way. I am, by the grace of God, as well as due to the lotus feet of the Gurus, always happy.

April 20th, 1961

[...] During the days mentioned in your letter I was really in a queer stage. Your feelings are worth appreciating. Almighty God is the sole creator of the whole world....

Some creatures, having no physical body like us, have been appointed by Him to take our messages from one corner of the world to the other, thus the spiritual Government is going on. There is never an error of any sort. We should keep in our mind that this world and all the things related to it are indeed for few days. During the short life, we are bound to realize reality.

During the days stated above, when the grace and bliss of God was coming in flood, most of the time you were not away from that atmosphere. I wish that you succeed in this life.

It is good that you have finished your book, and now you will be able to give your whole time to satsang.

May 4th, 1961

(In Kashmir, Lilian is worried about the war in Algeria, and thinks she will return to France, which surprises the Guru.)

[...] You have mentioned your idea of going back to France in May. How is it, I could not understand it.

May 24th, 1961

[...] You know very well that sometimes, being quite healthy, I become for days together like a human being without soul. It was a fact I remained under such state of feelings for more than a week. It is beyond whim and doubt you also pass through the same state to some extent....

In the last letter you have given some deep points. I have explained the same to you. It is brought in practice by and by. Swami Lakshman Joo also told you plainly.... One is supposed to remain with a high commissioned spiritual officer for a long considerable time constantly. Deep things are transferred or done away with the special moods.

In every respect experience is better than anything else. Spiritually and intellectually you are fit. I wish you success in every respect. May God bless you....

My wife says that she prays for your real happiness, while on the contrary, my opinion is that you should always try to face the sufferings, worries and difficulties etc. This is the way to reach the goal.

June 6th, 1961

[...] Lilian, I am very much affected this time through your letter; you are alone there, you are under sufferings and I am not at all helpful for you. Try to finish your work and remain near some hilly place. Really life is short and one has to do much....

You are remembered here not often but daily.

July 9th, 1961

[...] I do not want to trouble you in any respect. It is from heart to heart. You feel everything that happens here. The worldly worries always come in flood. We are supposed, or bound, to face them. It is a fact, constant peace with real happiness is found hidden there. Please never divert your heart towards this side. I wish you should pass your life quite joyfully.

It is good news, the Russian lady will accompany you here to this place in winter. One should have keen desires to learn something in spiritualism. No harm if one does not like the idea to have a Guru. I quite agree to it. Nothing can be learnt without a Master.

Please give up the idea of going back to your country so soon. Please pray for me.

August 5th, 1961

[...] You should keep in your mind that you are not an ordinary soul. You can bear any sort of trouble that may ever come in your way. I wish you success in life....

We should always keep in mind that life is very short and we have much to learn.

August 19th, 1961

(The Guru is planning to go to Kashmir in September.)

September 11th, 1961 (Pilgrimage to Amarnath)

[...] Whenever the idea came in my mind about your journey going to so high altitude, indeed it was troublesome and painful. No doubt your people took risk. I used to pray for you and for your friend, the Russian lady. Many many thanks to Almighty, you came back safely with your friend to your destination.

Well Lilian, your vision is quite correct. I am not feeling well for the last three weeks.

Really, peace with constant bliss is formed, hidden in worldly troubles and anxieties.

I wish to see your friend, the Russian lady. She must feel my presence in the heart of heart.

In every respect, one should try to remain in meditation most of the time.

Irina Tweedie, 'the Russian lady'
Author, *Daughter of Fire: A Diary of a Spiritual Training with a Sufi Master* (1986)

1962

IN KANPUR SINCE OCTOBER 1961, Lilian lives in the rhythm of her daily visits to the Guru which Mrs. Tweedie also attends. Sittings, diving, and walks are her main activities.

In the evening walk in the park: the Guru was not talking, same profound state, and I was in rapture, I was moaning: before being in rapture, sitting on a bench, I fell into this wonderful state, but after ten minutes he got up to leave, I couldn't follow, he sat down again, I mustered my strength; after five minutes, I got up and the walk continued.... Mrs. Tweedie, worried on my behalf as I was staying behind while getting myself together, pulled him out of his unconsciousness – it's unfortunate – otherwise he wouldn't have noticed my absence.

Philibert and Lilian

Lilian is waiting for the arrival of Philibert who stays in Kanpur between February 15th and March 1st. Philibert is eager and the Guru pays attention to him because of his very short stay.

After staying a year and a half in Kanpur and in Kashmir, Lilian flies to France on March 18th. So this year's letters are sent to Le Vésinet. There are six of them between April and December.

The Guru is seriously ill on two occasions: first in October, when he remains unconscious for ten days, and a second time in December when he catches the flu, and, as a result, December's Bandhara is postponed.

In these few letters, the Guru informs Lilian of his health problems and inquires about the progress of the friends around her.

Passages from the Guru's letters

March 23rd, 1962

[...] Mrs. Tweedie is going on well. She is feeling much change within her. She gives French lessons to dear Baboo daily [one of the Guru's sons]. You will see all your friends after a long time and you will never be alone (referring to Philibert, Marinette etc).

May 6th, 1962

[...] Since you left this place, you have not been absent, even a little while. Your presence is always found. In other words it can be said that you remain absorbed the whole time in divine bliss. It is a fact and one should not doubt; in deep love one does not want to write, to talk or discuss on any point. All these things disturb to some extent unless and until one is well balanced[43]....

How good it is that you are enjoying yourself there with your friends. My good wishes to you all. Please remember me in your life activities.

July 16th, 1962

[...] I have not been in writing mood.... I have tried to transfer the things from heart to heart....

Worldly worries must remain with everybody. Such things make a man quite complete. How kind the Almighty is to me that all sort of worries and difficulties come to me and they go away just like the waves of the ocean.

Keep in mind life is very short. We are not supposed to remain here forever. In case one is a true servant, he never dies.

Mrs. Tweedie is well. She is going very smoothly. She does not want to go anywhere. May God bless her with success in life.

October 11th, 1962

(Letter from a disciple: the Guru is ill.)

He remained unconscious for about 10 days…. Babuji [the Guru] says that in such a serious illness, you did not leave him but you remained with him.

October 20th, 1962

[...] Lilian, you cannot imagine how weak I am these days. At the same time people say that by face I don't look ill. How wonderful it is.

[...] Mrs. Tweedie for the last seven months or so is living in the same quarter in which you remained for some time.... She is a lady of peculiar type.

November 30th, 1962

[...] Nature has blessed you with a warm heart. On the part of anybody, it is not good to share. You can help others by inner power. Your dream in which you are cleaning my shoes is very nice and useful.

1963

AT THE END OF 1962, THE GURU wasn't able to attend the Bandhara on December 25th, and it was postponed until the month of March.

Lilian spends the year in Le Vésinet and works on *The Bhakti* that will be published in 1964. She used to say that the Guru would put her in the inner state corresponding to the text that she was translating and commenting.

In 1963, I was in Paris and working on my book about "The Bhakti." I wrote to my Guru so he could send me a good dose of Bhakti, which he did, but it really only lasted until the end of my work, thereafter its intensity diminished....

But in a way, these were wonderful months (I was in Chomérac, at Philibert's place, in Ardèche), the Guru was ill without my knowing but I suspected it....

And during the phase of "The Bhakti," constant moaning. And I had to press my chest against the table as if my heart was about to burst. It calmed down the uneasiness, but it wasn't the same sort of uneasiness as with the Kundalini.

The Guru says: "Whenever you experience uneasiness, dive deeply in him, and you will then be aloof from it."

We have seven letters from the Guru for this year. They outline his financial worries, banking problems caused by money transfers from Europe to India, and the necessity to build a bathroom to improve the Guru's comfort given his ill health.

The Guru follows the Western disciples very closely: Philibert, who he recognizes as having a "nice heart"; and he is expecting Gretty; he insists that Lilian come to Kanpur with her as soon as possible.

Passages from the Guru's letters

January 9th, 1963

[...] In the first week of December 1962, I got an attack of flu which was of serious type. I suffered from it for three weeks and for this reason the Bhandara was postponed. It will be done in the month of March before or after the date my revered Guru Maharaj left this world which was the 6th March 1952....

In this system the mind's function or "manas" is stopped and heart is opened....

Your presence is needed here much. Finish your work soon.

February 5th, 1963

[...] I was not at all in a position to sit and work properly during the Bhandara days. It is beyond expression, the whole function was done very nicely. There was a flood of Grace and vibrations. There was a great mob. Even now some people are staying. I hope you would have felt something more than usual....

Really I wish you in good mood and high stage.

You know, after Bhandara there comes a great burden....

If Mrs. X's faith is like this, nothing good can be expected. In this life, strong faith and undisturbed love is needed. My heart is still the same for her as it was ever before.

March 4th, 1963

[...] You are correct to say that during the Bhandara days you felt my presence there. At the same time, Mr Philibert is also right telling you that I was ill in those days. Sometimes it so happens when one is physically unwell, inwardly becomes quite well and stronger. Really, for some time I tried to remain with you both.

March 21st, 1963

[...] Really you are taking the same steps which a devotee, in real sense, usually does. Satsang is very essential.

June 13th, 1963

[...] Your presence is needed here earlier. It is a great pleasure for us that Gretty will come with you.

I am very sorry to learn that Mrs. Tweedie has written you a bad letter. She is a woman of peculiar type. You need not take ill of her writing. It carries no weight. You come here as soon as you can....

September 17th, 1963

[...] Your character and behaviour are praised by all.

November 4th, 1963

(The Guru is looking forward to the arrival of Lilian and Gretty.)

1964

LILIAN STAYS IN KANPUR UNTIL APRIL. Early January, she participates in an Indian Studies congress in Delhi. There, she meets P. Roux, a colleague from the CNRS. During the cocktail party at the French Embassy, a member of the congress was complaining about the terrible heat:

He had been right beside me for a few minutes, nothing surprising about that. P. Roux has told them that once, on the Vesinet train, he was complaining about a terrible headache caused by the meeting of the CNRS committee that we had just attended.

I said to him laughingly: "If I loved you more, I would take it on myself" (I had forgotten about this), and for the next three quarters of an hour that we were on the train, his headache totally disappeared, according to him, but it started again as soon as I left. After so many years, he hadn't forgotten it.

(The Bandhara seems to take place on January 18th and 19th.)

During the Bandhara, the Guru had the sheet cloth bequeathed to him by his Guru after his "adhikara"* – a sheet that comes from the lineage of Sufis and that had never before been bequeathed to a non-Muslim, thus implying that he is the legitimate successor of the lineage.

There have been several attempts to steal it from him, because it is filled with grace. During the Bandhara, he spoke for a long time with the sheet over his shoulder (an hour and a half, inspired) but I didn't feel anything much, at least at the moment.

My Guru tells me that during the Bandhara, when he came out of his absorption, Philibert was appearing to him, and sometimes Gretty, less frequently Mrs.Tweedie, which means that they were absorbed as well. "And me," I said, just to see. "Oh you, he replied, there's no need any more!*"... There's so much love in him!*

Re-reading this passage many years later, Lilian will write in the margin: *"I'll never forget the sound of his voice!"*

Wanting to note the effect of the Bandhara, Lilian writes:

Like the last time, this rare thing in the heart which isn't palpitation, a kind of strong indefinite vibration, like a bird trapped in the chest; but the heart itself doesn't pulse. Water boiling?

About the night of January 23rd, Lilian writes:

I woke up with a horrible feeling, a disgusting presence in my bedroom, by the bed, like that of the devil!!! I now understand Christian mystics. I had never experienced anything like it in my whole life. It lasted three minutes (less? a few seconds?) I was as if paralyzed, with my eyes open.

"Is it worth noting down?" I asked the Guru. "Yes," which only reinforces my assumption of some strange force, enormous and horrible. The further we go towards bliss, the further also into the awful, these are the two poles, the Guru explained.

Gretty arrives at the end of January. It is a period full of new experiences for her.

The Guru was saying to Gretty and I that if we always remain "alert absorbed to grasp the hint," he is there to help us cross the torrent: some cling to his back, climb on his head, and there's a risk of falling, but he grabs the others in his arms, those who love him and that he loves, and they cannot fall; they will surely go across, but they must be obedient, respectful (dead weight, if we struggle, difficult for the Guru: we have to hold on and do nothing).

At the end of January, Lakshman Joo comes to Kanpur for a day. The Guru learns that Lilian has already received the Adhikara but she does not remember when, maybe before her return to France.

Between April 10th and October 26th, Lilian is staying in Kashmir and receives about 10 letters, one of which is written by one of the Guru's sons who informs her that the Guru had suffered a massive stroke. About this the Guru will say that: *"the pain of the soul is unbearable, the soul leaves the body,"* but his Guru, like his father, sent him back to his unfinished task.

The Guru is slowly recovering, and also faces multiple difficulties, until Lilian's arrival in the autumn in Kanpur with Marinette who was waiting for her in Delhi. Marinette's stay is full of new experiences.

Radha Mohan and two disciples (1964)

One day, on the way back from visiting his father's grave where neither M. Bruno nor myself felt anything special, because the Guru absorbed himself immediately and too profoundly for us to be able to follow him, the Guru told us:

"I always try not to immerse myself."

But this time, it happened in spite of himself and, when coming back into his body, he suffers from gastric disorders, fever, nausea, and vomiting, etc., from which he recovers fast and well.

Samadhi

Marinette Bruno

Passages from the Guru's letters

Radha Mohan, his wife, Lilian,
and a servant before the

April 10th, 1964 (Lilian is in Srinagar)

[...] I am feeling very weak for the last few days. You need not to worry there, God is everywhere. My good wishes are always with you. Be courageous and try to face all the difficulties which come on the way. My B.C. to Sri Lakshman Joo.

April 17th, 1964

(Letter from one of the Guru's sons, announcing the illness of his father.)

April 23rd, 1964

[...] I got an attack at the heart with severe pain and the best doctors available were consulted who have diagnosed coronary trouble. I have been advised complete rest and am forbidden even to move....

It is all His mercy and we consign ourselves to HIS WILL.

May 6th, 1964

[...] I am better now but very weak..... Peace is so great and tremendous that worldly worries, troubles, etc. cannot overpower. His Grace remains and it is always needed.

You need not to come, pray for me.

May 19th, 1964

[...] I received your affectionate letter. It is always a great pleasure for me.... Where there is love, everything is tolerated.

(Desire to see Lilian's brother and sister.)

I am improving gradually.... The more I am in trouble the more grace and bliss there is....

After this serious illness, I am passing through a great

troublesome path. You have taken a great share in it.

My wife and children remain very anxious of me. I am not at all worried about me. One is not supposed to remain in this world forever. Everybody is deputed for some work and is supposed to finish it within time. This is the divine law.

May 21st, 1964

[...] It will be a great pleasure for me to see you both. There will not be the least tiredness for me. The worst thing for you will be the unbearable heat.

I am passing through a troublesome way. The more worries, the more grace and bliss. Pray and pray.

June 29th, 1964

[...] There is a great work before me. I wish to do it as it is needed but I am not satisfied as one ought to be.

Every 4th or 5th day, a letter of Mrs Tweedie is received. Now there is a great change in her. About ten or so people come to her for meditation.

It was very much troublesome to me during my illness. From worldly point of view, there is great burden.

July 25th, 1964

[...] I am sure sometimes you feel undisturbed peace, not only this much but it is full of grace and bliss. This is the way the soul of a human being comes to perfect realisation. One should always remain courageous. Nothing is difficult in this world. For a devotee everything is possible.

You may write whatever you like in your own way.

October 6th, 1964

[...] This is the world, sometimes such odd things happen which are never expected even in dreams. God is very merciful and kind.... You will know when we meet.

Never think like this, that you are spoiling the time. If one remembers Him in the heart day and night, the grace and bliss will not remain aloof. Our system is the best of all. Here nothing is required except love and service. Love is created by Divine Master. Service afterwards in every respect is done by the follower or disciple.

Winter season is said to be very nice for meditation. Blessed are those who have really a strong faith in Him. First it begins from the Divine Master. This is my unshakeable belief, everything concerning the path of love is detained through the heart of the Divine Master. On certain occasions you must have felt undisturbed peace and beyond reason complete nearness of an unknown thing.

One is supposed to remain on one thread physically, mentally and spiritually. For this, strong faith and intense love is needed. One reaches this stage unknowingly. When one becomes the master of the system, one comes to know it from beginning to end.

October 26th, 1964

[...] On 3rd November is Deepavali*. We will go to the Samadhi*, as usual.

An Australian lady, a friend of Mrs Tweedie, came here....

Your letter shows that you are in very nice state. I also think so, as the currents and waves full of peace, grace, bliss and love always go by. You feel accordingly. The more you go high, the more you will realise lower, blank and nothing.... Love cannot be conceded cheaper.

Passages from Lilian's notes

[...] The Guru tells me that he too felt desperate all his life: but isn't this strange? Even in bliss ... nostalgia for having lost one's true homeland that nothing can replace. This is why I cannot suffer from any other nostalgia.

The Guru tells us a story: A saint is followed by his disciples. On his way, a djinn takes the appearance of a snake. The saint orders the snake to disappear; he does not. So the saint asks his disciples to kill it. After his death, the djinn appeals to the Court of Divine Law, saying: "If I was on his way, it was to benefit from his presence and I was innocent. I wasn't doing anything wrong."

Divine sentence: the Saint was right, because he had given the order to disappear, he had to be obeyed.

1965

LILIAN STAYS IN KANPUR UNTIL THE MONTH OF APRIL. Some notes evoke the meetings with the Guru during that period:

The Guru spoke to me for a long time this morning: what is important is the sacrifice beyond merging [immersion in the Guru], etc. Accept everything from the Guru! Sacrifice that which holds on to identity, and where the ego completely disappears, then the Guru can transmit everything, otherwise a shroud will remain between them.

I have forgotten what he said about sacrifice which is essential. It isn't sacrifice of money, time, it's more than that: it's aiming at identification.

Then one morning, around January 15th, instead of waking up *miserable for the new day that is ahead, with the sole desire to go back to sleep and forget everything ... remain in a wonderful peace and a nearly unconscious state; everything seemed well again. Arriving at the Guru's, he tells me that he dreamt of his father, or rather that he spent the night with his father, and that I must be feeling good.*

I agree, and since then, everything is going well; doubts are overcome ... these doubts only concern the Guru's attitude that is so weak towards his children: he doesn't pay much attention to them, gives them everything, doesn't realize that they wander around all day....

Lilian notes a dream in the night of January 31st:

A dream that the Guru finds very interesting: a beach, the sea and an endless eclipse; it is very dark with the typical atmosphere of an eclipse. I'm surprised, as usually it doesn't last a long time, but this one does and seems to be never ending. I have lost all hope. The Guru says that it is a very good dream: not to have any hope– yes.... The eclipse: significant – emptiness, annihilation.

On February 24th, Lilian notes the arrival of Diana, from Pondicherry:

She looks like a man, shaved head, wearing shorts, withered, full of good intentions.

With the Guru she will return to life, as he will write later: *"She also realized that she was feeling more peace and bliss here than anywhere else."*

Before heading back to France, Lilian accompanies the Guru and his family to visit Durgesh, the Guru's eldest daughter, and it was a trial for her. She will keep a sad memory of all the discomforts and annoyances during those days at Durgesh's place:

At Durgesh's, end of my stay.... Feeling terribly depressed all the time and afterwards for the three weeks following my return to Kanpur. The Guru is ill, horrible journey in third class, all of us were separated, filthy and repugnant, no food from five o'clock in the morning until seven thirty in the evening.... The Guru rather rude with me, all the time; the dog bites me, does he have rabies? No one worries about it.

Is it a night? It seems to be, but my peace is so deep and permanent.

The Guru explains the reason ... he empties me of all "foreign matter." I feel such an extraordinarily deep and permanent peace without a shadow of variation, on which waves of dark thoughts are breaking: the increasing poverty of India due to speculation on sugar and grain, desire to return to France and finish my work, the Guru's lazy and spendthrift children. The Guru tells me that it's very good; those who have peace without depression (most of his disciples) don't progress, because anxiety on a peaceful background pushes you forward as long as mystical experiences attract you.

Another day, the Guru said that at the beginning, for several years, we are well absorbed (a gift of the Guru's, like candy canes to children); then the stage in the middle is very difficult because it's up to us to remain absorbed. I tell the Guru that I don't have any more hope; that's what it takes, said the Guru: from the beginning, we must abandon all hope, not want anything, even not expect anything: we rely totally on the Master. This is the way it has always been for him.

Shortly thereafter, Lilian leaves Kanpur. But just as she was leaving: *the Guru said to me:* "I keep you in my heart."

Once back in Le Vésinet, Lilian will receive around six letters. They echo the Guru's financial and health worries, as he is marrying his two sons Satyendra and Baboo in November, and is suffering from a knee abscess, a liver attack, and is weakening, but he remains very concerned about the celebration of the Bandharas and attentive to the evolution of all the friends around Lilian.

On December 15th, Mrs. Tweedie is back in Kanpur.

Passages from the Guru's letters

May 6th, 1965

[...] Really there are very few people who are interested in this life. Mostly people look outwards at things. They do not understand the value of peace, bliss and spiritual vibrations.

How good it is, your past! From the very beginning you caught the thread of the life without any breakage. I remember you were born on 19th February. There is something in you which will take you to the goal. One should understand without the least doubt that things can be and are transferred from heart to heart. I am quite satisfied that your every step remains toward me.

You are not only remembered here but kept in the bottom of the heart. I did not come to know anything of M., G., P. for long. They are all through you so they remain very near. They do not seem far away.

July 6th, 1965

[...] At every step there was divine help. The street of love is full of thorns. Nothing will remain except Him or His name. You have pointed out many things in your letter. The dreams mentioned are not only good but encouraging.

Philibert, Gretty and Mrs B. all have become one and the same, as well as part of my life, just like yourself. All are on one line. The difference is only of stages….

I am growing weaker and weaker.... Your presence here is very helpful to me in every respect.

September 16th, 1965

[...] Now from physical point of view I can't bear much heat.... During such time there is a flood of bliss and grace. It is beyond expression how you are remembered here.

I did not receive any letter from any of you. I have been trying all the time to transfer my thoughts. I hope you have caught the same. It is not at all difficult for you to understand. Hard time is going all over the world. Blessed are those who are going in the street of love.

When the heart is full of love and peace, each sort of service can be done easily. Really by doing true service we become nearer and nearer to Almighty God. Our hearts are awakened by the divine Master....

You may put the people there at any stage. It is our belief that He is very kind to us.

November 3rd, 1965

(Announcement of the marriages of Baboo and Satyendra, the Guru's sons.)

[...] You please, pray for me. At every moment there is Grace surrounded by bliss. There is a great encouragement. It is beyond expression what is going on and how it is done. For five days my condition was quite hopeless....

God was and is very kind to me ... I am only left at His mercy. I wish to see you earlier.

November 16th, 1965

[...] You know well the marriage ceremony is very troublesome here. Somehow or other one has to suffer. Divine help is needed.

The Almighty God who has always helped me, I am sure, must help me.

End of November, 1965

[...] The marriages of Baboo and Satyendra were performed on 5th and 6th of this month. Everything was done quite peacefully and amicably....

Really you have got a very nice heart. Your company is always welcome.... Keep in memory to pray for me. I assure you it is accepted.

Lilian's notes

[...] The Guru told me in January: "When real love (Bhakti or Mahabba) appears, the worshipper remains nowhere, afterwards he remains everywhere. Then, he's in the arena, stays there and enjoys everything in it. Bhakti is not easy, it isn't an ordinary thing."

"He remains nowhere." It's all there. Although it diminishes little by little over many years, at the end the ego collapses all at once. "He remains everywhere." As the boundaries of the ego are broken, it blends into the whole.

Nidra (Emptiness)

[...] It's a phase of darkness for comprehension and sensitivity, an entirely new way of understanding. This meditation is pure self-awareness, devoid of any object and with no diversity or variation; it cannot be called ordinary sleep, since we are awake and lucid; conscious of what, one might ask? Of our own bliss or of this consciousness itself, although there is no consciousness of consciousness, in the ordinary way by turning into oneself. It's a kind of uniform and silent dazzling, undifferentiated core of all consciousness, free from the ordinary game of subject and object.

It's a fundamental state, infinitely simple and peaceful, in which we don't know anything special, but we just rest at the source of consciousness. As this is general knowledge, it is deprived of any specific knowledge and therefore it can be called indifferently emptiness or fullness, as it is self-sufficient.

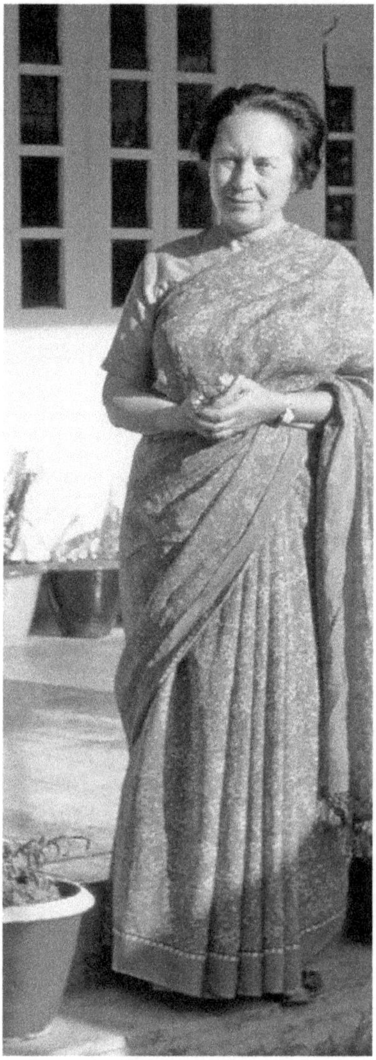

1966

LILIAN LIVES IN LE VESINET and plans to go back to India in November.

In the first months, Lilian receives five letters. They report on the Bandharas, mention old friends and react to the handwritings of friends to come that Lilian is sending to the Guru; there are constant worries about money and health, and in February the Guru is struck down by an attack.

Mrs. Tweedie gets back to Kanpur on April 26th.

In Le Vésinet, Lilian is working assiduously on *La Mahathamanjari de Mahesvarananda*, hosts some friends in the afternoon, and as of the month of May actively starts organizing Jacqueline and Henry Chambron's trip to India which is planned in August. Among other things, a complete list of all the members of the Guru's family must be established in order to bring a suitable gift for each one of them; it's a long list, a ritual, and has to be completed for each trip.

At the end of July, when everything is nearly ready, a letter arrives from Mrs. Tweedie announcing the Guru's death on July 21st, 1966.

Passages from the Guru's letters

January 5th, 1966

[...] I received your affectionate letter. I also received a letter from M. and P., separately, in the same light. They are following you step by step. I am satisfied with them. Really they are good and going on the real path.

The Bhandara in question was very successful (25th and 26th Dec. 1965). Everybody was in deep mood and forgot the world. It was full of grace and bliss.

Along with your affectionate letter there is the handwriting of three other people. You have written about each separately. They are all good and I appreciate them.

People are coming to you. They will be benefitted....We are always in the hands of Almighty.

March 1st, 1966

[...] On the 12th February I suffered from a severe heart attack. He was so kind to me and I escaped.

Really, you remain very busy and this is the reason you do not get time to write to me. Please do not forget we are in this world for a short time. His memory only will go with us. You are writing books on what subject?

The Bhandara of Basant was the best of all. There was a great mob and such was never seen before.

Really I was badly tired and remained unwell after that. Just after 15 days or so I suffered from a severe heart attack.

You people somehow or other come to know. This is one of the greatest signs of divine faith and love.

You are there. Give the people an idea of real peace, bliss and grace. This is a great service. It brings a good fruit.

(Undated Letter – Mrs. Tweedie is in Kanpur since April 26th)

[...] In the month of April, I went to Bhogoan Sharif and Fatehgarh. I attended Bhandara at both places. Mrs. Tweedie accompanied me. She was very much inspired at Bhogoan.

Really, if there is heaven, it is there. From the worldly point of view those people are very courteous.

May 5th, 1966

[...] I wish to see you earlier. Please come here and remain with me for some time.

In the divine life satsang i.e. company has got its great effect. I think of you much. Thanks to God you are in good state.

I am very glad to know that you are feeling undisturbed peace.

I received letters from your two friends. You have mentioned them in your letter. You are appointed there so you must do the needful.

July 15th, 1966 (the Guru's last letter)

[...] I am trying to write you this letter after a long time. I am very weak. I cannot walk freely even inside the premises. The heart attack in the night of 15th May 1966 was so severe that everybody became hopeless. Even the doctors were not ready to take the case in their hands. It remained for six hours.

The divine help was there which empowered all the members of my family to pass the time peacefully.... I wish to see you with your friends. Let them come in time.... During my serious illness you were not apart from me. I remembered Mrs Bruno, Philibert and your friends. Here everyone remembers you much. Love to your younger sister. Yours as ever.

[illegible] 15/7/66

8/223, Raghubar ~~[illegible]~~ Bhawan
Sant Shiromani Raghubar Dayal
Marg – Kanpur
U.P.

My dear Lilian,

I am trying to write you this letter after a long time. I am very weak. I can not walk freely inside the premises even. The heart attack in the night of 15th May 1966 was so severe that every body became hopeless. Even the doctors were not ready to take the case in their hands. It remained for six hours. The divine help was there which empowered all the members of my family to pass the time peacefully. [illegible] right above four hundred Rupees were spent. How [illegible] arranged only she knows. God helped her. The Grace of Almighty was with her. I have no appetite & take nothing except milk with dry grapes & juice of fruits. I am taking complete rest. Morning & evening for some time to get a change I sit outside. Mrs. Tewadia [?] informed you about my serious illness. She got the money from Shama [?] & gave that to me. Sometime she changes her mood. You know her attitude well. She herself wrote you a letter. She comes to me daily morning & evening.

Your very affectionate letter Babbo (Narendra Nath) received. He is impressed very much. Every thing from you, Mrs. Brown [?] & P. Philip [?] was received by me in time.

During my serious illness you were not apart from me. I remembered Mrs. Browne, Philip [?] & your friends. An early reply is needed. [illegible]

My good wishes to you & all. Love to you. Yours affectionately [?], Russell [?]

Death of the Guru

Letter that Lilian wrote immediately to Jacqueline [the author] and Henry Chambron, when she received Mrs. Tweedie's letter:

[...] I'm trembling, still under the shock of the news: I'm informed (writing it down makes it a reality that I still have difficulty to believe) that our Guru died on July 21st, in the evening (at around 4 o'clock in the afternoon our time).

The Guru had said to Mrs. Tweedie that, this time, she would stay with him until he dies. He died suddenly of his third heart attack. But he had told me, after the first one, that the impetus towards absolute truth is such that the body is unable to survive, hence it wasn't a heart attack.

I don't think that our plans to go and visit you will change.

Nonetheless I remain immersed in profound peace. That's the essential, in a way the connection isn't interrupted. These last days I was in a daze of samadhi, so to speak.

Then Lilian goes to Ayguatebia in the company of Philibert and Gretty:

[...] His presence is so alive among us. Oh! The joy of those days. No sad thought can slip through: I know that I won't see the Guru again in Kanpur, but I am not suffering from it and can no longer imagine how painful was the shock when reading Mrs. Tweedie's letter.

Lilian left for India in November and from Srinagar will write the story of the Guru's death according to his children:

[...] No one expected such a sudden death although he had announced it to each of them; on that day, he was particularly well and had taken a real meal, for the first time since May: the night before he had attempted death, but his son,

who was massaging his legs, hit one of the legs, thus forced him to come back; he was scolded by the Guru ... who, later, gave him a sitting for two hours and the young man is really transformed. The poor woman lost a lot of weight and doesn't eat much anymore.

The Guru died without anyone noticing it, painlessly. He looked at all of them, became luminous; ordinarily, his face was radiant, but that time his sons were not able to bear its brilliance, then he lay down. The doctor came to give him an injection. The Guru said to him: "Now your task is over." He lay back, and died. The peace was so profound that nobody was crying. He also used to say frequently that his task was finished.

Note written in 1967 (?):

[...] In 1962, I had a dream (I wrote it down) in which I was informed of my Guru's death (I was in France), and in my dream I was filled with so much bliss, that it was impossible to suffer: I was so sorry, because I remembered that my Guru had a lot of pain after the death of his Master. Under the shock, I woke up ... I related the dream to my Guru who said that it was a very good dream.

In fact, everything is given in advance through dreams. Thus, he knew how I would take his death. In another dream, he was dead and Raghunath Prasad too [one of the Guru's very close disciples]. I was telling him that I had enough, it was my turn to die, and he was in agreement. What a joy for me in dreams! Here again he thought it was a good dream.

Neither the Guru nor his father were there when the Sufi (Huzur Maharaj) died. My Guru, when a child, was dying, and he recovered as soon as the Sufi died. His father was only informed of his Master's death six months later and he fainted. His elder brother had been instructed not to reveal it to him. There is a subtle string of events of which I am starting to grasp the interaction.

Glimpse of the Stays in Kashmir

AFTER THE DEFENSE OF HER THESIS IN 1948, Lilian's first trip to India was to Kashmir, where she would go on various occasions for more than twenty years, until 1975. She was enchanted by the beauty of this valley of so called "wonders," but she had to put up with very difficult living conditions which seriously affected her.

Yes, everything is beautiful for those who are lucky enough to discover the site of Srinagar and its surroundings, framed in the distance by the high peaks of the Himalayas, crossed by the Jhelum River with its seven bridges and lined by ancient carved wood facades ... while a string of lakes unfurls nearby, bordered with lotus flowers and lush Mughal gardens.

On the lakes and canals, there is so much fascinating activity: we get around on shikaras, narrow Venetian gondolas, mostly hollowed out of tree trunks; there are many, of varied sizes, that glide silently over the water, constantly going back and forth from the shore to the houseboats, barges made of pine and cedar wood, on which Lilian particularly enjoyed staying; they also thread their way through a maze of floating gardens, islets of aquatic plants, lotus roots, covered with clods of earth at water level on which all sorts of vegetables are grown.

The pink rock of the mountains nearby, their blooming fruit trees dominated by the more distant mountain tops, snow-covered in the spring; the vast Mughal gardens in Shalimar and Nishat, with their canals and rose-flowered terraces gradually sloping towards the lakes nearby, while families and visitors enjoy the shade of the giant sycamore trees; the light varying according to the time of day, but often vaporous with a subtle softness; the *muezzin's* nostalgic voice that echoes at regular intervals: there is nothing, in this enchanting site, that doesn't induce a state of continuous contemplation.

Her wonder at this beauty is never exhausted throughout her stays and Lilian will be particularly happy to communicate her enthusiasm to friends who would accompany or join her, depending on the circumstances.

In the burning hot summer days, she will take refuge here, which was, to the Mughals, "the terrestial paradise of India," away from the unbearable heat of Kanpur. During the first summer she spent there, she discovered that her Guru had taken upon himself the heat that her own physical state was unable to endure, and she did not want this to happen again, at any price.

Always eager to admire the most beautiful views, and, if possible, in solitude, she will manage to have the house-boat maneuvered on the other side of the strip of land separating the two lakes, as far as Nishat.

This morning, I'm sleeping while I write, she notes in 1952. *The boat has that nice smell of sandalwood. Yesterday we arrived for lunch and I had the boat put in a magnificent spot, in the shade of willows, along a strip of earth, in the middle of the lake. I was lying down, not asleep and in dhyana. These boats don't hold in the water, and I had a view on both sides as well as of the mountains. It was a Monet and I was delighted.*

But at around five o'clock, storm, rain, hurricane, the rope of the boat broke loose, we had to reattach it under the rain, and the young servant boy was yelling desperately seeing his boat lost. We would need steel cables. At around nine-thirty the storm came back; the boatmen were thinking that, if the rope broke, we could capsize and sink.

So I put on my coat, took passport and money, and was preparing myself for disaster as there was a strong wind. Of course I was worried, my thoughts were dark but, nonetheless, sitting on my bed, I was so infinitely calm that I quite often couldn't think about the storm and the rope that was moaning. I fell sound asleep and did not hear the storm that resumed at 3 o'clock in the morning.

This morning, the servants demanded that I choose a safer berth. We're there now; it's beautiful too, but so much less.

In this solitary place, Lilian enjoys bird watching, thus combining the stillness of interiority with the love of nature.

I'm in the middle of the lake, birds are resting on the strip of land and my boat, the only one, serves as a perch for observation and fishing. At every moment, I can see three pairs of kingfishers on the foredeck: father, mother and the two little ones and two more on the left, two on the right closely bound together. They are so beautiful! The young ones are learning to dive and don't know what to bring back, sometimes a few blades of grass.... I hesitate to go out on the deck for fear of scaring them. When I sit there very quietly, in dhyana, the birds, busy fishing, brush past me, and almost bump into me. But the way they fish is cruel; they keep on catching fish and eating them in huge quantities. They shake the prey for a while, wait until it almost stops waggling and then swallow it whole. And I was thinking of God, the Supreme Kingfisher ... isn't he doing the same thing with me?

At another time she will write to Serge Bogroff:

Here, I don't have any more discomfort and I have never been so happy in my whole life: I am in a boat on the lake, in a Monet landscape: willows and lotuses. Yes, it's a paradise. Perfect weather. The mountain rises nearby and each morning, at around seven o'clock, I go all the way up to Lakshman Joo's and I am drunk....

This place, with its three or four beautifully kept Mughal gardens, its ruins of Buddhist monasteries, the Shiva Lingam stone, the rock on which Shiva wrote the Shiva Sutras: in only a few kilometers you visit all of this; the trail is high up on the mountain and from there we can see the mountains covered with snow and the lakes full of poplars and willows. It is beyond imagination.

She will also evoke the sight of nomadic people passing through Shrinagar:

Currently, there are some nomadic people with their horses coming from the border of Pakistan, Jammu, etc. They got on the road in April (the letter is from June). *India doesn't offer anything as wonderful: tribes of Judah or rather Persians from several millennia – on bas-reliefs – men with curly hair, very dark beards as well, women and their ornaments.... I admire them so much that I don't really see anything. They are not begging and have a lordly air. The Kashmiris, in comparison so lowly, say that these nomads are highly spiritual! In any case, they are imposing, smiling, beautiful, dignified, proud and charming.*

Through these few words, written hastily in a letter to a close friend, we can grasp the intensity of a temperament fond of beauty and greatness. She will continue to marvel at the infinite variety of the landscape, multiplying the destinations and timings of her walks, bicycle rides, or even bus rides.

Beautiful sun, wonderful bicycle ride of seven miles along the lake, with its mountains covered with silk, its blue waters, then the tough ascent and stunning view from the top.

Or, about one of Lakshman Joo's houses:

At noon, I would go and rest in the hills above the small thatched cottage, with just one single room that he puts at my disposal and which is very tempting to me as I know that I will have incredible experiences there. This thatched cottage is among the small trees, the silky mountain rising immediately, straight up. Then, going down towards Lasksman Joo, there is a mountain stream lined with very young poplars, and a wobbly bridge of intertwined foliage, afterwards hanging gardens, hedges of roses, fruit trees, with a footpath full of silver willows separating Lakshman Joo's house from its orchards. I spent three marvelous hours there.... Wonderful view of the lakes, flooded rice paddies, deep water of the frozen stream. But would I settle here?

Or again:

Long outing with some friends to Wooler Lake. I was calmly contemplating the landscape which was superb, lakes, mountains covered with snow, water everywhere among the willows, fields of blue flowers on the fields of golden wheat, carved wood houses, women with colorful clothes, far from Srinagar. The road was bumpy, spiraling, and it prevented me from fully enjoying my peace; this contemplative state concentrated on the moment intensified this bliss. No fluctuations of thought tarnished the reflection of nature. Inner peace and outer peace were but one.... Not a word on the bus.

Lakshman Joo (Swami Lakshman Brahmacarin, 1907-1991)

In almost all of Lilian's books, in the foreword, she expresses her deep gratitude to Lakshman Joo for all his help in her research and studies on Shaivism.

Lilian regards him as *"the very learned Pundit"* but also as *"a true yogin and jñanin,"* with the mystical knowledge described in the texts, of which he is one of the last to know the deeper meaning.

Over the years, she won't cease to compare the results of her research with the science of the Swami; the convergence of their views and their constant agreement give her great happiness and sometimes even some reassurance.

At the early stages of their encounter, Lilian writes:

I must take advantage of Lakshman Joo's precious help; yoga has given him a real beauty; his eyes are luminous like those of Radha Mohan's elder brother. He is the best of the Yogins that I have met, because he knows a lot, has read all the texts, and has experience....

In 1952, she remarks on her work with Lakshman Joo as a source of great joy:

His constant cheerfulness, our so perfect mutual understanding, his gratitude after our working together for an hour, as he is so appreciative of the task I am accomplishing regarding the Trika....

As soon as I arrived, she will write about fifteen years later, *I worked with the Swami Lakshman Brahmacarin who not only had the science of the Shaivist texts but also an obvious mystical experience. I admired the greatness and the simplicity of this very great yogin. Yet the monistic tradition of Kashmir Shaivism, still very much alive at the time of Abhinavagupta, had partly disappeared since the method, which is so important, of immediate transmission (anupaya*), had fallen into oblivion, as the lineage of masters had been interrupted. It is now up to the disciple to discover the Self through his own efforts, the master being only there to set an example, give some advice and explanations.*

Needless to say that Lakshman Joo is amazed to see what I have done in so little time, as such experiences have cost him twenty-five years of efforts, and he knows very well that his great master Abhinavagupta only recognizes one way to Shiva ... it is the "non-way": the one of our Guru. According to him, the Guru limits himself to teaching, to Pranayama*, and doesn't waver when the sisya* is unable to be put in Samadhi by the grace of Shiva. The *latter accomplishes more in one second than all other means in fifty years.* (Letter, 1952)

She immediately knew how to adapt to the Swami's character and teaching method, as shown by the following tips she will later give to a friend who had to come and work with him:

For many years, I was the only one (apart from his two female disciples) he agreed to teach, because I accepted everything, never criticising, not asking any questions nor exact references.... You see, this isn't an objective science, but he teaches you without any discussion what he received reverently from his master. He refused to teach Shaivism to an intelligent man who stayed eleven years with him as a servant for the only reason that this disciple was asking him questions and discussing.... He transmits a life, a profound understanding of the texts that he loves, and doesn't coldly break them down in the Western way, but deep down he knows, he understands.

Her sense of humor will always preside over their exchanges, and throughout her visits to him she made a point of distracting and amusing him with all sorts of fantasies and surprises, thus revealing a natural cheerfulness that some of his devotees doubtlessly did not always admire.

Since Lakshman Joo intensely enjoys my every word and laughs to tears, it's a pleasure for me to amuse him. He is kind, candid, simple, and his eyes are luminous. (1952)

She never arrived from France without a huge quantity of gadgets collected for her by her friends and which, unfailingly, delighted the Swami with hilarity. Lakshman Joo, if not his devotees, very much appreciated her taste for jokes. One day, for example, she hid herself under a chair and acted out a wacky scene without Lakshman Joo recognizing her; it was all very cheerful. Some devotees still remember it. She liked to say that, in reality, they both had the same age, which is three years old.

One year however, she found him in deep sadness, evidently in the throes of his inner darkness. She proposed to give him a sitting, which he accepted; on that occasion, she said she felt the earth shake:

I had asked Radha Mohan if it was possible, since Lakshman Joo is more advanced than I am; would I be struck down by divine energy or the Guru's power? Radha Mohan told me I should try, that everything was possible for me in this path since I'm merging in the Guru. I will never forget that morning: I wasn't concentrating well enough and all of a sudden I felt a terrible earthquake, the house was disappearing under me.... I opened my eyes, panicked, and everything was calm ... but it started again; in addition, I was burning with heat (heat of Kanpur) and Lakshman Joo did not feel anything more than usual, although he was magnificently concentrated; but it is love that I wanted for him, and maybe he did receive the subtle things that he needs, as he already has Samadhi.

That same evening, another sitting for a woman and earthquake again (did the Sybil from Cumes feel the same things?). An hour later I was in bed when, once more, earthquake; as I wasn't giving a sitting, I couldn't understand. Then, people from the houses around were yelling, so were the animals, and I thought the house would collapse: this time, it was a real earthquake of one minute (my first one and it was on the front page of the Delhi newspapers). Well, I could compare with my illusory tremors (which are spanda according to Lakshman Joo) and the latter are infinitely more terrible because they are interior and exterior.

In 1964, on the occasion of a trip to India, Lakshman Joo made an unexpected visit to the Guru in Kanpur:

One single day in Kanpur, he said that I had a wonderful Guru and he intends to come back next winter. Will he do it?, she writes in her notebook....

He did not come.

The difficulties

But Kashmir wasn't only a source of great joy: materially, Lilian was to lead a difficult life there, a rough life, as she will write. *"I lived in incredible poverty in Kashmir (in Kanpur as well) without realizing it,"* she will admit in a letter to H.C., in 1967.

At the beginning, her resources were very limited and money circulated badly from France to India. The different accommodations proposed by the Swami were, for the least, without any comfort, no water, no light, an earthen floor, rats that were hiding her modest underwear in holes; thus she was forced to hang her underwear from the ceiling so that she could find it again. She finished the *Vijñana Bhairava* sitting on her trunk, wild beasts roaming the night.

During the first year, referring to the uproar that her neighbors are making, she writes to a lady friend:

I asked around, and I was told that it's to keep the beasts away. Very often, I hear the jackals; as for the other sounds, I don't know to what beasts they belong.

And two years later we read the following in her notes:

Monday: along the torrent, I went to my former house in Gogitirtha. There was such a beautiful view! And all these rocks ... (a young sadhu* lives there now). He's terribly frightened where I've never been afraid, even though I was living there in November with long cold nights and big cats.... He says that there are big cats in the garden at night; he can hear them panting, and not long ago, one of them devoured the shepherds' mare; he offered to show me the bones. In the morning, there are still tracks in the garden, but it's true that I didn't really look for them ... as I couldn't believe that big cats infested *such a quiet place.* (1952)

Furthermore, Srinagar was far from her residences, more than ten kilometers away, which made it difficult for her to do any shopping. Sometimes she used a bicycle, but on the way back, it was heavier with the load of her supplies, and she had trouble getting it up the steep slope leading to one or the other of her lodgings.

On this subject, she liked to tell a strange anecdote. One day, when she was particularly exhausted, struggling along with difficulty, pushing, pulling the bicycle and provisions, a man suddenly appeared who picked up her load and brought it to her door without saying a word. She never saw this man again. But curiously enough, Lakshman Joo himself was surprised because, in this isolated area where everyone knows everyone, there was nobody matching his description.

The hostility of the population and its wiles, against which she often had to defend her modest interests, should also be mentioned.

We would have to live with demons before venturing to go and live in Kashmir, learn to whirl around with a cane and to laugh cynically. (Letter to A.C. 1958)

As a joke, she will write to P.'s children:

Lakshman Joo, the great Yogin, is turning me into a fish and all I see are fish everywhere. It is true that in Kashmir people all have fish heads. (Letter to A.C. 1958)

But she was also facing violence as she had to endure stone-throwing by the children of the neighborhood:

This morning, I was going to Lakshman Joo's. An hour later, I was absorbed, I didn't understand anything he was saying to me. I sat down under the willows and the view was magnificent, the snowy mountains, the stream near me, the lake; I was overlooking all of Srinagar. But I wasn't able to remain absorbed any longer, children surrounded me, begging, and then threw stones at me: they are twelve to fourteen-year-old kids with vicious looks on their faces, shepherds of the mountain.

We should mention here the episode about the young boy who on this occasion did not participate in the attacks with his comrades. It was however difficult to communicate with him because he did not speak English and one day there was a funny misunderstanding.

The other day, I was on the mountain path and the little shepherds were throwing stones at me. Then comes a kind young man. But he didn't understand English and I wanted to ask him to scold the children; so to show him, I pick up a big stone and, still furious, pretend to throw it in the direction of the children.

But now he's scared, thinking that I want to throw the enormous stone at him, and it would have killed him a meter away! – He protects himself with his arm imploring "nahi mensahib, nahi!" and, terror-stricken, tries to run away. But I run after him, still with my stone, yelling "no! no!" as I was afraid he'd say everywhere that I wanted to kill him. He finally understood, laughed a lot, and then I heard him screaming and the children ran away.

She always told a thousand and one episodes of this kind with a lot of humor, whatever the difficulties described in the story.

During her last stay in Kashmir in 1975, Lilian even tries to find the one who, as a child, had dissociated himself from these attacks. It was no small matter, as she knew neither his name nor address, but only the area where he could have lived and where, of course, nobody spoke English.

It was picturesque and quite a pursuit, but we succeeded!

Finally, it was the father of a family that we found, who was working in his mountainside garden, in a beautiful golden light.

He was happy to see her again and despite the difficulties in communicating, he seemed to remember very well; and a picture was taken in remembrance of this very special moment.

Amarnath Pilgrimage

In 1961, Lilian undertook the Amarnath pilgrimage. Amarnath is a cave situated at an altitude of 4,250 meters, and it is inside this cave that Lord Shiva explained the great secret of the world to his consort Pãrvati; but, like a weak woman, she fell asleep, unable to resist the boredom of metaphysical speeches.

However, while Shiva was reciting the great Amarkatha to her, a parrot was listening, hidden in a crack in the cave, and when Shiva discovered his intrusion, he couldn't do anything about it as, having heard the Secret of all secrets, the parrot had become immortal.

The journey to the holy cave which houses the lingam, a block of ice whose dimension varies depending on the year, usually starts six days before the August full moon; at that time, sadhus*, devotees, pilgrims of all ages and of all conditions, set off to undertake the arduous mountainous trek to the top of one of the peaks of the "Roof of the World." It is a challenging and dangerous climb, at times life-threatening, and some pilgrims, hoping to never come back, even dive into the icy waters of the lakes just before reaching the top. Lilian's Guru assured her that her heart would stand such a high altitude; he had given her the necessary strength for it.

Shiva protected me well during the pilgrimage despite exceptionally bad weather conditions. I was never out of breath at an altitude of four thousand meters, whilst I am in Paris or in Delhi.... I wasn't cold.... The last part of the trek to the cave – of twelve miles there and back, in slippery mud, did not give me any trouble, whereas my Russian lady friend – who has a strong heart – fainted in the cave.

One day, she was bumped into on the narrow trail, and caught herself taking three steps into the void, over the precipice, before getting back on the firm ground of the trail, and this in a sort of trance: then she had the certitude that her master had protected and incredibly saved her without having had a chance to be frightened, as if having slipped from the natural to the supernatural, without one plane eliminating the other.

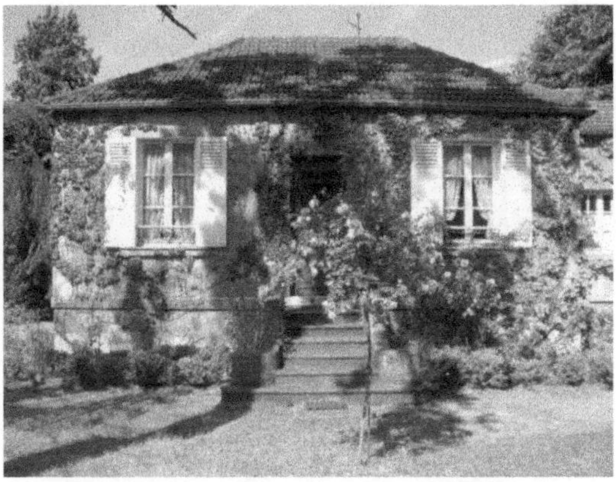

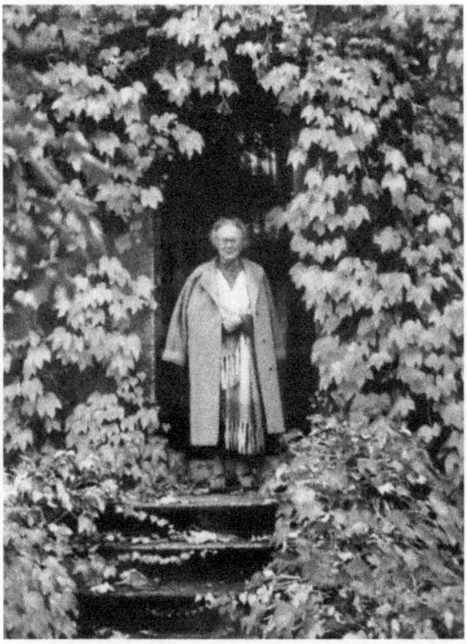

Life in Le Vesinet

WHAT LILIAN SAID ABOUT CHACHAJI clearly applies to herself:

"But the moment you are grasping how exceptional is his personality, you realize that he had lost it, that very loss being his greatness."

During the first part of her life, all Lilian longed for was the absolute. She was also very much concerned about sharing her experience with others so that they might benefit. Therefore, from the very first days, she sought to assure herself of the Guru's path.

If life was sometimes so hard in India, it's because the Guru was preparing her to transmit, in turn, to others. Accordingly, despite the level of her first experiences, the Guru made her go through all the inferior levels to enable her to accompany others in full awareness. Therefore, he had to put her through an intense, thus exhausting training, as he had very little time in which to do it.

After the Guru's death, only one thing would count for Lilian: to transmit what was revealed to her in Kanpur. We will try to evoke the essential highlights of this period that we were fortunate to share with her during so many years. We will also offer testimonials of those who met her and benefited thereby from her efficacy. On this part of her life, we only have a few personal documents (her diary and various notes). However, we can quote excerpts from letters and scattered notes.

We can also refer to her long introductions to her books on Kashmir Shaivism, subtly imbued with her mystical experience. The articles that she published in the journal *Hermes* are also very precious.

In the following sections, we have inserted certain testimonials according to the date of each initial meeting with Lilian.

Testimonial

A few childhood memories...from S. G. (1954)

"I was five when my parents met Lilian. She appeared to me as a surprising character, even somewhat of a magician: she was sometimes wearing a sari, had a cat, a tiger skin on her bed (or was it a panther? I don't remember well) and was always sitting on a rocking chair. Was she English? Was she French?

"When we paid her a visit, while the grown-ups 'dove' (to what depths?), I went to explore the garden: a big, mysterious garden with a large pond, a grove of bamboo thick enough to hide in at will, and a kiosk (for what, music?). Sometimes I met other children there. She had one day exhumed some old costumes from the basement for us to disguise ourselves (to tell the truth, she was gifted with the ability to enter the world of children as if she never left it, naturally). One day during vacation, I received from her a postcard addressed to:

>   The little mouse   Hole number 6
>   Under the weeping willow   Big Earth.

"Indeed, there was a large weeping willow in the middle of the garden in Sèvres! This postcard, posted from Majorca, featured two Flamenco dancers. It was her dancing with her brother, she wrote.

"When it came to the traditional tea time, Lilian was very present, attentive to everybody, inquiring for news, and commenting on daily events with simplicity and humor. She made us laugh very often, but was joking without ever hurting, mocking herself without hesitation but without dwelling on it. For she was extremely discrete, somehow always avoiding to be the center of the conversation.

"At other times she was lively, discussing texts, manuscripts, and proofs to be corrected. Unknown words flashed out of these debates, mysterious words coming from India, such as the saris ladies wore on feast days.... One year, she sent me a postcard showing the houseboat she lived in during the summer in Srinagar.

"And so distant India progressively felt a little more familiar to me. Later, she would bring me back silver jewelry and an embroidered shawl from Kashmir, for she was living sometimes in India, sometimes in France which at this time was rather original, especially for a woman.

"Another source of wonder: her ability to transition in an instant from the funniest remarks to the deepest silence. She then seemed entirely absent ... or rather 'elsewhere' ... with closed eyes, sometimes twitching like some others 'diving' around her, which left me in these moments with a deep feeling of oddness.

"Lilian loved the sea. She often spent vacations in Brittany with Miss Esnoul. One summer when she camped with Philibert at La Grande Côte, near Royan, I was invited to join the children. It was for me a memorable Dahu [an imaginary animal] hunting game, in the middle of the night, in the large pine forest near the beach!

"Sometimes on Sundays, in the middle of winter, my parents picked her up in their car and we went for the day to the coast of Normandy, not far from Dieppe or Etretat. These unplanned getaways near the sea were an immense joy for me.

"So were some outings on the Seine aboard the Pirate, our little inflatable boat on which she never feared to embark!

"Lilian also liked music a lot. I think she played some too (piano?), although she never spoke of it.

"Lilian greatly appreciated magic and magicians too, who, while amusing us, were surreptitiously introducing doubt in the middle of our certainties and in fact questioning reality. What did we see?

"Many years later, I was then a teenager, we did a wonderful tour of Corsica with Lilian. She did not hesitate to camp one night with me in the eucalyptus forest bordering Porto's beach. At night, we went to walk on the beach. It was a night without a moon. Lilian chose the darkest place on the beach to show me the phos-horescent sea: we entered it walking, and the wake of our arms and legs was punctuated with tiny fleeting stars, renewed with each movement. It was Mediterranean plankton illuminating the sea. But only a dark night would let us see it.

"Light, at night...

"These are already not entirely childhood memories.... But 'the essential is invisible to the eyes.' How would I say?"

Death of Louis Renou

Back from Ayguatebia, a village in the Pyrenees and Chomérac, at Philibert's in Ardeche, where she spent the first days following the announcement of the Guru's death, Lilian has another shock upon her return to Paris: the death of Louis Renou.

Lilian had a lot of admiration and gratitude for this scholar who had helped her at the beginning of her career and with whom she collaborated; she also shared a great and deep friendship with Mrs. Renou, and was very fond of their children.

Letter, September 1st, 1966:

On the 19th of August, I had another shock: Alice informed me of Louis Renou's death. I'd known him for more than thirty-five years, the greatest Sanskritist in France and such a friend. I also like his wife very much. I hurried back to Paris and went to stay with her and her children in Vernon for a few days. Mr. Renou died of acute appendicitis. It revived the pain of my Guru's death, and I don't clearly know who I am crying for anymore. Louis Renou was high-minded and friendly, very much appreciated by all – India and Japan.

But in November, she will write to a friend:

I haven't been disoriented as a result of my Guru's death: he is more present than ever. Thinking of him is like sinking into bliss. On the contrary, Mr. Renou's death leaves a great emptiness and I can't bring myself to go back to the Institute of Indian Civilization right now....

After a stay in Brittany, Lilian leaves for India in October 1966 as planned, stops in Kanpur to visit the Guru's family, attends December's Bandhara in Bhogoan, but stays in Kashmir for several months where D. joins her. She is back in Paris in September 1967.

From there on, Lilian lives in LeVesinet, leading a simple life in the small house that she shares with her sister, on Avenue des Pages. She now spends her time between her sister, her research work on Kashmir Shaivism, and the new friends who come ringing the bell, at the door of Avenue des Pages.

As we mentioned earlier, her sister Aliette had a very different character: shy, retiring, she led a very ordered life. She worked at the National Library where she was responsible for Tibetan manuscripts and printed documents. In Avenue des Pages, she prepared meals, but was very anxious about managing the house and its big garden. In addition, she stood totally aside from Lilian's intellectual and spiritual universe, never expressing herself on that subject. Despite these incompatibilities, they both did their best to respect each other.

Work

The house that Lilian shares with her sister is small, and she has a modest bedroom. She works there most of the time during the day, assiduously typing her translations of scholarly works and their invaluable comments. When she has visits, she covers her big typewriter and clears her desk to the great surprise of visiting academics, amazed at such simplicity. She goes to the Institute whenever necessary and participates in the various meetings at the CNRS.

> From A. P.: "The little house on Avenue des Pages was surrounded by a big garden and, somewhat surprisingly, enclosed by high railings – which apparently were re-covered from the destruction of the Tuileries; it was at once her place of work and, from the 1950's, the haven of peace where, as an Indianist, one would come and work with her (she guided and advised like researchers) and where also – or particularly – one could come to her looking for spiritual support, the impression of a Presence whose source – if the source could be so pinned down – was in India and to which one could hope to find access through her.
>
> "A working session on a Sanskrit text (notably of the difficult and subtle Abhinavagupta, whom she knew better than anyone) could just as well end in a shared time of silence in which one immersed oneself with her, by her. Lilian did not present herself as a spiritual master: nobody played the Guru less than her! She knew of course, as she lived it, what she had in herself and what she could bring to others, but she achieved this by her sole presence – nothing more.
>
> "She presented herself as what she appeared to be and was officially: an Indianist and member of the CNRS, pursuing erudite research, a simple person, certainly very reserved, but delightfully welcoming and extremely kind. She had a great sense of humour. If one could feel in her a strange force, one could (at least in the beginning) also be with her and not notice anything in particular...."

The new friends

Before the Guru's death, when Lilian discovered that one of her friends was sensitive to the currents flowing though her, she only had one idea: to put him or her in contact with the Guru, initially by writing a letter, and afterwards by going to Kanpur. This is how many of her friends went to Kanpur, with varying results; all of them didn't have fervor as ardent as Serge Bogroff's.

But after 1967, things change: strangers of all ages and from diverse backgrounds are prompted to request a meeting with her after a lecture or a chance encounter. Those lucky enough to be accepted – not everybody was – suddenly find themselves sitting down, having a cup of tea with a leading Sanskritist, who tells them about Kashmir, India and the extraordinary master that she met over there, all this combined with a long moment of silence.

Their vision blurs, they don't really know what is going on anymore, intimidated, they stutter and leave, incapable at that moment of saying what happened; later, coming back to their senses, they are conscious of having heard the first chords of an unknown music of which they haven't seen either the musicians or the instruments, but from this point, they are ready to sacrifice everything to listen to this music again and again.

They will discover that this music is called "grace," and understand more or less rapidly that it is through Lilian's heart that they will be able to access it from now on. They recognize her in the secret of their heart as their Master, and, although they don't really know it yet, as the successor of her Guru whom she talks so much about, while remaining his disciple; but it will take time before they can start using all these "grand" words.

The presence of newcomers subtly changes the atmosphere of the gatherings. Their eagerness and connection with Lilian, being only interior and wordless, inaugurate a new form of relationship. Lilian is no longer the friend who went to India, but the one through whom we can reach the Grace, the one who opens our heart; some of the old friends will have difficulty recognizing this. The sessions become more frequent, silence essential. Aliette must get used to new faces.

But there weren't only silent gatherings. We could also get involved in various tasks with Lilian. Whenever she could, she tried to make changes to modernize her house. We would help her convince Aliette, and this is how she brought in an electric cooker, a refrigerator, and a television set!

Lilian was able to paint or wallpaper a room. She was quick, skillful, efficient. If we had the chance to be invited to help her, it was a pleasure to take part with her in this outburst of activity. But –and this is somewhat difficult to suggest – the more we engaged in simple tasks of everyday life with her, only concentrating on doing our best, the more our inner space was broadening, and after a few moments of activity during which we didn't seem to be conscious of anything else, we collapsed annihilated, and totally absent: wonderful life, indescribable, so far from major stories with a capital S, so much beyond what we imagined. We were in this state only because of her mere presence, propelled into a profundity only matched by the simplicity of the actions performed.

Passages from letters

On the occasion of the first experiences of new friends, Lilian refers, here and there, to her own experience:

All that you are experiencing is normal. You are not wasting any time! No, there is nothing to know "when these phenomena occur" other than not to give them too much importance; what counts is the inner attitude, the meditation. It is up to you to discover what they mean. As for myself, at every turn, I'm still discovering a new sense or rather a deeper one.

Don't worry: ordinary life can no longer pull me out of my state. I've been in a slack sea for a long time; sometimes I come back to the surface, just for fun, tossed on the waves; at other times I try to reach the depths – or I let myself sink – but this isn't really important, the main thing is to flow directly into the sea, the ultimate merge into the Guru. (1966)

This wonderful awakening that you are currently experiencing doesn't make sense to me any more; I only retain the memory of a memory. As for the nightmare (that my life was about) before I met the Guru, I have really forgotten it; I only have a theoretical knowledge of it. I understand Saint John of the Cross who never talks about his life "before"; he had forgotten it, hence couldn't mention it. You have left the banks, you have entered the river and it is carrying you, taking you away rapidly: the banks are still visible, but you have already forgotten how you walked there. The river is the enlightenment – the path of energy (saktopaya). Then, when the river widens, the waves calm down, you've reached the sea: the banks have disappeared – forgotten. And the extra-ordinary mystical experiences fade away.

You don't really know where you stand any more: it is so silly, simple, absurd. The clearing happened of its own accord, without you even realizing it. This is the stage of Atman, no longer glimpsed but realized.

I think that beyond this huge peace of the infinite sea, slack, self-evident, and once we are well accustomed to navigate it (without any landmarks), it is the beginning of the vivacious flame of love or the gallop (as my Guru would say) which would be impossible without the slack sea or the equalization between samadhi and ordinary state. We then completely forget this great peace: all that is left is this gallop (I met my Guru at that stage). Beyond that, I don't know: a divine cosmic reassurance, and further beyond, the prodigious leap?

I understood this from reading your letter: total forgetfulness of the previous level. This is why I'm starting to understand the utility – for those who will be guiding the others – of writing down what is happening each day, even if it's only a few words, otherwise the transitions just don't stand out. I wrote my notes during the first years. The Guru insisted a lot on this. He used to do it: it seems useless, fastidious, but it is useful from many points of view which you cannot yet glimpse. (1967)

You write "coexistence of levels of consciousness – of the illusory and the reality." But there's nothing surprising since the fourth dimension has opened up and the commonplace has disappeared. As consciousness coexists with everything, if it subsides into bliss, we [can feel] a great pain [the loss of someone] and at that same moment[44] an even greater bliss. The highest point (not accepted by Vedanta scholars) is the coexistence between nirvikalpa and vikalpa; we are thoughtless and thoughts are just passing over an undifferentiated background without binding to it, like drops dripping on lotus leaves (on young leaves, it really amuses me...). (1967)

On this matter, Lilian used to tell the following anecdote:

The evening when my Guru passed on the wonderful thing to me, he had received a shock in the afternoon: his salary and the rest of his money for paying the expenses of the bhandara (500 Rs. in total) were in a safe in which he thought he had put them; suddenly, the judge called him, and when he came back, the money was no longer there. At first, he was devastated. But then he bathed in that bliss of which I only had a faint echo that evening. God wants him poor, there is nothing to do about it! But what is worth noting down, is that during painful emotions, the divine grace also flows. (Letter, 1952).

At that time, Lilian also discovers new demands related to her emerging role:

One day, in his youth, the Guru threw himself on a bull who had penetrated the garden while they were all meditating, and was dangerously charging them.... He grabbed the horns and pushed it back out; it was a feat, yet his father pointed out to him that one must not use the force that his masters have filled him with, against either animals or people.

This teaches me one thing: we can't do anything (except giving them peace) with people we are not sure of, I mean those not obeying totally and in all circumstances. If they are not ready to sacrifice their own ideas and impulses, and ask themselves what their master would do in their place, then to bestow knowledge and power upon them would end up leading them to catastrophe.

I sense here the importance of tacit and constant obedience which enables the Guru to bestow everything without any hesitation. (1968)

Sometimes, she sheds a light on what will be her situation from now on:

So when I'm alone, I bathe in a state of bliss – but I must come out of it in order to transmit at all levels.

Avenue Maurice Berteaux

There being more and more visitors, the house on Avenue des Pages gets crowded rather quickly, which makes things difficult for Aliette whose space becomes increasingly limited, and her fixed timetable is thus disrupted. Therefore, Lilian seeks a solution; and this is when the house on avenue Maurice Berteaux comes into play, as one of us quickly decided to buy it in 1972, at Lilian's suggestion.

It was an adventure, as everything inside had to be redone, and funds were scarce; but it interested Lilian passionately, and she did not hesitate scraping the stoop's gate, wallpapering the hallway, and exploring demolition yards to find an entrance door befitting the facade. She had great interest in her friends' real estate projects which she did not hesitate to support, in her great generosity. As a matter of fact, some of them did come to live in Le Vésinet and Chatou in order to be closer to her.

From there on, the gatherings took place at J. C.'s [the author], at Avenue Maurice Berteaux, and once a week, at J. S.'s, Allée du Lac Supérieur. These were long-awaited moments. Lilian always arrived highly spirited, looking happy to see everyone, and applied herself to bringing life and cheerfulness before silence set in, which everyone was waiting for to continue on their own inner way.

As the number of visitors increased, expectations were of different intensity and tonality, and Lilian subtly managed this. There was the inner circle, the starving, the big guns, the unwavering, those who heard nothing, saw nothing, engulfed in the magic of her efficacy right from the doorstep, but also a more light-hearted section, more fascinated by her knowledge and her dazzling and imaginative personality, than by the mysteries of a silent initiation.

Once established, which didn't take long, the silence was surprisingly dense, with a total stillness. Currents were flowing through the hearts and transforming them, but the alchemy was different for everyone – a mystery of the diversity of effects within the unity of consciousness.

Lilian was frequently bothered, as inwardly she had to come down to the level just above the one of the participants, but no one noticed. At other times, she was physically shaken by the forces of the currents, but tried to make it as discreet as possible. At one time or another, Lilian would interrupt and launch a theme, asking questions to the one whose eyes were more open than the others. She would've liked to convey a message, give an indication about the nature of the path, but she complained that instead of paying attention to what she wanted to suggest, the conversation ended up in an ordinary exchange of opinions, and it wasn't what she was looking for.

But there were moments which were particularly blessed, one might be tempted to say, moments when it was heaven on earth. A certain quality of silence suddenly emerged, Lilian hidden, lost in a memory of the Guru from Kanpur, would first refresh it within herself, and some of us, feeling the change in vibration, would go quiet before Lilian could say one word. At that point, once in this state of internalization, Lilian would tell what she had experienced or heard. What she evoked about the previous masters rendered them present, and her words echoed in a silence whose intensity stiffened our bodies.

In this context, moments of her life with the Guru, in Kanpur, came back to her memory when being "interiorized," and transfigured the most ordinary scenes:

One day, the Guru and his children were having their meal and offered me some tea, which I refused pretexting that it was another kind of food that I needed, reminding him that it was the anniversary of my first unforgettable visit, the first day of my life. Immediately, the Guru, smiling and continuing to eat and to talk among his noisy boys, immersed me in a samadhi overflowing with Self bliss, of a quality so different from all that had preceded. Substantial and light state ... indescribable immensity....

Testimonial

Some memories from here and there... From M. T. (1971)

"I was only twenty-two years old when I first met Lilian. I was sent to her to find a thesis subject in Indianism. Very shy, I didn't speak much and I came back with a Sanskrit text to translate. On the station platform, I felt very queer, I was seeing lights, and for a minute I wondered if she was not their origin.

"I met Lilian for a second time, and suddenly she said to me with a little smile: 'We are going to try something.' She put her armchair in front of me and, to my big surprise, she shut her eyes. I'd already had some beautiful experiences on my meditation cushion, but the powerful vibrations which bombarded me that day, I'd never known before! Fortunately, I understood that I had to give way to them and that's what I tried to do. Afterwards, she offered me tea and said: 'Maybe you could come and join us: it's very simple, we take tea and we try to catch the currents which are passing....' This way of framing things left me very puzzled. I realised afterwards it was an exact description of our meetings.

"One day, we were sitting around the table at Ayguatebia and Lilian was speaking about the Guru: her face shone with light. Streams of Love were passing and we looked at each other, amazed. We shut our eyes one after the other.

"Lilian was very cultured and at times labored hard to find someone to speak with who was at her level.

"We often heard music when arriving at her house. She initiated me to baroque music: Monteverdi, Vivaldi.... I have a memory of being greatly moved by these concerts to which we went with her and where the vibrations were so strong.

"Lilian was very experimental and realistic: she believed in nothing except that which she had verified by experience. She said that she even verified what her Guru was saying. An event was supernatural or mystic only in the last resort, if another explanation was not found, and yet there was a doubt!

"Very interested by science, she would have liked to find somebody qualified to speak to her about modern discoveries: black matter, vibrations.... Very free, she had no taboo about mysticism: she wondered if science would ever come anywhere near to that which mystics are sensitive. She had much fun looking to see how long the grace stream took to pass from one to another: a quarter of second between each jump?

"We felt she was trying all sorts of ways of transmitting, always creating. She was at the same time completely in the service of the grace passing through her and sovereign when she was pouring it on another.

"Although she was quite small, she was very impressive. Particularly her eyes were formidable: I sometimes felt reduced to a little pile of ashes! On the other hand, they could fill you with love and you were full....

"During a stay in Kashmir, Lakshman Joo asked her how she was from a mystical point of view: 'Oh! I'm very withdrawn, very withdrawn, but the Lord is very good to me....'

"If she wanted to start something and the grace was flooding her at the same time, she would sigh, protest ... and smile. It was like a love play between the Lord and herself; she resisted but was only too happy to let herself be conquered. 'The best,' she would say, 'is to dive with your eyes open and to close them only when forced by the grace.'

"Sometimes she was animated by such energy that she wanted to move all these 'sleeping' people: she was very hard to follow!"

A scientific experiment

In 1971, Lilian is sought out by a team of researchers: J. G. Henrotte (CNRS), P. Etevenon (INSERM) and G. Verdeaux (Faculty of Medicine in Paris V). Their purpose is to record brainwaves while in meditation.

Always curious of any discovery in this area, Lilian agrees.

Previous attempts of this kind with the Guru in Kanpur had always failed, but the means used at the time were less efficient.

So Lilian went twice to the Sainte-Anne hospital center in Paris, with different friends. What she was particularly interested in was to find out if signs of direct transmission could be captured live in the recordings. The staging of the experiment amuses her a lot. With her head bristling with electrodes, she's full of joy, and her cheerfulness contrasts with the austere reserve of the scientific body that she doesn't manage to cheer up.

Results were published in December 1972 in an article in the periodical, *Research* entitled "States of consciousness voluntarily modified." They state that the participants in this study generally present a trace characterized by alpha waves, but one of the tracings, Lilian's — as P. Etevenon specified afterwards[45] — contains some specific characteristics.

On one hand, "a slowing of the trace within a few seconds, without loss of consciousness, was observed several times during the same recording." Retrospectively, these episodes are described afterwards as a state of "wonderful rest," but nonetheless a conscious rest. On the other hand, they also observed in Lilian "several times, very fast rhythms of great amplitude which lasted a few seconds" which correspond to "different subjective states." The *Research* article specifies that "these variations of the E.E.G. don't seem to correspond to disorders observed in neurological or psychiatric pathology. They can be activated at will by the subject. They don't look, either, like tracings done on healthy volunteers who have taken psychotropic substances."

Tea

Meals were of little importance for Lilian ... she easily neglected them, but there was a moment that she considered of prime importance, no matter the circumstances, and that was tea time. We would never go anywhere without taking the "tea basket" with us, and organizing secret teas in hotel rooms was quite an achievement.

Prepared and served according to the state of the art, tea was served with a few biscuits, but, above all, it was an opportunity for exchanges full of joy and fantasy, whose contents varied according to the guests. If it was a distinguished visitor, Lilian would listen to him with great interest if it was a new subject for her, and with patience and courtesy when the person had spiritual pretentions. On such occasions, there was no question of the close friends closing their eyes, impressed as they were by such a lesson of tolerance and modesty. On Sundays and holidays, Aliette, always so discrete, would join us and we had to make special efforts to find suitable subjects, in the conversation, that would interest her. Despite all our efforts, there was always one of us who ended up dozing off; an amused sparkle, a bit ironic, pierced Aliette's eye as she discretely disappeared, going back to her manual chores.

In the summer months, tea was served in the garden to passing visitors coming from Paris, who appreciated the charm of tall trees and roses in full bloom. It was a friendly atmosphere and if one or the other wished to have a more personal conversation, Lilian would casually take this person for a tour of the garden; strolling along the pathways, she listened to unexpected and often painful confidences which saddened her, but her companion would come back with a smile as if their worries had suddenly eased.

When a new friend came, after meeting with Lilian he would join two or three elders for tea, around the table of the small dining room; a bit dazed, he generally had difficulty speaking, we could understand. On that occasion, Lilian liked to evoke her own beginnings in Kanpur of which we so often heard, but it was livelier each time and the assembly was shrouded in a pervasive sweetness while the meaning of our words became blurred.

The most intense teas were those shared with the closest friends, a relaxing moment, between two silent dives. Lilian talked, laughed, questioned one or the other with humor, but always with a daunting relevance for the one to whom she was talking, who alone was able to understand the implications. During these gatherings, there was no risk of falling into a sterile emptiness, as vibrations intensified and silence always managed to take its course in a new vibratory mode where we would each pursue our inner adventure within a unity of our hearts.

But we must also mention the Christmas Tea, an annual ritual. It was restricted to single women. It was "for Aliette," but wouldn't Aliette have said that it was also "for Lilian"?

The table was extended thanks to a board that was only used once a year, sumptuously covered with cakes and china; but there was also the traditional pudding that would appear, wreathed in flames, in the darkness of the dining room, a trial for vegetarians who did their best to smother it in custard.

Exchanges were cheerful, warm, on a background of subtle and contained inebriation which had nothing to do with vapors from the flaming rum, but originated from the Sufi's Bhandhara, celebrated thousands of kilometers away, in Bhogaon and to which hearts were secretly connected.

Bhandhara in Le Vésinet

In this tradition, in India, each year for the spring festival, all those benefiting from his blessing gather around their living master. On those days, we commemorate the late masters, worship them, and whenever possible, go and pray on their grave.

The word "bhand" means: reservoir, treasure, a "reservoir of divine energy" from which the Guru draws at will; these Bhandhara days, dedicated to the memory of the late masters, take their name from it, because it is said that the reservoirs of divine energy are then fully open and, through the Guru, spill over the disciples the seeds of life that will develop during the year. Thus it is important to immerse ourselves together, at the same time, in oneness. As we can read in one of the Guru's letters:

"I have not seen people coming there unless we are all one – ever united together in the bigger and more permanent realm of spirits." [Guru's letter, Feb 27th, 1954]

During the Bhandhara, the Grace overflows and floods the whole body of the Guru who generously redistributes it. Lilian specifies:

Disciples and their families come from Uttar Pradesh and other towns in India, peasants, small shopkeepers, intellectuals, rich and poor gather together and most of them in Dhyana... The Guru is nearly unconscious, intensely radiant, with a divine touch. Everyone draws enough from him to subsist spiritually during one or for several years.

Basant's annual Bhandhara represents a big expenditure for the Guru who must bring together and feed all the participants, and sometimes some unexplainable interventions occurred which were somewhat miraculous.

Each year, in Le Vésinet, we took part in the commemoration of Basant. But the manner evolved over the years. At the beginning, a very small number of people were invited, the right amount that could fit in the small dining room of Avenue des Pages. A letter from India would give us the exact date of Basant, which was different every year, between mid-January and beginning of February, the heart of winter for us.

On those days, we gathered morning and evening around Lilian, happy days when we benefited from her continuous presence. Each day was specifically dedicated to late masters, one for the Guru and his father, the other for the Sufi, and if the letter from India did not specify it, we recognized to whom the day was dedicated just by the tonality of the current. These days were intense, some had difficulty containing their reactions, surprised as they were by new experiences.

Over time, the number of participants increased, some coming from provincial towns, filling up one large room in Avenue Maurice Berteaux, and then two. At tea time, we moved around a little. Lilian went from one to the other, much to everyone's great delight, but we couldn't go into the garden because of the cold. But how can I resist telling about the ending of some of the Bhandharas? With only a small number of friends gathered around her, in the dimmed light of a lamp, after the intense moments of silence that punctuated the day,

Lilian talks ... talks about Kanpur, Bhogoan, the Bhandharas in India, of her Guru, and eventually answers some questions; but we hear without really hearing ... we don't know, we're floating, dissolved in the vibrant, evanescent and inexhaustible sweetness that emanates from her; there is no longer a soul or body, nor subject or object; everything seems to be made out of this subtle and infinite sweetness....

But Aliette is waiting ... and Lilian must leave; the driver gets up, resigned!

Ayguatebia

AYGUATEBIA IS WHERE LILIAN GOES on the day after the Guru's death, faithful to the plans made before the fatal announcement.

Ayguatebia is a Catalan name, given because of a thin stream of warm water gushing out of the mountain side. The village, which was almost completely in ruins at the time (1966), is located at an altitude of one thousand four hundred meters [4,593 feet], facing Mount Canigou whose peak can be contemplated under all kinds of light from the stepped terraces at the top of the village, right after the last house where a couple and their four children would take refuge for the holidays. Magnificent view, and a total lack of comfort, as suggested by the photos from that time.

For fifteen years, in August, Lilian spent her summer vacations in Ayguatebia. Surrounded by a very small group of new friends, who are unfamiliar with her tastes, her habits, or her experience in India, she dedicates herself to initiating them silently, heart to heart transmission.

She recalls some of the Guru's words whose full scope comes to light, and, as days go by, faced with the magnitude of the task, she experiences an increasing feeling of great solitude. Thus she appreciates Philibert's brief and rare visits: as he went to Kanpur, and knew the Guru, so a fraternal sharing of experiences is possible.

Nevertheless, indifferent to the difficult material conditions, and ignoring the frictions between some friends with incompatible characters, Lilian continues, imperturbable, determined, cheerful, with her good sense of humor, and many projects.

The following activities would take place, alternatively or successively: visits to Romanesque churches, Type or Character studies, swimming in Font-Romeu's olympic pool, picnics and daytrips to the surrounding lakes, particularly Lake Bouillouse, but especially long collective silent gatherings (satsang) or individual meetings (sittings), not forgetting the stories of her Indian experiences or her life in Kanpur with the Guru.

And at the same time, as our daily life was shared with children and teenagers in the first years, we had to ensure day-to-day food supplies, the nearest shops around being as far as twelve kilometers [7.5 miles]; this is to say that it wasn't at all a question of immobility or retreat in a "closed box," but of opening ourselves up to the inner dimension in the midst of everyday life.

Be it in silence or activity, Lilian operates ... her "efficiency" works on the heart, and at any moment one of us could be thrown into a new experience, all of a sudden becoming profoundly silent or moving away discreetly to deal with it. Thus hearts open up to the revelation of divine love whose symptoms vary: moaning, dark night of the soul, profound dreams, as well as a rise of Kundalini, but also violent purifying coagulations. Which just goes to show how intense days and nights could be....

Lilian doesn't sit on a platform, nor does she formally teach, but she participates in all the activities, except cooking, as this is where her skills fall short. Usually, mornings are spent on the main terrace which is always sunny, under the shade of screening reeds. We gather around her, and everything is an opportunity for her to stir the spirits and the hearts.

During the first years, Lilian draws inspiration from her old repertoire: a quiz on the village explored with Serge Bogroff, and "Type" analysis of which she elaborated the characteristics and classifications with her friend Anne-Marie, and in the practice of which she trains people around her. The detailed presentation of each type generates all sorts of comments and reactions.

Through cheerful dialogues and spontaneous remarks, more than one of us was led to hear, through some happy pleasantries, certain truths that they would have willingly repressed, and this often without Lilian's knowledge, as she was only concentrating on the Type's description. Fruitful experiences of self-awareness occured that way, even if they were sometimes painful.

During the stay, there was a particular time, that of heavy work, reserved for the gentlemen, of which in fact there were only two, occasionally three. It consisted, for example of designing the descent of a few stone steps, or consolidating one of the barn pillars which was about to collapse, but always with the means at hand, which required a minimum of inventiveness. The ordeal was more about the multiplicity of suggestions and comments rather than physical effort as such, thus making it easier to assimilate high doses of vibration.

For the ladies, the tasks could seem lighter but they did, nonetheless, require both submissiveness and risk-taking. It was, for example, making a dress for Lilian with just enough material. Any error of measurement when cutting the fabric was fatal, and the material would have been useless. Such was the exploit to be accomplished by the dressmaker with shaking scissors.

Thereby, the acts of everyday life remained simple, natural, but were always an opportunity to go beyond oneself without it being noticed. In Lilian's presence, the most apparently insignificant things could only be experienced with intensity.

During the stay, there was a critical moment for one or the other, even more so when the sky darkened (which was rather rare), as retreating together in a rather confined space generated a certain tension. In that case, we would notice all of a sudden that a particular person had disappeared, having gone for a run in the mountain for the rest of the day to calm down over-heated energies, and would come back more or less late, once relieved of what had been suffocating and was mysteriously becoming conscious. Upon this person's return, no comments were made and life continued. Each had their own way of "coagulating."[46]

There were also great scenes of laughter, a sense of humor being a must, and everyone would contribute in their own way, for whatever reason. But the wildest fits of laughter could stop abruptly, and in an instant a complete silence set in and absorption resumed straightaway.

Every year, there was the time when we all climbed together to the top of the mountain overlooking the house. Upon his first visit, at the time of the Guru's death, Philibert climbed up there with Lilian and Henry:

Jacqueline S., Jacqueline et Henry C.

Philibert "recognizes" the path in the pine forest, writes Lilian, in her small notepad. *When we reached the top, the three of us sit down in the sun, fresh air, and I pray the Guru intensely, so that he gives us all divine love: my prayer wasn't finished when Philibert was already sobbing loudly, experiencing the same opening of the heart that he had had with the Guru in Kanpur, tears were flowing, I was in awe of the Guru's immediate answer.*

Thus this place became Philibert's mountain.

Once we reached the said place, facing Mount Canigou, we "dove" profoundly, sitting more or less comfortably, in the greenery, among the rocks and tall grass. The rocks were rather poorly padded, the grass tickled, insects, flies pricked, but very quickly everything faded into the unconsciousness of some or the moaning of others. It even happened to one of us to rush forward, feeling like she was flying from rock to rock, under the pressure of the inner state.

The last year, Lilian wasn't able to walk to the top, so the gentlemen built a makeshift sedan chair, which was an occasion for a lot of laughter. Lilian was always willing to take part in new trials and that year, she did a triumphal climb, the last one, to "Philibert's Mountain"!

Each summer had a different coloration, depending on each other's life. In 1975, there was no summer session. Lilian was away on a mission in Kashmir for her research work on Shaivism.

Over the years, activities evolve and reduce. Lilian's health begins to fail; we fear a relapse of tuberculosis. The treatment is heavy; those summers, we could enjoy long "samadhic" naps on the terrace. The rhythm slows down, we travel less; in the cool of the evening we sometimes go for walks in the vicinity, but strangely enough we still have a difficult time following her; on the paths she seems so light and agile to us who are having a difficult time just keeping our eyes open and would so much like to sit down!

But with Lilian, there is no indulgence; we learn at the same time to let go of everything when the "grace" falls, whatever the daily emergencies may be, but also not to cling to states of softness: subtle dialectic indeed, but a living one, that is taking us always further.... Mornings spent on the terrace become more industrious; Lilian resumes her research work which she presents to the thinkers, while the "non-thinkers" plunge in the softness of dhyana or in the depth of samadhi, closing their eyes.

At the end of August, Lilian needed to get away; it was a rush to the sea, the ocean, never the Mediterranean. "Finally," she whispered one day, despite herself, when the car was about to leave for the Island of Oléron! Thereby we revisited all the beaches of her youth: Noirmoutier, Northern Brittany between Cancale and Trégastel, the island of Bréhat, but also the Spanish Basque country. One year, she wanted to visit the different places frequented by Saint John of the Cross. It was a wonderful journey which led us all the way to Granada.

Because our "driver" was part of the Department of National Education, we had to return to Le Vésinet in time for the start of the new school year, and more than any of the teachers, Lilian complained about the changing dates of the new school year which were earlier and earlier!

Testimonial

Memories of the "Holland campaign" – R. B. (1974)

"It has often happened like this and, this time, it was during a trip to the Netherlands she took with Jacqueline for spring holidays. Lilian had invited me to join them. We were visiting the country by car and, every night, we looked for a hotel or a guest house.

"Throughout the whole journey, we were plunged into such a

deep state of interiority that it sometimes totally immobilized us during museum visits, in the hotel room or even in the car, which formed a sheltered area, a sort of traveling lounge, the hull of a ship floating on the world's ocean.

"On the road, Lilian usually stayed awake, like a captain in charge of the crew, discreetly directing the operation. Our sense of the right destination or of the daily activities relied upon her intuition. We were going with the flow and it was smooth sailing. Jacqueline, who was overloaded with work and responsibilities in everyday life, was resting on the back seat, enjoying these rare moments. Lilian was keeping a prudent watch over me; I was driving as if in a trance, focused on the road, aware of my responsibility, but at the same time overwhelmed by intense vibrations.

"One of the excuses to go on this break had been the visit to museums that Lilian wanted to see or see again; she intended to re-examine works she admired and talked about enthusiastically. We were wandering from one room to another. Lilian was walking at a lively pace while we were struggling to follow her, as if sucked into the depths of our inner emptiness. We were craving so badly for a seat! But there was no time for that and we had to resist the siren-song of the chairs opening their arms to us. Lilian, with a knowing laugh, was taking us from one masterpiece to another, inviting us to tilt our head so we could admire them from a fresh angle. She was most assuredly at home in the vicinity of these geniuses who had been able to communicate to the world their vision of the invisible.

"Then there were the guesthouse experiences; these encounters with our hosts regularly forced us to emerge, to find snatches of conventional conversation while remaining inwardly absorbed. They were like a breeze blowing on the sea of tranquility on which we were sailing. We rang the bell. When the door opened, the man who answered looked like an alien compared to our usual hosts: a sort of cowboy with tattooed arms who had just climbed off his Harley-Davidson. He spoke to us with a familiarity which was probably a mark of hospitality or was meant to make us feel comfortable. He was certainly surprised to see us on his doorstep. Obviously we were not here to buy some weed. Together with his wife and daughter, both in harmony with their man, we soon found ourselves sitting on high stools, leaning on the bar in their living room, where the posters on the walls allowed no doubt as to their interests.

"I had never imagined I could have found myself in such an unlikely and comical situation with Lilian.

"Once again, without showing the slightest embarrassment, she demonstrated her natural ease in facing whatever came her way with simplicity and fluidity.

"As with all those she usually welcomed – spirituality seekers, academics or friends – nothing seemed to embarrass her, any discomfort being quickly dissipated by her humor and spontaneity. Like a ship drawing in its wake objects abandoned to the flow of the sea, her fervor was effortlessly dragging us into the stream of grace."

1975 – Last trip to India

After traveling to Kashmir so many times for over twenty years, Lilian visits Lake Dal for the last time in 1975.

That year, as CNRS' official representative, Lilian actually spends three months in Kashmir, happy to be accompanied by friends, some joining her later. She is going to make them discover and appreciate what she has been telling them about for such a long time. It is her last visit before the publication of her latest texts: the *Śivasūtra* and the *Spandakārikā*.

After passing through Delhi, she goes to Kanpur where Pushpa is waiting for her. In Kanpur, Lilian is deeply moved to see Pushpa and the Guru's family again after an absence of eight years. The Guru's children, now heads of families, are very happy to welcome her. They have known her since their childhood, and were always looking forward to her visits. They know how important she was to their father and to the path, thus they keep on repeating: "She has all the permissions."

It saddens Lilian to see all four of them confined to a third of the house after the settlement of the inheritance. In fact, their father had actually bought the house but always refused to put it in his name, despite the entreatment of his father.

Lilian has a good time with Pushpa and her family, but it's the monsoon season and she is eager to get to Kashmir, especially as she is planning to come back through Kanpur before returning to France.

In Srinagar, she rapidly settles again on her preferred house-boat, on which continental food can be provided for her guests. From there, for two months, she will take her visiting French friends around to discover the beauty of the site, rush to see LakshmanJoo, and make new arrangements for her return to Le Vésinet.

It is always with deep joy that Lilian shares what she discovers and what marvels her. In her company, we tour the lakes on shikaras, discover the floating gardens, the sculpted facades surrounding the river, and, we take a rest in Nishat and Shalimar gardens. Lilian trains us to observe *"the colorful birds, the resplendent dawns, the sunsets, the blue-tinged, pink mountains"* by the water's edge.

In the vicinity of Lakshman Joo's dwellings, we could descend the slope rather quickly to reach a narrow path separating the lakes, bordered by willows and lotus trees, and we were staggering, feeling dizzy, and not knowing whether it was due to the effect of the surround-ing mirror-like waters, or inner rapture.

During these walks, Lilian liked to draw our attention to the beads of water sliding on lotuses in full bloom without permeating them, an image of the consciousness of a liberated living being on which mirages of illusions just slip away.

But one should not forget that the main reason for her presence in Kashmir was her work and her meetings with Lakshman Joo. At that time, the Swami lived in a delightful ashram in Nishat, full of flowers and birds, among which were the famous "bulbuls" that Lilian found so charming.

Soon after she came to Srinagar, Lilian arrived unexpectedly one day at Lakshman Joo's when he was giving a class on Śivasūtra, in a small building next to his house, where no one entered except his two closest disciples, Sharika and Praba. He hadn't been informed of her arrival. While commenting on a text among his devotees, he stopped from time to time to express his astonishment and his almost childish joy to see her there all of a sudden!

That year, the Swami is particularly sought after by an American couple and their charming little girl whose birthday is celebrated cheerfully. Everyone also participates in the rice harvest. These are colorful and joyful moments.

But Lilian would like to work and she often moves around in a scorching heat, in vain.... She always had to announce her imminent departure for the Swami to decide to work, read the texts, and answer her questions.

The Swami's delays and lack of punctuality were a source of difficulty for Lilian and, at times, of discouragement:

The Swami has lost weight, we do the drawings for him, D. helps me a lot and paints gods and goddesses for him, but we still haven't started working on the Trika philosophical texts.... Nothing before the 7th.... As I am only staying a limited amount of time in Kashmir, I am worried.... (Letter, May 1967)

She didn't like feeling that she was wasting her time, but her patience was inexhaustible, her kindness boundless, and she was full of indulgence for the Swami.

In some way, he was a brother from the depths.

Letter addressed to Le Vésinet

In the middle of her stay, Lilian goes for a week to Pahalgam, in the mountains, with her friends. She wants to think about the decisions to implement upon her return. She also wants to enjoy the coolness of the mountains, and the walks along the powerful torrents with deep blue running waters.

It is at that time that the letter from myself, Jacqueline C. to Jacqueline S. is written:

Pahalgam, September 25th, 1975

"Dear Jacqueline,

"Lilian asked me to inform you of some important decisions that you need to share with each and everyone.

"Lilian had a dream: the Guru came out of this grave, he wasn't happy with most of his disciples ... and Lilian sadly agreed. The Guru was greatly respected, the Sufi even more so, as never did the Guru, nor his father, or his uncle actually say a word to him. As the Sufi told the Guru, mores had changed greatly in the Western world, and we could no longer expect such great marks of respect; nevertheless, Lilian had hoped that all of this would be spontaneously recovered in-depth and this is what happened for some of us. But now, she is afraid that young people will have trouble adopting such an attitude by themselves, given that the spirit of their generation doesn't really prepare them for that! However, this is crucial in this path where the Grace is the absolute Master.

"The other day, the Swami cited a verse about the non-way:

'As long as Shiva is not fully satisfied, he does not grant his grace ... and even if the Guru would give it, it would make the one who was unable to please, fall into evanescent pleasures.'

"Roughly speaking: the energy coming from the Grace vanishes into all sorts of excitements, whereas all effervescence, on the contrary, should normally be transmuted into divine energy.

"In the absence of a path, it is essential to attract the Guru's love. He is the first one to love, the one who grants peace (dhyãna); but if we sink into it without expanding our limits, without a glance at the Guru, we squander the Grace or even worse, the Grace can turn against the one to whom it was granted.

"What is essential is the transformation of one's being, the breakdown of all limits. In order to facilitate the process, the Guru welcomes with open arms, puts into samãdhi, and guides up to a certain stage as fast and as far as he can. At that point, it is up to us, and only us, to overcome the obstacles: doubt, indifference, attachment to dhyãna, lack of fervor, etc.

"The Guru doesn't impose anything, he has no will of his own, but asks that we don't impose ours on him. He follows the hints from the Grace and we the ones of the Guru, but the Guru's hints are subtle, we need to listen carefully, seize them on the fly, and for that, silence our own desires. It's the only way to extend our limits and come out of ourselves. Through this ever renewed attentive listening, we are gradually opening ourselves up to a new and full life which is offered to us. The most important sign of such understanding is the intense perception of the greatness of the Masters' lineage. It is in this spirit that Lilian made some decisions:

"You, Jeremy, Marinette, if she can free herself, and I, must back her up from now on. According to her, this will be very much an advantage for all of us. She will have more free time to address everyone's real needs. If we serve as intermediaries, she won't have to come down to the beginners' level which is physically exhausting for her, and we are now able to do this: it's time that we fully dedicate ourselves to others, as we have received a great deal. Therefore, there won't be any more meetings at her place, but at Donatienne's, at your place, Jeremy's and mine. For each of us, there will be some meetings to which Lilian will participate, and also others with fewer people, some more mobile ones with one or the other among us, according to affinities or convenience.

"Lilian is responsible for each one of us; she does her upmost, but we must trust her, wait for her invitation and not impose ourselves on her, thus forcing her to say no, and reply to a lack of courtesy by a lack of civility, which is contrary to the path. She asks that we stop phoning her at home, that we don't intrude with unannounced visits. She always says that there is no bother, since it's already done, but each one of us can appreciate the great trouble that such incidents can cause as they break the momentum of Grace, or simply the rhythm of family life.

"So this is what Lilian asked me to write to you, Jacqueline. There is no doubt that these few lines will encourage each of us to question ourselves, but it should not be to stir up a false sense of guilt. On the contrary, we must rejoice deeply as if the Guru has a more severe gaze today, it is because his love is becoming more insistent!"

"Ye companions up in the morning,   Which one of you will see the dawn   That will overwhelm us   Like flying specks of dust?" (Rumi)

But bad news awaited Lilian upon her return to Srinagar. Her brother was in a car accident and, after a few days, she left for South Africa, thus shortening her stay without going back through Kanpur where she was expected. Her brother died a few days thereafter.

Alongside the work on Shaivism...

In parallel with her scientific work, Lilian agrees to supervise the production of a book on Buddhism. Her personal contribution is particularly important. The book, *Buddhism,* is published in 1977 and will be re-edited in 1997 with the title: *The Sources of Buddhism.*

The preparation of this book provided numerous opportunities to meet and exchange with others and with great enjoyment. Lilian worked very hard on it. She tried to draw some of us in her wake, inviting one or the other to participate. Always optimistic, Lilian was committed to push everyone to the best of their abilities; she helped, encouraged, pushed forward and shared the profits evenly! Her generosity was unequalled....

In 1982, she succeeds Jacques Masui at the head of the journal *Hermes.* Already in 1969, she had actively contributed to that year's issue of the journal dedicated to Emptiness. She published an outstanding article: "Emptiness, Nothingness, the Chasm."[47] Through a scholarly presentation of this journey, we can catch the echoes of her own experience up to that time. She also participated in the issue *The Spiritual Master,* in which she evoked the subtle atmosphere around the Guru in Kanpur.[48]

In 1982, she re-edits the issues published previously on *The Spiritual Master* and *Emptiness,*[49] and completes them with new articles.

The issue entitled *The Mystical Paths*[50] is an entirely new publication. Lilian is always concerned to highlight the similarities between the different mystical traditions. On such occasions, she can outline the aspects of inner experience in a more accessible fashion than through her scientific work, which everyone is not always able to comprehend. The parallels that she points out, as well as placing similarities into perspective, expand the minds and nourish the hearts by directing them towards tolerance and the universal.

Unfortunately, her deteriorating health and loss of vision get in the way, and will prevent her from publishing the issues of *Hermes* that she had planned. After a publication dedicated to *Tch'an*,[51] she was thinking of an issue on Taoism.

Walk to Ibis Park

After long hours of hard work, Lilian needed to move. At that point, she dragged along the occasional visitor to Ibis Park's lake, near Avenue des Pages.

Despite her lack of attraction for all that is artificial (which was the case for the lake), she always found something to marvel at: a pink tree in spring, new plantings made by the town's gardeners, the autumn colors, the frozen lake in winter....

After a quick march two or three times round the lake, and exhausted by the mental effort, we could finally collapse on a bench and enjoy a well deserved moment of silence.

Testimonial – by R.C.

The Ibis Park (1976)

"A promenade proposed in the beginning
Accepted with enthusiasm...
In the gardens of the Ibis, step by step...
A spring perfume is in the air
On the newly opened flowers...
Bit by bit a haze blurs everything
Spots of vivid color, in a light mist...
My steps unsure,
In my haste and torpor...
Her clear, far-off voice...
The sparkle of her words, of hidden meaning

Bright laughter, unsuspected fullness…
I was bringing some of it back with me, stunned,
The faint echo of the ripple of the waters,
The thin, sharp trills of the birds,
The fresh odor of spring rediscovered
And a radiant quiet…"

"Another time, a new meeting in the park (Ibis) lit by the colours of autumn…. Of the conversation that we had, nothing remains…. I was once again enthralled by the vivacious nature of the Master, her familiarity, her simplicity, her tact, her discretion, her sense of humour, her infinite but subtle attention, almost detached, that she showed in her relation with me. Despite the intense force, at once dense and sweet, which emanated continually from her, there was nothing strange about her, nothing strained, exalted, intolerant or extravagant…. I felt, on purely human terms, an extreme admiration for her uncommon equilibrium, for her intellectual and spiritual strength, without visible prestige, disdainful of appearances, and who went so far beyond me without ever crushing me."

"With empty hands I advance To murmur my gratitude
To this immense heart that fulfilled me
For so many years…
This immense heart generating such fulfillment
And wonder
Which transmitted to me the breath of the Spirit…
Which made me hear and live…
That which had never been said to me…"

Other things said over the years...

Lilian never ceased to tell us about the exceptional greatness of the Guru and his "efficiency," so different from all the others that she had the opportunity to meet in India:

During my numerous stays in India, for the purpose of my philosophical work, I was led to meet many famous scholars, Pundits, Vedantins, Lamas and Buddhist monks from Ceylon and Tibet, and, through various chance encounters, I got to know Bhaktas, Shaivites, Vaishnavas and Jaina devotees, Yogis of all religious backgrounds, and ardent Muslims. Everywhere I came up against a certain narrowness of mind or heart, ritual practices, use of special means, postures, concentration of thought, breath control, which somehow did not fit with the high opinion I had of the Absolute. I also met saints who were constantly absorbed in an ecstasy of love, unaware of the world and its worries. Kind and humble, they spread peace around them as does a flower its fragrance; but they weren't able to actively deal with disciples and pass on mystical states to them, ,over which, despite their experience, they had no control. Nowhere, be it among Jñānins, able to explain the Scriptures, or among saints and devotees, did I discover a man capable of transmitting peace, bliss and knowledge or ensuring a quick and easy progression.

Lilian never missed an occasion to awaken us, wake us up, stimulate us, drawing at the same time on her memories, texts, images and her own experience, inviting us to let go of our habits in any possible way:

Basically, according to an āgama* Sanskrit text, the Guru only has one task, which is to make you understand what is water and ice: living water, flexible, fluid, the undifferentiated mystical life –and hard, sharp ice, fragmented, the ordinary life, which must be restored to its original nature, fluid and which carries you. We can also make a comparison with volcano fire, incandescence and fusion, in which everything is stirred into one single flame, furnace (of love), and the lifeless, frozen scoria (of our ordinary feelings).

According to Sufis and Trika, we don't operate on the lower plane but, starting from the higher plane, we fill up the lower plane with grace – water – to level out its asperities.

The Heart has to melt, the entire being must become more flexible, habits, rigidities, ruts must disappear, so as to always remain malleable and flexible: we can then obey the divine hints at all times and flow spontaneously in accordance with their directions, without even being aware of it.

The Buddha himself (who believed neither in God nor in the Guru) pointed out the great flexibility of the saint which depends on dhyana, peace, and which, in turn, deepens the peace: childlike trust, certitude, conviction and letting yourself be carried, it's all there. During the effort, it is necessary to have a fervor that is never stiff or tense, that is continually reborn, hence tenacious, unwearied, lively, in harmony with flexibility, fire in water, maximum fervor within maximum flexibility.

To progress, cultivate sweetness and flexibility. You will then be able to receive what is given to you. Be flexible. No asceticism!

The Guru continuously offers new occasions to sacrifice yourself. What he does and says is only for that purpose, and he doesn't act for self-serving reasons.

What we really desire, we obtain in an instant, because we are ready to do anything for it; if it's money, we prostitute ourselves without any hesitation ... if it's the Absolute, we forget all the rest that is detached from ourselves and we have exactly what we constantly desire.

Impulse, fervor

The biggest obstacle on our path is artificial emptiness; all previous preparations, techniques, preconceived ideas about what should be done, achieved. I asked all the followers of this form of meditation. They are all used to concentrating and creating a vacuum. Abhinavagupta and Ruysbroeck rise up violently against such quietism which is empty, without any impulse or spontaneity, and I now understand why a bad sort of emptiness, wrong attitude from the start, becomes an insurmountable obstacle, (that of) self-control as well, while on the other hand everything that is "life," passion, natural obstacles are not insurmountable.

One must not get into such emptiness, the ordinary path for many, out of which it then takes several years to come out; it's all a question of momentum, of love. Mystical life is made up of alternations of fullness and absence that cause a desire, a calling, a dialogue without duality!

Introspection is also essential if it isn't too self-centered. It must become more and more subtle and sensitive; intelligence is exercised and asserts itself in an obscure area where everything is yet to be discovered.

The essence of the path is to give fully of oneself, to swim towards the river. Once the river carries you away, you've won.

The spiritual path is like a series of stairs, sometimes with gardens on the different levels; we mustn't lose ourselves in those gardens; we can get lost on any level; we must go up as fast as possible!

Lilian gets impatient sometimes

Like a fountain, the Master wants to give, put the gushing living water into his disciples' mouths, but they just turn to avoid it, running, making lots of efforts and moving constantly. Can't you just keep still for one minute, so that I may give to you?

If you only understood, one minute would suffice....

Every event was a chance of inviting us to freedom, and to stress the importance of ordinary life which, in itself exempts us from mortifications, as the path is not a refuge:

Saints of this lineage must appear like beings full of worldly worries, like an ordinary man, so that only those seeking Reality can recognize them for what they are.

Work, family, needs of the family, etc.: everything is given to face what is essential in everyday life. But any activism goes wrong.

Different occupations only get in the way if they become a priority.

There should not be a separate life. No hermits! There are many people who would like to have the tranquility of a hermit. This is not our path. I insist on this, as I have already done.

No free will of our own – it's Grace! It's all about letting ourselves be carried by the river – consciously. No morality! It's the downfall of religions.

Do nothing, above all, no technique whatsoever!

What matters is peace, bliss, if possible a state of dhyana. Then, certain events may occur. Such peace depends on untangling inner knots, not on external conditions. So we must first eliminate all complexes to allow peace to be established.

Prayer

If something is not going too well for you, the best thing is to pray. but while in dhyana, only then will the prayer – simple heartfelt impulse – be effective and immediate.

My Guru said sometimes that we should pray God to give us the love of the Guru, and pray the Guru to give us the love of God.

Collapse of the ego

The Guru puts the disciple into a state in which he detaches himself from everything; he first plunges him into bliss which makes him even forget his own self, then into emptiness where he loses his ego. The self disappears, but the reality of the higher Self remains. The real always remains, the unreal vanishes.

Love of art

Painting

Lilian appreciated all forms of artistic expression, particularly music and painting. Her criteria were vibration and resonance; she would teach us to recognize vibration even in sculpture, which was a revelation for most of us.

Her paternal grandfather was a painter. In her youth, Lilian showed a lot of talent for drawing. Painting could have become a passion for her, hence the reason why she gave it up to avoid being distracted from her essential quest. In her diary during the years she was in India, we can grasp the acuteness of her gaze:

The vibration has almost disappeared, as well as the lights, only the ripple of the fire snake remains. But nature is bathing in an incredible peace. As night was falling, the red flower against the dark green made me understand Monet (his Nympheas) much better, as well as other artists. The greater ones are those who, through a long contemplation during which they forget their own self (such as Monet, Titian, Rembrandt, Van Gogh), end up expressing that peace: but to be able to understand their peace, we must have been immersed in a great peace ourselves, for a long time. There is no movie nor photograph that can reveal this peace and sweetness. Now, each time I open my eyes in the countryside, I can see it through the eyes of these masters, which is with endless patience. Mystic and artistic contemplations converge. (September 1950)

Lilian had several painter friends and she followed their progress and exhibitions with interest; and as long as her health and sight permitted, she took us to all major Parisian exhibitions, especially those of Impressionists. Monet had all her favor: light captured in the moment fascinated her.

For us at the same time, it was a great pleasure and a trial. We could say that in her wake, we experienced the ordeal of "seeing without seeing." Happy to have been asked to accompany her, we were ready to share the enthusiasm that she wished to communicate. Lilian encouraged us to close our eyes in front of the paintings and to reopen them abruptly so as to grasp the work in an initial burst, prior to any mental construction. We were trying our best.... Apparently, in this operation, those who were near-sighted were in an advantageous position.

Pleased as she was to contemplate what she enjoyed so much, she was radiating such a special intensity that some of us were quickly encouraged to close our eyes, with no desire to reopen them, whilst others, more resistant, carried on, tilting their heads to the side, from right to left, to vary the viewpoints.

This is how we've glimpsed works by Chagall, Monet, Rembrandt, Turner and others. I do mean glimpsed, as, despite our good will, we collapsed one after the other on the first bench in sight, being too young in the inner experience to combine open eyes, aesthetic discoveries and jolts on account of the Grace, as Lilian would give, or transmit, in all circumstances.

In London, we spent quite a long time admiring the Turner collection, another magician of light. In Holland, it was Rembrandt's interiority and Van Gogh's intensity. On the other hand, she was much less sensitive to the art of Picasso, except for his blue period, which strongly displeased some of our painter friends who were muttering. Despite our vacillating gaze, we learned a great deal and from then on we look at these paintings differently, certainly with an interiorised look, but with our eyes open!

Music

While talking to Mataji [the Guru's mother] *during our walk, I felt a sort of anguish: I needed Occidental music and I said that, to me, music was the closest thing to my current state of bliss. An hour later, as I was lying down, not really concentrating, I suddenly heard the music that I love, Mozart, J.S. Bach and first of all, Daquin's piece, "The Cuckoo." I first thought I was dreaming. It was coming from a house nearby, so I sat in the garden at night for an hour, and more than ever I enjoyed the music infinitely, as I am entirely living in the present moment and every sound is a delight. There is only peace in the background instead of agitation as in the past. For three days, I listened to the best records by the best performers: the records belonged to a young Bengali couple who were brought together by the love of music.* (November 1950)

Lilian loved music. She loved it deeply. She knew it intimately.

She would listen to a lot of music at night and with her friends during the day. She stopped going to concerts as she did in her youth ... essentially because she feared receiving any clumsy knocks on the back of her chair. They could trigger a sudden Kundalini rising followed by a feeling of queasiness. But nonetheless, we still had pleasure in accompanying her to a few concerts: Jean-Pierre Rampal, Alfred Deller at Royaumont Abbey.... We could then close our eyes in peace!

Lilian loved classical music. She found Baroque music and Debussy's dissonance particularly charming. She introduced many of us to Monteverdi. She would listen attentively to the interpretation of the various performers and could perceive their most subtle differences. This is how she discovered the exceptional playing of Clara Haskil, certain of whose interpretations have remained unique until today. "She plays with her whole body," she observed.

Lilian was also very sensitive to the human voice. She particularly appreciated singers such as Kathleen Ferrier, Elisabeth Schumann, or even Marian Anderson. She was also fascinated by the voice of the counter tenors, Alfred Deller being her favorite.

She also listened to Indian music. In her youth, she had been courted by one of Ravi Shankar's brothers. "What tempted me (she said) was the family, a family of musicians." Later on, she enjoyed the ragas of Hariprasad Chaurasia and recitals by the Pakistani singer Nusrat Fateh Ali Khan. Over the years, she equipped herself with the latest equipment and made non-stop audio cassette recordings which we could take with us when traveling. This is how, in addition to the tea basket, we got a second little case for audio cassettes.

If Lilian did not often take us to concerts, she often invited us to listen to records or music programs. Especially on Sunday afternoons, we would listen to a program which proposed different interpretations of a same piece of music. However, it is far from certain that we could really grasp any of the differences, caught as we were by another sort of vibration.

The Marseilles wave, 1980-1981

On two occasions, in 1980 and 1981, Ram introduces many of his students from Marseille to Lilian. Ram, an eminent teacher of Tai Ji Quan in Marseille, has a deep veneration for Lilian as he is aware of her efficiency. He has his heart set on introducing to her those amongst his students that he feels are up to following the path she offers. So he arrives with a group of students who are all very different one from another.

After a solemn demonstration of Tai Ji in the garden, the newcomers pile up on the armchairs and benches, and it is difficult to tell who is the most intimidated. Lilian does her best to relax them by dint of cheerfulness and simplicity, showing interest in each and every one, demonstrating an astounding insight.

Rams' intuition and Lilian's magic proved to be very effective. Many of Ram's students became friends, and faithful friends of Lilian's. And so the circle of close friends became bigger and daily life was punctuated by the Marseillais' visitors who became unconditional users of the TGV [High Speed Train].

Three of them are the authors of the following testimonials.

Testimonials

Memories of an exceptional meeting – S.A.

"I met Lilian Silburn in September 1980. During all the years I came especially to see her, I never exchanged more than a few words with her like: 'Hello' or 'How are you?'

"This was a deep mystery because very often I would come to Le Vésinet with my head full of questions that seemed very important to me. I was trying to find the very best formulations to clarify the nature of the Way.

"Each time, without any exception, all these questions dissolved, like salt crystals in fresh water. At each encounter, I was overwhelmed by an immense peace and a total absence of will to try to understand or grasp what was taking place. The experience of silence, and the depth of self, imposed themselves above all else.

"One particular memory, however, which I experienced many times in the same way, concerns the precise moment when Lilian entered the house. Sitting on a corner of the sofa or on a chair, my head buzzing with thoughts, I remember it as if it was yesterday, that magical moment when Lilian's laughter and presence was spreading through the house. A total upheaval in my state of mind was taking place. A luminous wave of lightness, gentleness and silence, elusive yet manifest, invaded the space with an energy of love.

"This extraordinary instant, without beginning or end, indisputable evidence of another dimension of being, made me think of the beginning of everything, the beginning of life, the innocence of early childhood.

"One day, sitting next to her in silence, Lilian spoke to me, surprised at never hearing the sound of my voice. I was unable to answer a single word, but she assured me that even without ever having heard me express myself, she knew me very well from the inside, perhaps even better than I knew myself. This, far from seeming exaggerated to me, seemed so right that I felt myself blushing to the roots of my hair.

"I had never talked about these few scattered memories until now. They remain in my heart, along with many other moments, witness to my immense gratitude to Lilian.

"To find this spark of life in this total, gratuitous and selfless love is an unforgettable experience, which, at that time, allowed me to reconnect with the real meaning of my life, which had seemed impossible.

"And yet...."

The grace of Lilian (met in 1980) – C. D.

"The grace of Lilian seeps through all the chinks of everyday life. Just walk with her and the slightest surge of love is increased tenfold in the simplest gestures.

"For example, I reach out to Lilian to help her put on her jacket. Immediately, her presence draws me in and, at the same time, disappears as I move forward.... Suspended in a dizzying emptiness, the jacket is slipped on in an impulse of love of the whole being. There only remains the vibrant delicacy of this fading through Lilian's eternally present smile.

"Another time (in 1984), in the car, contemplating Rotheneuf beach, Lilian told me that, after her illness, she regretted not being able to swim anymore, she who loved it so much. Touched in my heart by this regret, I didn't even have time to react before she suggested I go in swimming.

"Without any other thought than to follow this incitation which propels me into the water, I cross the bay in an unforgettable state of exhilaration. Swimming becomes pure abandonment to the movement of water, air, light, no effort needed, with ease, flexibility, and infinite joy.

"When I got back in the car, Lilian said to me mischievously:

"'That will give you memories for later!'

"What a memory! Seized by the moment, keenly touched by the grace of abandonment... as if it was nothing! ..."

Holder of a fundamental mystery – From C. P.

"It was on All Saints' Day 1981 that I first met Lilian Silburn. At a friend's initiative, we were a few from South of France coming to meet her, to simply taste, through her presence, a silence of a peculiar intensity, a transforming silence. It was, in any case, an experience such as this that I aspired to at that time, definitely not knowing how things would go.

"That afternoon Lilian Silburn, with a few friends, greeted us; she radiated a joyful, serene and intense presence. After a few friendly exchanges, an incredible silence spontaneously arose, and carried us to the depths of ourselves.

"This experience proved to be decisive for many of us. Lilian Silburn came back to the conversation after a while. No heaviness, no injunction, no advice, only the enthusiasm of joy, a lively humor, full of insight, permeated her words; everything, in her attitude and words, expressed sincerity. What had just happened seemed like wonderful evidence and yet was as unusual as wonderful. As pure as the intangible atmosphere of the highest peaks, space seemed transformed on emerging from that silence by which we were inexorably attracted.

"As holder of a fundamental mystery, free from all individuality, Lilian Silburn stood among us, connected to a pure stream of light and love, making us live directly the essential experience of the formless, of the limitless. I knew immediately that I had found what I had always expected, thanks to the state of fullness, centered, appeased, which had spontaneously been established; I also understood that, to the extent of our receptivity, a kind of osmosis was taking place, of which this simple-looking woman was the origin. This first absorption in silence was followed by many others; it was the beginning of an inner journey that cannot be told because it doesn't belong to the registers of thought. What can just be said is that through her presence, thought and its dilemmas were dissolved; then arose the perception of deeper dimensions, full of rivers of light, and, above all, an infinite agreement with the nature of things, broadening the current of life, suddenly more intense and conscious, permeated by a feeling of universal life.

"During the next twelve years, I also had the opportunity, apart from those blessed times of silence, to meet with Lilian Silburn several times about my research in the field of Indianism. In spite of her very bad health during the last years of her life, she always revealed sincere interest and always provided answers of striking clarity and depth. She was concerned to shed light on the authentic, infinitely precious legacy of Kashmiri Shaivism on the level of mystical life. Besides her knowledge in that field, she enjoyed sharing stories about her life with Lakshman Joo in Kashmir, or with her Kanpur master. The profound experience that inhabited her, then rose spontaneously through any memories, bringing up the silence of the depths.

"I remember her enthusiastic comments on the concept of vibration during the 1980's; because of her passion for all areas of knowledge, she considered this central notion of medieval Kashmiri Shaivism of great relevance, in resonance with recent discoveries in physics. She cherished the experience of art because it can lead to contemplation, and so to a saturation of bliss, until a fulfillment of consciousness.

"How essential the encounter with Lilian Silburn was, words could not express it. However, one aspect seems important to me to mention: it is not so much her person as such, even if she was admirable, that captivated, but her ability to bring to life in herself, through herself, forgetting herself, an immemorial spark, transmitted from heart to heart. That is why, for those who came to taste her silence, life took on a special flavor, the gaze returned to the essential, suffused with light, the whole body became again but a fragment of universe."

Puech Redon

After a cardiac incident during a stay in Dinard, at Easter 1981, Lilian was hospitalized in Saint-Malo, and, as it was suggested to her, she agreed to the insertion of a pacemaker. Thereafter, because of the altitude, it became necessary to give up the holidays in Ayguatebia. So instead, Lilian opted for the house of a lady friend, in the South of Auvergne: Puech Redon. Another adventure.

From the outside, the granite stone house looked beautiful, but the inside was totally dilapidated and occupied by owls. As we already mentioned, Lilian disdained luxury, and this was confirmed once more.

Uninhabited for several years, uncared for much longer, the house was without any comfort.

Never mind! Within two months, two basic bathrooms were improvised, a pump installed on the well which had been miraculously dug a few years before, and we were able to penetrate into a place swarming with multiple lives which hadn't been disturbed by any human presence for a very long time.

Like savages, we were upsetting the balance of a natural universe of which Henri Bosco has the secret and the sensation of which we rapidly lost. Nonetheless, owls, bats, grass snakes, lizards, accepted the cohabitation without any problem: a source of mixed emotions for city dwellers.

Yielding to the visualization of an expanded space, Lilian gave a great number of invitations in the first year, and a new generation appeared to colonize the out-buildings: barn, attic and former hen-house.

Lilian occupied the first floor with one or two ladies. Thus she could work in the morning and avoid the length and agitation of group meals that she dreaded. Guests managed life on the ground floor.

The inaugural year was very cheerful. Lilian, always very active, suggested all kinds of sketches and, if necessary, there was even a costume trunk transported from the cellar of Le Vésinet in case of need. The gentlemen surpassed each other in funny inventions, and Lilian was laughing wholeheartedly.

But there were also working sessions on a new contribution to the journal *Hermes* of which Lilian recently took charge, and as usual, she was seeking young and inexperienced collaborators that she would stimulate, anxious to give them some recognition. That year, the young and not so young were cheerfully engaged in the leveling of a path: fragile ankle sprains had to be avoided. However, at tea time under the old apple tree, silence regained its place and, in an instant, everything would disappear but the rustling of insects or the chirping of new-born birds nesting in the hollows of the façade.

Yet it wasn't the same rigor and intensity as in the first years at Ayguatebia. Fifteen years have passed, Lilian has strengthened herself in the role of the elder, she has trained a first generation, and from now on newcomers are discovering the depth into which she plunges and from which she pulls herself out only with more and more effort, but no one notices. She gives, in an instant, her full attention to each one.

But she can also bustle about when everyone is together. She can be cheerful and get interested in the most external of problems like making improvements to the place. This is how she encourages us to purchase an old spiral staircase to connect the two floors, a staircase which wouldn't have continued to serve its purpose in this house, without her.

She will never lose her taste for what is original and comical. We narrowly avoided the purchase of a pulpit or even of an altar that a neighboring church was renewing! Such eccentric projects, fortunately without outcome, had at least the merit of stimulating discussions and provoking liberating laughter, between moments of deep silence that profoundly affected hearts and consciousness.

Like in Ayguatebia, her efficiency is continuous but it is exercised through much less active forms of daily life: slower walks, various presentations in the shade of the apple tree.

In the first years of course, we explore the surroundings: Conques, le Puy Mary, but it doesn't last. As Lilian is becoming less and less nimble, outings are limited to the close environment and above all, by car, in an old Renault 10 which was her favorite because we could comfortably dive in it, with our eyes closed, in a landscape carefully chosen beforehand! If we left the car, we would look for gentle descents for Lilian to walk on.

Under the apple tree or inside around the table at tea time, she tried to initiate the ignorant – and there were many of us – to Kashmir Shaivism; it was an opportunity for various exchanges punctuated with bursts of laughter. Jeremy, our artist, immortalized the painting of the three paths on a couple of old wooden planks that were used as a table....

There was another activity appreciated by everyone: television programs, many of which were of great quality at the time, particularly on nature like "Cosmos," or the seduction mode among the different species of birds, a series of Shakespeare's plays.... We appreciated such silent moments when, gathered around Lilian in front of the screen, we would sink into the depth of our states, in total forgetfulness; only a few among us actually followed a whole program even if eyes could see from time to time. It was very difficult to get up when the screen shut down. Happy interlude, a time of rest and forgetfulness, when everyone had the feeling of having been somewhere, having followed Lilian in her breakaways.

The memories of India were always there. Lilian liked to revive them from time to time by wearing a sari, especially when she was giving an individual sitting.

It's in Puech Redon that, for the first time and perhaps the last, she wore her Sufi outfit, remembering the words of the Guru: "Now, you are one of us, dress if possible like me." (January 1965) The isolation of Puech Redon lent itself to it.

But whatever the moment, Lilian was always ready to please! As much as she was rigorous, even demanding, probably without her knowing it, for those who wanted to follow her path, her patience and kindness were unlimited for other people. This is how, at an advanced age, she would be hoisted on to a jolting tractor trailer to explore the woods of a friend who lived nearby: it was so important to him! Some passing visitors who come to meet her, knowing her work, have trouble concealing their astonishment when they discover the rusticity of the place and the extreme simplicity of reception.

Lilian will spend ten summers in Puech Redon, until 1992. But conditions evolve according to her health. Her period of availability is reduced, but she wants to work until the end, and the unfinished texts are read to her, in this case *"The Tantrāloka."*[52]

Her sight is failing, osteoporosis develops, nights are difficult; we stop going to the seaside at the end of August but we extend our stay until the end of September, in a small group. The group is becoming smaller and smaller, Lilian more and more silent.

A passing visitor: Minouche

Lilian protected dormice, welcomed mice, fished tadpoles in the garden pond before emptying it and taking them to Ibis Park's lake, and recruited an escort to accompany young ducklings, brooded in one of our gardens, to the nearby lakes. But this had more to do with a respect for life than a so-called "love of animals." However, there was Minouche, a happy episode.

Attracted by Aliette, when he was crossing her garden, Minouche, as we called him, soon became a regular member of the little household, for the greatest joy of the two sisters. He didn't make much noise as, once he passed the threshold, he would lie on Lilian's bed, completely relaxed, turning into a soft and flexible mass, unrecognizable. At other times, he'd fall asleep against Lilian's shoulder, completely still, frozen in his position. He neither disturbed Lilian during her samadhi, nor the silence of the meetings, until we started to realize that he might actually be participating too. Effectively, whenever the Grace took the form of blows in the heart, he was obviously whining at the same time. Everyone was thrilled.

Minouche

When he'd been missing for a while, it was a joy for Aliette to find him sleeping under some ferns in the garden.

Thus Minouche was the star of a time. Cameras clicked toward him and he was photographed in all his ecstatic poses. It greatly amused Lilian. But one year, coming back from vacation, we didn't find him. We waited and hoped, but in vain. Lilian didn't say anything but, apparently, she was sad.

Aliette and César

Some time later, Cesar appeared, russet and slobbery. He wasn't a nobody. It happened to be M. Gotlib's cat, who lived in the neighborhood. But the cat of the cartoonist who designed *Fluide Glacial* [a French comic magazine] remained insensitive to the vibrations of Abhinavagupta's devotee ... unless it was the opposite! Nonetheless, he did not enter Lilian's bed room and remained under Aliette's sole control. The spell was broken.

Contrary to what some might think, all cats are not ... mystical.

Testimonials

From F.P.

"From our first meeting (1983), I immediately felt an intense presence in she who was to become my spiritual master. With an empathetic smile, she said to me, 'you're crying already!' I had been touched in my heart and my mind was freed from all confusion.

"Probably because of my Italian roots she talked to me about the stigmata of Saint Francis of Assisi, about her experience when she visited the burial place of Saint Claire, and of Padre Pio's gift of ubiquity. 'You must know that,' she said teasingly!

"During the interview, I was filled with the deep presence of life, this Reality which I did not know; I fell into a state of torpor. I didn't understand what was going on: 'It's the grace,' she said. A deep peace came over me. Lilian Silburn, who was grace itself, had put me in this state despite myself."

From A. M.

"What struck me the first time I met Miss Silburn (in 1986), under the appearance of a 'beautiful, smiling, modest and welcoming grandmother,' was the intensity of her presence that was hardly apparent to outsiders.

"She revealed no sign of the richness of her inner dimension. She had a piercing gaze that testified to her keen perception. No need to hide it from oneself, she could 'read' the depth of one's heart.

"Very subtle, full of humor, she could express, with infinite courtesy, an incisive truth that shook the strait jacket of our own convictions.

"Always attentive, she brought to each one a kind word and the comfort of her infinite compassion accompanied by a vibrating current that ran from head to toe, invisible to others ... as if to show the way forward.

"Whoever remained connected heart to heart with her was protected, as if by a shield, in all situations.

"Her modesty and discretion were commensurate with her effectiveness. It was enough to dive in her presence to experience the power of her Love. Sometimes, I came to her, my mind tortured by all sorts of problems ... without a word everything disappeared in a burst of her laughter expressed with incomparable gentleness and cheerfulness. I was then carried in the current of her purest and most efficient Love!"

From E.M.

"The first time I met Lilian I was impressed by the youth of her voice and by the playful lightness that emanated from her person despite her age. Her face was lit by an inner clarity which was accentuated by her blue eyes and high, clear forehead.

"Her courteous and attentive attitude should have made me feel quite comfortable. However I was having difficulty speaking, I couldn't find my words. Touched in my heart and with an empty mind, I felt a great respect as well as an almost incredulous gratitude.

"I had had the opportunity to see her handwriting in which perfect harmony and dancing fluidity were clearly evident, reflecting an exceptional personality. Her enchanting sense of humor, always ready to burst forth, could be wicked or wise according to the circumstances. And what about the peace, limpidity and intensity of her presence? When you were staying with her, all questions and worries vanished, existence took on a subtle flavor. Her vivacity of spirit and penetrating intelligence were reflected in her clear and refined voice, whereas the power of the grace was revealed in the secret silence in which you aspired to merge with her.

"If her spontaneity, her humor and her cheerfulness filled us with wonder, it was because they expressed an absolute freedom. And such a freedom can only spring from the Reality in which Lilian was living and still lives for us."

From S. T.:

"The first time, I arrived to meet Lilian weighed down only by my preconceived ideas and an overload of illusions.

"Then I found myself in front of an elderly lady, very simple, natural and almost modest. She did not correspond to the erroneous idea that I fabricated of a Master. I am struck by her sobriety. She bids me to sit beside her. I am incapable of remembering the questions I'd prepared or even to articulate any phrase. In front of her, I find myself destabilized, confused, as naked. She asks me some simple questions to which I try to reply. I am aware only of my ignorance, my incapacity, I lose all control. This little lady had, in an instant, reduced me to nothing.

"Then, my eyes close; I don't know what's happening. Later, on opening my eyes again, I discover the greatness of the Master.

"In a session where Lilian was surrounded by a lot of people, I had my eyes closed. At one point, I open my eyes: we are alone in the room; those around her had disappeared. However, several moments later, they were still there, they hadn't moved...."

Time is passing...

Lilian becomes more pressing. She tries to stimulate people, by all possible means, and in meetings she often uses the image of the river and the sea into which we enter progressively:

As time is limited, I strongly insist on what is essential; later on, some of you will regret not having understood this when it was time: You must be convinced that the path you are following is the best for you, the only one that will carry you and take you as far as you would like, and beyond what you could ever hope. Otherwise, what is there to do for you?

Your obstacles, so you think, lie in fear, complexes, etc., but they are secondary compared to that conviction that can sweep them away, all of them, at once.

The path is like a big river capable of throwing you into the sea. You can see the progress achieved as a result of simply recognizing the river: some know almost in advance that it's the only path, and without any hesitation, with full certainty, they go into it, letting themselves be carried along, with complete confidence, without even knowing how to swim.

Others, full of complexes and inner problems, cannot remain constantly in the river, but each time I reach out to them, they follow me without hesitation, and because of their absolute faith they benefit from as much advantages as the first ones. Thus the biggest obstacles do not prevent us from diving in the river, but only from remaining there for a long time.

Certain ones remain on the shore, hesitant, with their feet in the water, and I sprinkle them: they don't have complete confidence and are moving forward slowly, either because they are scared, or because they can't see the greatness of the river and its outlet to the sea.

There are those who don't get wet and who even turn their backs on the river, dreaming of small streams at their level (past or future) where they could safely splash about at ease, according to their own will, and get wet from time to time. They lack confidence; we won't be able to draw them into the river.

Indeed, being interested in two or more currents at the same time, going from one to another, will not enable them to reach the sea. We can then only sprinkle them from time to time, when they momentarily have trust, but it isn't enough, as they quickly lose the benefits as soon as they run away. At the right time, they always run away.

Testimonials

From E. D.:

"Emanating from Lilian was a force so soft yet so powerful that from the first instant of the first meeting with her (in 1989), any doubts evaporated as if they had never existed. Encouraging with kindness the newcomer by this simple word 'So?,' she listened attentively to the awkward words which, in front of her, came without thinking and described for her an existence, hopes, worries. Quickly the silence installed itself. She knew. Words were unnecessary. Time stopped. A sensation of eternity filled the consciousness of those she had welcomed. The invitation to unite with her in silence engulfed every sense.

"This dimension deepened with each visit. The individual conscious, superficial and limited, came to receive and benefit from being with hers, profound and generous. No words, but the absorption of perceptions and thought in the mystery to which her presence alone gave access. This mystery was so tangible and surprising that it encouraged the temptation to address it explicitly. Lilian then laughed gaily, avoiding with humor the devotion but encouraging us to recognize and deepen this mystery. *'It comes in its own way,'* she said one day, *'like a good surprise.'*

"The moments passed with her left in my heart a germ of a new peace. The experiences of rapture would traverse our daily life. The senses would no longer function in the same way. A paradise glimpsed from the window plunged us irremediably into the mystery of the moment. A peace appeared suddenly in moments of ineffable sweetness when confronted with the beauty of a flower, wet from the rain or the corner of a wall so sharp against the far off sky. The silence arose from the depths. A calm slipped into apertures in the conscious. 'These are the most important moments,' Lilian would say. Elusive, the desire to recapture them was no good. Something always evaded our grasp, pushing us to question more. The simple and concrete answers that she gave would bring us once again back to the unfathomable sweetness that emanated from her. Only the abandon of self opens up to peace.

"Her presence was of an intensity and purity such as it was difficult to imagine Lilian simply as a person. Her human form dissolved to let appear the profound light which shone from her and only at her side was it possible to live and feel. This intensity permeated those that aspired to it and nurtured from it. Learning that, in her youth she liked to pass holidays alone in a grotto in Corsica, and she loved to take long walks in the Mediterranean, the sea, the waves, made me think inevitably of her.

"In time, the transformation deepened and revealed to disciples more and more profound layers of their being. Sometimes uncovering long forgotten, painful traces that had affected them in the very early years of their lives. The evocation of Lilian sufficed, the grace of her presence offered a profound peace.

Pain was no longer of any account. Life rejoined forever something larger, deeper than oneself."

Memories of my first meeting with Lilian (1989)

From F. P. (Twenty years later):

"One day, I had just walked into her entrance hall, when J. playfully said to me: 'I've got a surprise for you!' she then re-opened the door.

"The clear memory that remains is that I had to make an effort to lower my eyes towards Lilian, because her presence was so great, despite her small stature, that I naturally looked upwards.

"I then had to keep myself from falling at her feet, finally understanding how one could do that, as I had spent all my life thinking of everyone as equal.

"I was really impressed by her greatness.

"As she laid her eyes on me, I felt that she knew me to the deepest point of my being.

"Later, J. sat me next to Lilian, for the three of us to meditate.

"Here again, I had to restrain myself from slipping to her feet as I felt unworthy of sitting so close and at the same level as she. I felt from within that she wasn't expecting that sort of behavior from me, and little by little, the silence soothed any questioning.

"From that first dive with her, I keep the vision of our three hearts linked together, vibrating in space.... "

From C.S.:

"After having a dream, I asked a friend if I could attend a meeting with Miss Silburn; I thought I was going to an anonymous teaching, knowing nothing about transmission from heart to heart.

"I was surprised by the simplicity of the meeting and by the deep silence surrounding us. Then I felt the joy and a tremendous happiness flowing over me. I said to myself: 'So, there is a hereafter?' deeply moved by the presence of this radiant person.

"From this very first encounter, what were hopes and expectations became faith and certitude within me.

"At the end of the meeting, she asked me what I was looking for; I mumbled a shy 'who I am'; *'seek rather who you are not,'* she laughed.

"At home, the presence of her grace was catching me everywhere, regardless of time or place. As I was not living in Paris, every time I came up to meet Lilian, I was plunged into powerful currents the days before and would arrive in Le Vésinet filled with love and thankfulness.

"A memory of her effectiveness: arriving at the maternity hospital for my daughter's birth, despite the shyness she always inspired in me, I phoned Lilian to inform her.

"I had an unusual experience: between each powerful contraction, I was carried by a breath that brought me deep peacefulness and confidence: a rhythm settled in me, like a regular, healing and efficient wave, until the child was born.

"Later, I heard that Jacqueline, who had been talking to Lilian at the very same time, was surprised to be told, *'Be quiet! I'm giving birth!'*

"Meeting Lilian gave me faith in a *'garland of love'* within reach: seized, lost ... always offered."

From M. G.

"The first time I met Lilian, in January 1991, I knew nothing about her except that she had translated and commented on many texts of Kashmir Shaivism, of which she was recognized as an eminent specialist. It's thanks to her works that I wanted to meet her; they aroused mystical intuition. Without revealing anything of its author, there was a strong attraction. It appeared to me that such frequentation of these mystical texts, such a science of commentary could only emanate from a person with real knowledge of the experience related in these writings. It went far beyond an intellectual and scholarly approach.

"At our first meeting, however, there was hardly any mention of her books. Lilian went straight to the point, questioning the underlying reason for my coming. Then very naturally and very simply, she invited me to let myself be won over by Silence. The ensuing peace was her work, without her mentioning it. Her secret action, her incitement to grace, operated in silence. I perceived them all the more efficiently as I had arrived already plunged in a very great confusion linked to an emotional distress. The awakened peace remained for several days, recognizable by a silent vibration.

"The next few meetings were also very simple, neither education nor technique. In the presence of Lilian, it was enough to remain seated, eyes closed, back straight and supported, heels on the ground, and thus installed, to let the impersonal work inside. Little by little the body was won over by an increasing immobilization and an ineffable peace enveloped us.

"We arrived as we were, no need to convert, to abandon our religion or beliefs. These would leave us of their own volition if necessary. At the same time, Lilian greatly appreciated the discernment that, in fact, she encouraged. It was about apprehending things as the consciousness awoke. An immense freedom reigned, nothing was imposed, which, moreover, could be very disconcerting. Lilian in no way adopted the posture of the Guru, as one could imagine it. And, in her presence, the representations fell away one after the other.

"Despite being over 80, she amazed with her playful and witty humor. But what was even more remarkable was the impersonal and immense love that she spread.

"Once, while I confided to her my lot of difficulties, she invited me to *'not worry about the lesser, but only to be won over by the more,'* or evoking an author of Kashmir Shivaism,

Vasugupta, '*Pay attention to the best, the rest will fall by itself.*' She invited us to consider that it was not 'we' who were intervening, but the force of Reality. She insisted on the true Subject, which is the Consciousness of the subject, on the threshold of all mystical life.

"Among the great mystical currents, she told me that she had deep affinities with Taoism, '*so simple to understand*' ... the true mystic.

"The last memory that I keep was of the *Bandhara*, in January 1993, a perception forever fixed in an eternal present, of the luminous vibration of Love, which when in contact, revealed itself in all its evidence and enveloped us. It allowed access to this space inside, but neither inside nor outside, which revealed the link between consciousness, light and love. And her efficiency is such that it allows it still."

From C. G.:

"That garden, flowers, alleys, a kiosk, water, a tranquil place.... A room, people sitting, my mother who does not reply, and Lilian who turns to me. Her gaze....

"Her gaze, another time, on a pavement, so piercing, so acute, so penetrating.... A meeting in my adolescence, tea time with the "friends of Le Vésinet," two ladies talking about Yasser Arafat, one of them so fascinated by uniforms that she would marry a soldier. My thousand questions before the meeting, freezing when facing Lilian, that silent question 'is the exterior so important?', and that perplexity thereafter so disconcerting....

"And yet, during the first dive with Jacqueline, that feeling of recognizing something, of finding a frequency again, a vibration.... That long search, trying to free myself on Saturday morning to go to Le Vésinet.... It was almost unconscious, a deep desire, incomprehensible, untold...

"Those messages from Lilian afterwards, with a particular tone, short, two or three words, direct, incisive, which stop me in my tracks, freeze me, shake me, submerge me in perplexity.... That gaze, sparkling with intelligence.... That gaze I see sometimes on Jacqueline's face like a wink. Thank you, Lilian."

The last days

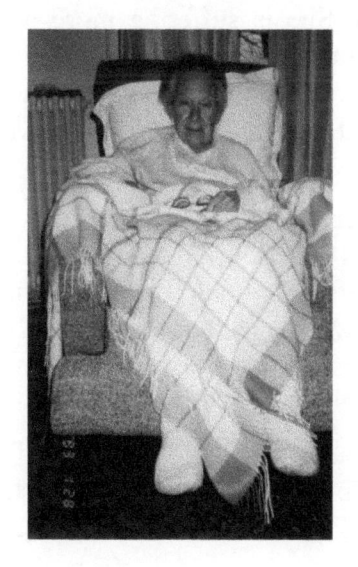

At the time of the Bhandhara in 1991, Lilian, tired and emaciated, decides to move into avenue Maurice Berteaux for a few days: this will enable Aliette to rest and avoid Lilian the discomfort of comings and goings. In fact, she'll never go back to avenue des Pages, without ever having expressed a clear decision on this subject.

Her health is slowly deteriorating, but she continues to work with the assistance of those around her.

André Padoux visits her regularly. They are planning to publish together the first chapters of the *Tantraloka* [posthumously published in 1998].

She can't see anymore. She has osteoporosis. She has violent pains. But despite all these difficulties she continues to work and conduct meetings, true to what has been her life since the Guru's death. She even receives newcomers, but less and less often, always ready to open a heart to the great current of grace, and perhaps with the hope of finally discovering the "great" mystical experience of her dreams!

But it becomes increasingly difficult for her to be present for passing visitors. She must be warned well in advance of a forthcoming visit, to give her time to "come back," as she put it. Her absorptions are getting ever deeper, reaching increasingly higher states. We can't follow her anymore. But we also sense that secretly, deep down in her heart, she is going over her life with such humility that strikes those around her whenever she lets out a few words on the subject.

Her difficulties continue to worsen. She is suffering more and more, can no longer sleep in her bed nor go downstairs. In 1992, Lilian solemnly went down the stairs, carried by some gentlemen in an armchair especially designed for this purpose; it was cheerful.

Nonetheless, she spends the summer in Puech Redon and will preside over the last Bhandhara in 1993 from her room, where she invites everybody to come, one after the other, paying special attention to everyone's concerns, which, without showing it, required an enormous effort on her part, as she had to "come back" from very far, so very far!

She will live her last days on the ground floor, with the help of a home care scheme. From the depths of her suffering, she welcomes visitors, still anxious, until the end, to flood with light those who approach her.

She passes away on March 19th, 1993.

Testimonial: In the continuity

From M. B.: 1980 and thirty years later:

"I met Lilian Silburn almost thirty years ago, in a sunny garden of Le Vésinet. I was about forty at the time. I had just read her book about the *bhakti*, and she, whom I saw as an unreachable scholar, agreed to see me, a stranger, simply because I asked. From that moment, I should have known what she really was.

"What remains of this first encounter is the memory of a welcome of great simplicity. I don't remember a word of the conversation, but I keep, deep inside of me, a lasting impression of vibrations passing through me in soft waves, as we were speaking of the most ordinary things. It was not a problem, although I had never felt anything like this. I hadn't had the wit to ask her what was going on, but perhaps it was for the best. As we went our separate ways, she invited me to come back, on days when a small group of people gathered around her.

"I met her a second time and, as I was alone with her, she showed me the picture of a very beautiful face, full of light and serenity. Then, she whispered: 'It is the face of my Master, during his last moment. He is a Sufi.' She was no longer a scholarly, enlightened pundit of Abhinavagupta's work, so knowledgeable about Kashmir Shaivism. No, in this instant, she was simply a woman, showing me the photograph of her worshipped sadguru. Between us, a tangible love, like a real presence, was manifesting itself inside of me. I was flabbergasted: her master was a Sufi? What a surprise! This unexpected revelation moved me deeply, although I was not yet aware of the connection between this confidence and the experience in the garden, that I had lived a few days earlier. Twice, Lilian Silburn shared with me the most precious, intimate, living part of herself. How I wish now to cherish what was given to me that day!

"I would come back to her only thirty years later, as the seed she had planted in me spontaneously germinated, opening a breach in the last, most solid wall of resistance left in me. All of a sudden thirty years on, I absolutely needed to seek her out and find her. And, miraculously, wonderfully, it was possible, I did. All I had to do was ask and 'knock' at the right door and, on my first try, the door opened, wider than I could've ever dreamed it would. I saw this as the third sign, thirty years after the first two, and I followed it, without the slightest hesitation. Despite her passing in 1993, the link I established with Lilian, all these years ago, never died and, today, the light from this undying path guides my every step.

"Today, here is my own humble testimony: far from enrolling me in any sort of system, my meeting with Lilian opened an invisible door inside me. Without any word, any artifice, she guided my hand to the 'unreachable,' and now it is anchored in my ordinary, day to day life. All is clear. Everything makes sense, truly everything. What survives inside me, inalienably fixed in the intimacy of my heart and taking root far away from any convention, is an immense sense of gratitude.

"It has been, now, three years and it feels like I have come home. I am surrounded by friends, who participate, as I do, in this spiritual current which Lilian Silburn so deeply personified. What made the 'unreachable' accessible? No need to ask further. It is the certainty of the bond and its grace that takes away any doubt there could have been. All that remains is a deep sense of infinite gratitude toward the powerful and patient masters on the Path. This thankfulness inhabits my silent testimony."

We only know the state of freedom
When our love for You is truly ripe, O Lord
But as soon as it comes into our hearts
We are almost already freed!

  Utpaladeva ("*Shivastotrâvalî*" *XVI-19*)

The Mystical Dimension

THIS CHAPTER IS COMPOSED OF TEXTS written by Lilian.

Mysticism should not be considered as a mere extension of the most noble experiences, religious fervor, love, heartfelt impulse, sense of beauty and understanding, etc., as it isn't a matter of a different intensity but of nature: the mystic penetrates into a new dimension of reality that, so far, nothing permitted him to even imagine, and in this new total life, his whole being will be transformed, hence it really is something totally different than just a new vision of the universe as is commonly believed. It's a very pure and undifferentiated energy, inexhaustible reservoir and source of efficiency.[53]

In fact, all conscious beings are eternally immersed in the beneficial energy of Grace, but they seize it in order to use it for their own profit; they separate it from its source and thus deprive it of its real efficiency; they restrict it, individualize it, directing it outwards in connection with feelings and individual desires. The single energy divides into multiple energies, the cosmic body into various bodies, the supreme Vibration (Spanda) into limited movements, and life (Prana) into vital breaths; then the energy in itself, infinite and undifferentiated – the absolute Self – appears fragmented within one self, finite and dependent....

But since a human being doesn't really separate itself from its own essence made of Grace, he can regain self-consciousness and recover his initial freedom: to this end, all of its dissociated energies will have to converge toward their center, the Heart.

The Guru's essential task will be to facilitate such a return to the source, by penetrating the disciple's body in various ways: through the breath, joining every breath he takes to his disciple's in order to reawaken his dormant strength and enable him to regain the undivided breath which will reintegrate him into total life; through the heart, he enters into his heart to arouse the vibrations of the cosmic Heart; through the consciousness, by combining consciousness with consciousness, he sparks the recognition of the Self. So these are the different aspects of the return to unity: insertion into the breath, awakening of the vital strength (Kundalini), and enlightenment.

We thus understand that the disciple must follow blindly the trustworthy guide and not his own impulses and desires, if he wants to return to the origin, to the divine hint residing in the depths of the Self. As, in fact, such an incitement predates the formation of the ego and its artificial structures of a self opposed to the non-self.

The Guru

Words sung by the Guru: "He gives water but he must not touch it. He gives the fuel but he must not be burnt."

It's the presence of the Guru but not his person that should be evoked. The Guru doesn't have a body and this is why he isn't actually in this body; he's beyond time and space. (Diary, 1952)

The Guru doesn't try to generate considerable force; on the contrary he is only a pure instrument, like a dropper which limits this huge force regulating it at the level of the sisya; but the Guru himself sometimes gets knocked down by this force. It isn't a question of projected force but of channeled, dominated force. (Diary, 1952)

It isn't the meeting of two "egos" like in ordinary life, but something beyond where any way of being has no importance. (Notes, 1956)

Necessity of the Guru

In her diary, Lilian expresses how the necessity of having a Guru imposed itself on her:

Here is what I knew when arriving in India. I was fully aware of the walls of my caves – and how to shake them up. Once, an enormous piece collapsed but I didn't realize it immediately. I replastered it. The Guru's help was necessary; on my own, I was too weak and too ignorant. Perhaps I know better than him how to put up walls and structures, but he forcefully pulls them down, and the wonder is that I have no reason whatsoever, nor do I feel like reconstructing them.

Reach my goal, the absolute through silence, solitude, renunciation, the greatest simplicity; but a silence, solitude, an asceticism reaching the heart of being. But this will come spontaneously. Any effort on my part is useless and here, the Guru is essential.

All my efforts in life were aimed at developing a greater personality, fully conscious of having been this way originally, and expressing such a personality in a strong and unique way. From now on, like Buddhists – I must forget this personality and blend into the unknown. But how? My ego struggles against extinction.... Only my Guru can do that, push me towards the unlimited.

My Guru often talks about veneration and surrendering to the Guru. I really don't have any problem of surrendering myself. All I want is God and I'm ready for all sacrifices to reach Him. My Guru knows the way better than me. So I follow him, hoping that I will always abide by the highest ideal, and the most difficult things. It isn't to a man that I must submit myself, but only to God. One must avoid following one's own will and desire, but if my will is only directed towards my goal....

As long as the Guru expresses himself and lives according to his own realization rather than to what he heard, studied or picked up from tradition, I follow him with blind faith. But when he starts to speculate, discuss philosophy, make decisions about worldly matters, I keep my own opinion ... but a great Guru will never do that, and that's why silence is so important. (1950)

The Guru was saying that if, truly, I could only love God, I would make dazzling progress. However, I fluctuate: I haven't found the point where love of the Guru and love of God converge perfectly.

A few days ago, I forgot to note a dream I had while in a sleeping experience of dhyana, as intense as reality; here again, the demarcation is very blurred. Love, extraordinary veneration for the Guru, a sort of infinite respect induced by his presence ... a feeling that I hadn't experienced before, and which cannot be compared with any of my usual emotions; it's the calmest and most powerful thing I have ever experienced in terms of feeling, like an invincible rising which has dredged the bottom of the unconscious and is growing roots far beyond my self.

For the Guru is the means, and he emphasizes this aspect of being God's instrument. To reach God, I must go through him. But it is true that he would dearly like me to go directly to God as in that case, I would make faster progress.

The Guru said that now I'm always immersed in him, in such a way that whenever he plunges deeply, he takes me with him. This is extremely important, hence the necessity to remain perpetually immersed in one's Guru. (1952)

The Guru was saying that, at the beginning, a constant presence beside the Guru is necessary, but afterwards (when we easily merge into him) the Guru does anything he likes within a few seconds. Yet if we live close to him, alert, we can enjoy godsends, provided that they can be kept, which we don't do....

Before, Gurus used to order, but who would obey nowadays? So the Guru gives unconditionally, without narrowness, only for the sake of people – no longer imposes on his disciples what he had to do or has done for his own masters: he adapts to new conditions. (Undated notes)

The help of a guide is essential in many respects[54]

He is the one who adjusts the Grace to human frailty. If Grace is very strong, man cannot bear it, he suffers from mental and physical disorders, and the Guru is there to take it back.

It is true that if his flow of love is excessively powerful, and he is unconscious at that precise time, the disciple, immersed in him, will be unable to bear it, but the Guru will remedy this as soon as he returns to outer consciousness.

As I understand it, the Guru only serves as a dropper for divine Grace. He has to get to the level of the disciple, leave the higher state where he remains permanently and come down much lower, so as to give the disciple only what he is able to bear. This represents a great sacrifice on the part of the Guru.

Once, the Guru was in a deep state of unconsciousness and during a large gathering a disciple happened to meet his gaze; he jumped up in the air and a British lady friend of mine who was there was extremely impressed (I wasn't there). This disciple landed a few meters away, at the Guru's feet, which cushioned the impact. It will take him years to digest what he received inadvertently. (Letter, March 2, 1956)

On the other hand, all along the path, it's through love and devotion to the master that one can forget oneself. So that the personality re-emerges with increased stature, transfigured, and endowed with unlimited faculties; one's limited self, one's own will and knowledge must be annihilated; perfection is at that price.

Furthermore, one who has a guide remains humble, for he can constantly observe the guide's superiority; he knows that he owes nothing to his own merits and efforts, and doesn't tend to boast in the manner of Indian yogis. Neither does he imagine having reached the heights of mystical life, whereas he is only on the threshold of the path, and experiences for the first time, in dhyana, fulfillment and serenity of the self. He doesn't confuse intellectual intuition with purely spiritual enlightenment like so many of the ignorant do.

Nothing in the world is more difficult than to melt a man's heart and immerse it permanently in dhyana: wisdom, knowledge, intense and unlimited effort won't do it; but it only takes a few seconds for a good and complete master, in contact with Grace, to awaken the heart, "better than one hundred years of japa, tapas...."

The Guru's presence is no less necessary at the moment of Self-realization or enlightenment, which passes like lightning, and that the guide will have to put within the disciple's reach again and again. Later still, he will help the disciple balance enlightened stability and ordinary states.

Throughout the path, without wasting time and in an easy manner, he leads him to the goal as if guiding a blind man in the dark, for the path ahead of the disciple is entirely new: he must learn, in silence and darkness, a new way of knowing, of wanting and loving, and this path is so subtle and unfathomable that, on his own, he would never venture there. Neither feelings, intellectual faculties, nor senses, imagination or speech can access it. He would like to succeed by himself, according to his wishes, his discursive knowledge, and the ideal put forth by his imagination, but all these can only lead him astray and hide the true, undifferentiated path (nirvikalpa) from him, the one of the void in which, destitute, we grope our way along.

Even with the help of a Guru he trusts, he feels constantly disoriented and progresses in a state of doubt, sorry for having to let go of his most intimate possessions, his knowledge and previous spiritual experiences, thinking he is lost, hanging on to what hasn't any value, the charms of the path, but, carried by the Guru, he moves on, and continues to explore with courage. Moreover, his personal effort and concentration are even the biggest obstacle as they imply that one is clinging to a goal fiercely pursued, a targeted end; we become attached to what we have thus acquired and when time comes to move on to a higher level and abandon dhyana or samadhi, we refuse to let go of what cost so much trouble to acquire.

But with the Grace and trust in our Guru, we let ourselves be carried along, unattached to what we want or what we have already obtained, the most important is to progress constantly, spontaneously, not knowing how and without looking either backwards or forward. The vigilance required is, here too, without any effort; it is by no means directed towards something that has to happen, the most harmful attitude of all, because it is only an impulse toward the future, and doesn't allow keeping to the present, the only time when imagination is likely to gush forth. It's a vigilance of pure consciousness or of the heart, which doesn't expect anything, but only listens to a silent Guru, well immersed in him, following him step by step without knowing where he's going: in other words, such vigilance is sheer verticality and not in continuity like vigilance specific to will power.

There's another obstacle on the mystic's path: doubts and scruples. At every turn of his dark path, the mystic is worried, wondering what he did wrong to lose the state he's been in for such a long time, filling him with joy, and how he can recover it. If he has a Master, he will be spared all these torments. Otherwise, how would he know that he must leave a lucid and soothed consciousness far behind to sink into a desperate night and void? Due to the fact that he is progressing, past states' experience no longer apply to the present situation, and only a Master who has experienced and overcome these various experiences can help him.

The Master also subjects the disciple to repeated trials, seeking to shake his faith to make him stronger, as it is important for the disciple to overcome his doubts, called Vikalpa in India, the alternative that devours his life, exhausts his strength, disperses him in the phenomenal, preventing him from remaining stable in the present moment.

There's another important point, so subtle that it is difficult to describe precisely, as it relates to the Grace, and concerns what the Guru suggests (his hints) without ever expressing it: it is his purely inner promptings that a vigilant disciple, well merged into his Master, catches even unknowingly, doing spontaneously everything that his Master wants of him....

This is how, for many years, the Master trains the disciple, by patiently repeating his hints and, once the latter becomes well trained to grasp them, he will be able to catch the Divine Hints which pass faster than lightning and don't come back. These hints, sort of invitations from the Grace, are present throughout mystical life, as they last as long as human will hasn't fully merged into Divine will.

[Elsewhere, Lilian specifies: *They represent in terms of the will the dark side of the path leading to the unspeakable, the Nirvikalpa, and, as Divine hints, seem to correspond to the subtle and fleeting divine touches of Saint John of the Cross.*]

From another point of view, the Guru's help is also necessary for the one who experienced a spontaneous revelation of the Self (Atman) and this for two major reasons. First of all, his body won't be perfectly purified or deified: without love for the master and constant immersion in him, the foundations lack strength and no monument can be erected. Enlightenment is not all; it should be associated with power which is only achieved if body, heart and mind are purified. Thus, for many years, the Guru will purify the disciple's body by giving him power over his body and organs.

Secondly, while it's true that the one who spontaneously enjoys Self-revelation is capable of transmitting peace to those around him, he still isn't an accomplished Master, because he neither has the science nor the control of such transmission, since he hasn't been trained by a Guru.

All along the path and from the very first stage of fullness and bliss, there is a great danger of stopping too early, and later on as well, after Self-revelation when we are sincerely convinced to have accomplished everything. Then, the Guru's task is to take you beyond.

To train a master, the Guru does it in silence for many years, without explanation, the disciple not even being fully aware of the work that his Master is accomplishing within him. However, before dying, the Guru leaves a letter for him, that defines his mission.... The true Master who inherits tradition carries out his mission in silence.[55]

Difference between a saint and a Satguru*

The perfect saint shows himself as he is. He serves as an example. The Guru fulfills a function. Being in charge of the disciple, he must destroy his ego at all costs and in any way he can. He provokes problems (preferably against himself, otherwise life will take care of it more painfully; there are also nightmares). These vary depending on the disciples. For someone who is honest, the Guru can pretend to be a liar and be caught in the act. He can talk about sexuality to those who dislike it; he may seem angry....

If the disciple goes beyond the stage of doubt or difficulty (by innate instinct, deep insight), he then progresses rapidly as he must never stagnate in effortlessness and enjoyment. He must awaken, excitement plus fervor.

Therefore, the Guru only cares about the benefit to the disciple rather than himself and his good reputation. He never defends himself, regardless of the accusation....

A Guru must be tough.

Dreams

For the dreamer, as we already suggested, a dream can be a source of insights, but above all an opportunity for a real experience. For the Guru, the disciple's dream is a source of information. *"Through these dreams,"* Lilian would say, *"your Inner Selves want to give me certainty."*

Lilian pays attention to dreams but not just any dream, to mystical or initiatory dreams, those expressing a true experience and recognized by their symbolic content and the state we're in when awakening. Furthermore, she considers that it is up to the dreamer to figure out the message, thus she avoids interpreting: *"You'll see, you'll see later,"* she would say, with a little smile.

Elsewhere, she will specify that no explanation is to be given; work must be done in the unconscious, as clarifying things prevents profound development and nourishes the ego. We must let ourselves be invaded by mystical life; it's on a background of Grace that consciousness-raising experiences occur spontaneously.

In a letter to a friend (in 1970) we can read:

We highly value mystical experiences that we have in dreams ... it has nothing to do with a waking dream. It's usual to first experience in a dream or when half asleep (that is in relaxation) what we will later live in samadhi and, finally, when fully awake. A dream, its contents, its atmosphere provide me with precious insights on the mystical states of people; I know if the subconscious has been touched, even if the dream presents the mystical content in a slightly odd way. And if something from the dream remains for a while, peacefulness, sweetness, bliss, it's a very good sign.

When I was twenty years old, I had a wonderful dream with a dazzling bliss that I found more than twenty years later with my Guru.... Nightmares or horrible dreams can be very precious as they are signs of a deep purification. Dreams and impressions, if imbued with mystical life, are often like a prefiguration of the future unless they purify the unconscious by an explosion of nightmares.

She specifies to a correspondent in 1976:

In our path, the Guru can induce scary dreams which prevent you from going through painful experiences in everyday life – saves time.... And yet, the drama is experienced with as much intensity and reality as in real life."

But long before, in 1952, she had already written in her diary:

The Guru was telling me about a disciple who had a dreadful dream about a sexual relationship with his mother during which the pleasure exceeded what he had ever experienced [so far]. Desperate, he wrote to his Guru who replied saying that this was a good dream; it meant that he was about to become a mahatma as this dream is sort of a last purification, like when a man heaps up all the dust swept through the house to throw it away. And such relationships focus on the dearest, the most sacred beings, he added.

Yes, purification through manifestation of what is hidden, repressed, and expulsion. And, as it seems, sublimation of what remains.

Some mystical dreams

The following is a selection of a few mystical dreams from one of our friends (J.S.) which Lilian had suggested collecting. She appreciated their simplicity, their clarity and their general scope. Each time, they illustrate the mystical overcoming of an inner difficulty.

The monster

I was in a dark, medieval town, and in unknown streets. I was looking for the exit. I knew that there were monsters behind me, prehistoric-looking monsters, which were running, not only after me but after all the people who were fleeing. I was really scared, imagining that these monsters were going to eat us. I was running and running, without looking back. I was moving forward, in a maze of old streets, not knowing where to go. At some point, I was so afraid that I entered a house, hoping that I could shut the door and lock myself safely inside.... But there was a monster behind me who had passed through the door. I found myself back to the wall, unable to go any further. So I had to turn around and face the monster, there was no other solution. There was no way out.

And the monster arrives, he comes in the room, facing me. What am I going to do? Terrified, I don't know what to do. Then, all of a sudden, it's clear: "I must accept it!"

I say to myself: "Well, he's going to eat me, he's going to kill me, that's the way it is, I must accept it." I open my arms, ready for anything, especially the worst, he comes, he gets in my arms and caresses me ... he is nice.

He didn't eat me at all, it was a very nice animal, very gentle. And we get along very well. And I realize that what I was scared of wasn't a horrible thing like I imagined. On the contrary, it was a very gentle and loving animal because I faced up to it and had accepted.

The exam

I was dreaming that I had to pass the baccalaureate again. I was in front of my blank page, everybody was answering the questions, it was an exam ... and I thought I could respond. I thought that I would be able to write on a blank page. Instead of that, nothing could be written down. I knew the answers, but they just couldn't be written down. At the end, the examiner collects the papers. I tell him: "Listen, I'm sorry but I wasn't able to write." Then, the examiner says to me: "But that's wonderful!"

I was the only one in the class who hadn't answered the questions, with a blank page that I hadn't been able to fill in.... "But it's wonderful, it's good, you've succeeded because you weren't able to write, and you're returning a blank page!"

And afterwards, thanks to this exam, I was being told: "Now, you must go to the other exam." And there, I am told, or not told (you know how dreams are), I knew that, literally, I had to cut my head off. It wasn't enough not to write anything, I also had to actually get rid of the organ that generated, so to say, useless answers.

I was very embarrassed, asking myself: "How can I cut my head off?" Then I look around, and can see a basin and a chopper above it; it was the image of a toilet cistern and bowl. It did nonetheless make sense that it was a toilet bowl and cistern.

How was I going to do it? And I find a button for making the water fall (actually, the chopper); I bend down over the basin to cut my head off; I had to do it myself (in the dream, I was told that I had to do it myself, nobody would do it for me). So how am I going to do it? I press the button, nothing happens. And then, all of a sudden, illumination: "Ah! Of course, I have to let go! I have to let go of the button.... Stop pressing on it, and effectively...." Afterwards, I woke up.

The spiral staircase

In this dream, I had fallen down a hole, as it happens in dreams. I was very scared, and when I arrived at the bottom of the hole, I found myself in some kind of black cellar. There, some people tell me that they'll hang me by my feet and soak me in a vat.

When they pull me out, they say to me: "Ah, you've changed, it's wonderful! You have changed color. You leave right away. Well, take the stairs." So I climb a spiral staircase, that goes up and up.... While ascending, I felt an invisible presence beside me who was encouraging me, as it was high and arduous....

I could see a sort of wheel with blades like those of water mills, and people on it. They appeared as being very small. In fact, it was humanity ... with the wheel turning, they passed through the water, or in I don't know what, they died, and then it all went up again.... They were desperate. I too was desperate to see them. I was saying: "But it's terrible, those poor people, can't we save them?" And then the voice was saying: "No, there's nothing we can do." "But it's not possible!" I was desperate to see this world so miserable. And it kept on turning, like a wheel, endlessly....

I said: "Can't they come down from this wheel?" But no! They just stayed on it, stupidly. And they went back into the water, and it went back up again.... It was endless. It was really upsetting! I was fascinated. I was saying: "It's not possible, we must do something for these people." And the voice was saying to me:

"No, leave it, it isn't up to you to do anything. There's nothing anyone can do. It's the world. Well, let's continue...." So then, I struggled peacefully, leaving that area. And the more I went up, the more the anguish I felt for these people went away. I was moving up. I didn't feel them in the same way anymore. Then, myself, I climbed more easily, it was getting lighter. The farther I went, the lighter I was and the more I forgot ... I forgot that wheel of doom. And then, at that moment, I was encouraged by the voice of the invisible person who was next to me.

Then I went up the stairs, almost without putting my feet on them. And the more I went up, the more I was filled with a great inner joy, it was wonderful. And a moment later, I arrive on a final level. And then, there was no way, I didn't know where to go. I said: "What am I going to do?" And there, I see a door. It was like a door, but with no lock, no key, no handle, it was smooth. It closed on I don't know what. "And now, what am I going to do?" And it suddenly came to my mind: "Of course, there's no handle simply because there is no door!"

And it ends there. Of course, I knew that there was something behind. Afterwards, it was really inaudible, inexpressible. We were entering into the inexpressible; it was another journey maybe.... I have no idea, never mind.

The golden thread

I was in a room with other people ... we were in a circle and everybody was knitting. The knittings were all different, more or less beautiful, some very badly done, coarse, others very fine, others very beautiful, with a nice color, others dull.... Basically, everyone was knitting their own life. It's true that there are all kinds of lives, beautiful ones, ugly ones....

When they had all finished their little work, they said to me:
'So, what shall we do with it now?'
'Well, we unravel it.' So, we were unraveling.
'And then what do we do?'
'Well, we put all the wool here, in the middle, between us, all mixed up.'
'And then?'
'Afterwards, we search, we spread the wool....'

And among all of these shuffled yarns, in other words all the mixed lives, what do we see? A golden thread.... "

The white eagle

I was in the countryside, in a magnificent garden, everything was beautiful, splendid. I was very happy in this flowered garden. And then, little by little, I realize that the garden is withering; it was like in winter, everything is dead, plants are dead, it was terrible. I say: "So, is this life? Is everything going to die this way? Well then? And what's next?" And I was so sorry to see the desert I was in, all the plants completely dead....

And now, I'm being told: "Good, look up there." There was a hill, and at the top of the hill, there was an eagle, but a disproportionate one, very big and all white, with outstretched wings and a ferocious beak.

So I say, "But what should we do?" I am told (or I think, we can't really tell in dreams): "Well, you must go see the eagle. That's what's important, not the garden, it's the eagle that's important. But you must dare to go."

I had to go up there, on the hill, and I had the courage to go: "Good, I'm going!" He could kill me. There were reasons to be afraid because he was ferocious with that beak and those eyes.

I go there and dare look him in the eye. At that moment, I was filled with courage. I look at him in the eyes, he leans towards me with his threatening beak, he touches my forehead, not at all to eat me; all of a sudden, I was filled with I don't know what, one could have said an enlightenment, a really wonderful state. I turn to the garden, go down, everything was flourishing again, everything was truly wonderful, everything was really beautiful. It ends here....

Comment from the author of the dream: "It was an inner state; one mustn't get discouraged even if everything seems dead. The garden was dead, nature was dead. You must go up the hill and face the fierce eagle which gives new life. We must face far superior forces."

The non-way

FROM THE VARIOUS WRITINGS AND REMARKS that Lilian left, we offer an overview of the main aspects of this non-way.

"The best one way if one leads somewhere.... [as originally written in English] (Diary 1952)

It's a mystical path and not a religion; it doesn't require any conversion, any belief, not even faith in God, but thanks to the Guru we are more and more immersed in a life imbued with the divine presence. Mysticism without esotericism, as everything can be revealed to the disciple, but we don't talk about colors to a blind person....

A living path

A master who is dead can only transmit through a living disciple that he has trained. A concrete living contact is necessary ... the body counts. But the Master's Master can give something extraordinary. According to the Guru, the Sufi would often say: "A live fox is always better than a dead lion."

An intense living system, hence of living beings, a living system that has withstood centuries.

But if there is no one alive, no complete Master, then contact with deceased Masters is very useful.

Over time, Masters accumulate an increasingly simple and efficient science. Accordingly, the Guru has developed a new system which enables one to receive a little at a time.

The path is based on experience. The Guru often states:

"Example is better than instruction and experience better than both; this is why we must follow a complete guide."

This path transforms profoundly:

Yesterday, my Guru told me important things about the school; the practices taught by [...] and so many others have no lasting effects, the effect only lasts for a while and then we go back to being the same. (But the process of the Guru's school is totally different. It operates from the inside, in depth, and has lasting effects.)

On this path, there are no interdictions or directives: no injunctions, no rites, or any practice which, if avoided, are a source of guilt, thus cutting off the life of Grace. Nothing is forbidden, but certain habits stand in the way of the necessary availability to mystical progression.

Never did my Guru give me any advice; he never makes the slightest reproach to his disciples. [...] He would let me commit a murder without lifting a finger. Of the Guru, he only possesses the perpetual gift, but there isn't any personal interference. (1951)

Life on this path is led through normal activity, family obligations, attention to others, activity that doesn't hinder contemplation. Therefore, from the beginning, the Guru ensures that the disciple's mystical states happen anywhere, anytime, in noise, bustle, rather than a quiet meditation in a chapel. For we are entering into a new dimension of being where opposites reconcile. We suffer physically, we're tormented morally, while the heart is melting with stillness and sweetness or even bliss: it happens that joy is proportional to the pain endured. It isn't an exalted mental joy, but something not in the order of just ordinary life.

Path of transmission from heart to heart[56]

Everything takes place between the Guru's heart and the disciple's heart. The Guru first starts to work on the heart of the heart, the best of energies. Concentration of mind follows and unconscious layers become conscious.

"What's in the heart of the heart can never be written in books; although educated people have done their best to explain, even then it remains a secret." (Excerpt from Guru's letter, 12/09/56)

Only one thing: silence and love. No effort is required, the Guru is the means. Everything happens spontaneously, without any effort. So all you need to do is merge in the Guru. (1952)

But the Guru already loves you and if you too have love for him, that's the essential point, the rest automatically follows; it's more important than Samadhi, as this love is the mainspring of mystical life. (1956)

And what is so very special and precious about this school is that the Guru, when entering into union with God, not only enables grace to descend upon the disciple while preventing its excess, but he may also confer this same power to the disciple – I dare not say who is worthy as no one is worthy – but as this is done automatically, any danger of pride is averted.

Lilian's initial transmission experiment:

To begin with, I prayed God for ... I forgot who, but [this person] felt all that I had desired. About that, the Guru told me that I shouldn't want anything, but only pray ... and in a way, I didn't want anything, I just prayed at the beginning. It seems that I was in a superficial state; therefore doing absolutely nothing in this case is wonderful and we can talk about grace. (1952)

Path of silence

Transmission takes place in silence, in a silence without object, in a silence without mode. Without the help of physical postures, without breathing or concentration exercises, with no mantra, without exchanging a word, without advice, without philosophical explanation. Mind is more of an obstacle than an aid.

Only silence corresponds to the divine grace. The Guru is only an instrument, he doesn't say, he doesn't think: "I'll give to him"... He gives automatically. (Diary, 1955)

Later on, Lilian will address the necessity of silence in a text that she distributes to those visiting le Vésinet:

"The system is based on silence and the intimate life of the heart that everyone discovers according to his own rhythm and which takes different modalities for each; therefore, making comparisons is worthless, chattering is useless.

Mystical experience is too deep, too real, too intense to be the subject of any form of discussion or talks. It can only develop away from any discursive language, any objectification; exteriorizing it is to lose its fragrance and even its reality; it's taking away any chance of developing an intuitive discernment that must accompany all new experiences.

Many are stalled in dhyāna for not developing this capacity. It makes my head swim when, listening to everybody's words here and there, I discover what I can actually say. What I say to one at a given time only applies to that person, not to others, hence repeating it indiscriminately leads to misinterpretations.

It is also important to exercise a great discretion in relation to each other. Names of those met in Le Vésinet should not be mentioned outside, their initiative being strictly private and personal. There also shouldn't be any proselytism, propaganda, conversion, as what is essential will always be recognized by the one who is able to attain the secret of the heart.

The silence of the path isn't a silence of secrecy or exclusion, but one of shared evidence; we don't talk about it, but nonetheless it isn't concealed; the path is open for whomever opens up to it by abandoning themselves. But it's a silence of vigilance, guarding the treasure. The path is simple, bare, and as long as we won't have understood the dimension of silence, we will not be part of the path.

There is no teaching on this path. As transmission takes place in silence, any teaching, any word is useless. Radical rejection of any teaching as the life and reality of the path are discovered within oneself and in line with our development whose form varies for each of us.

Usually the Guru doesn't explain what will happen to avoid influencing the disciples' imagination and to prevent them from comparing their states and falling into spiritual pride, as the experience takes different forms for each one. He only gives explanations very rarely; he only gives some to those lacking mystical intelligence and sensitivity. The others must discover everything by themselves, otherwise their intuition would not develop.

When she was discovering and going through this aspect of the path, Lilian protested in the intimacy of her diary:

My Guru doesn't give any explanation, putting them off "until later".... And I feel lost ... he forces me to find out and discover every single thing by myself. One day I will rebel and tell him that he doesn't know and that I must explain to him and make him discover; and then he'll have to be explicit and take part in the work. (June 1950)

Path of surrender

At the beginning, these Sufis require that the disciple put his Guru to a severe test, with a sharp critical sense, as blind faith exposes to some danger; then, once convinced, he has absolute faith in his Guru and follows him blindly sometimes as the path is dark and we grope our way forward. This obedience is the first step towards a complete submission to the divine will.

The Guru was saying that (up to now) the required surrendering was a simple, voluntary, intellectual consent; but now, it involves the abandonment of the whole being, the abandonment of the subconscious as well as of the conscious, absolute faith in him, love. (1953)

The aim: achieving oneness. "Surrendering is not slavery." (1964)

*In fact, surrender is only deep love. Thanks to it, the Master can carry you in his arms and take you across the river. The Master never says "*surrender.*" But we forget ourselves: "You put yourself somewhere else and you have surrender."*

But at the end, these various relationships come down to the essential: faith and fidelity, or rather, the disciple follows the Guru faithfully, obeying the slightest hint, as he tends to identify with him and follow him in all his various states.

Path of love, path of non-doing

The whole path is contained in this: seizing the thread of love ("mala of bhakti"), being always ready to seize it, as it is constantly put within our reach by our Masters. We seize it and then we lose it. We must remain vigilant to seize it again and again, day and night, conscious and unconscious, always, without respite.

We need to remain constantly in a state of meditation, without wasting one second of this so short and precious time. [...] Only a great love can enable you to realize this.... First of all, love of the Guru, then later love of this wonderful presence within yourself. But such love itself, is already divine or is a gift of the Guru.

I told you many times that there was nothing to do on our path: it's only true in a certain way, but I don't really know how to explain what you should be doing ... and this is the most difficult task in the world.

Nevertheless, we can already try to meditate, to remain peaceful, to merge constantly in the Guru, to think of him ... alert, vigilant, intense at any time – like the married woman who has a lover and never stops thinking about him despite all her occupations, or like the mother who rocks her child with one hand while doing a continuous gesture with the other: a momentary lapse and her hand would be crushed by a pestle ... or also the woman carrying a vase full of water on her head and remains attentive, despite the stones on the road, that not one drop of water is spilled.... Such are the examples from India that the Guru reminds us of. (Excerpt from a letter)

In the mystical experience of this school, there are arrows of love that pierce the heart, cooing of love, even frequent heart pains, of a spiritual nature. Remarkable concordance with Saint John of the Cross, especially in relation to nothingness or emptiness (nada) and its two aspects:

- Destruction of the self, of its selfishness, its limited desires and self-esteem ... and also:

- Nothingness insofar as it being a perpetual surpassing of

oneself, the Buddhists' method for attaining absolute emptiness (sunyata) and which is also the Sufis' Fana; we mustn't dwell on anything and especially visions, not even the bliss of mystical states.

This slow destruction explains the depression and suffering, loathing of life, and other states that some go through and that seem to correspond to the Dark Night of Saint John of the Cross, but with the exception that the Guru can shorten them as, according to Radha Mohan, this night can last for a whole life without the Guru. But this depression is good in itself as it is due to love.

Despite it being imbued with peace, love can be absorbed into passion, given that it doesn't allow any expectation or intermediary. It's neither the love "for," nor "of," or "in," but pure and simple love. Unifying love, intensifying, the shortest way to where its exclusiveness is its strength: at the same time universal, global and whole. We are carried by love, we no longer carry it in ourself, it is no longer at our disposal.

Path with no proselytism

Each time we make a gesture to someone, everything goes wrong. You must let people come to you, even the closest ones; this is one of the rare recommendations of my Guru's school. (Letter, 1968)

Path of humility

As on the first day, my Guru told me that only the grace of God could do something, that he could do nothing – as he was only a means ... he didn't know anything ... and his humility contrasted sharply with the spiritual pride of India's ascetics and mystics.

Besides love and limitless patience towards all (ksanti), humility is the essential virtue that is required. The disciple knows that his spiritual progress is not of his own making, since it's the Guru's work, and that he makes no effort himself. He constantly feels that he's at the beginning of his career.

It should be noted that in this system, there is no sense of sin or of those scruples that make us go round in circles around "the humble self." Self-forgetfulness is the thing to reach. We know that we're unworthy, but we suffer patiently.

Universal path

The Guru's uncle and father have innovated; they have set the seal on the universal path. Yes, eliminate all sense of belonging, override civilizations, fly over beliefs and religions, no syncretism, as everything is rejected as a whole for being merely traditional beliefs, sometimes useful, always wrong for being delimiting, separating. (Diary, 1952)

The Guru questioned me about Christian Saints, as he says: "Only what is universal should be accepted as certain." *It's a rule of conduct for him, as it was for his father. What saints of all religions accept as right by common consent [can be recognized], but what is accepted by some and rejected by others must be scrutinized with great care. This attitude seems right to me.* (November 1955)

And in a word:

Way without limits

And now:

Forget everything, your heart will remember....

Lilian Silburn's Publications

From Colette Poggi (Indianist, Sankritist)

The Indian-sounding titles that are referenced here might sound strange, even obscure; most have, in effect, Sanskrit names, a sacred language, extremely ancient, but still used in India. However a reader, even without much knowledge of Indian culture, will find precious and substantial sustenance principally concerning the internal experience and the ways of the mystic.

Lilian Silburn lets appear in her translations and her commentaries a light that goes beyond the conventional sense. Drawing on her personal experience, the same as is described in the nondualist texts of Kashmiri Shivaism, her understanding illuminates the original depth of the texts and of key terms, as she knows how to portray a breadth of meaning which remains obscure to the best technicians of Sanskrit. It's this rare alliance of erudition and inner realization gained through her Masters, which give her work force and originality.

The themes which she constantly brought into the light, throughout her research, find today resonance with the scientist of the infinitely large, infinitely small, and of that other infinity, so mysterious, the consciousness.

Let us cite for example, cosmic vibration, the original emptiness from which came primordial energy, as well as the consciousness defined as light-energy. Such notions, present throughout the work of Lilian Silburn, are in a common vein with new intuitions perceived today on trying to understand, or to express otherwise, the nature of the universe, of consciousness and of life.

Lilian Silburn, philosopher and distinguished Sanskritist, devotes herself, from the beginning of her studies, to Indian thought in its deepest dimensions. Pupil of the greatest masters of the age, such as Louis Renou, Paul Masson-Oursel, Sylvain Levi, Emile Benvéniste, she quickly collaborates with them and belongs to that generation of pioneers who knew how to let their imagination flourish in true liberty.

Lilian Silburn thus brings together excellence in the practice of the Sanskrit language and in the interpretation of the texts of ancient India, as witnessed by her doctoral thesis, "Instant et Cause." This landmark research still remains indispensable and is recognized unanimously by the whole scientific community in France as elsewhere in the world.

If the worth of a publication can be measured by the enlightenment it brings to the world, no one would doubt that this work, a pioneer in the domain of Kashmiri translations, continues, as an inexhaustible spring, to quench the thirst of searchers seeking a living knowledge.

Books (in French)

Aitareya Upanisad (French translation of original), Paris, Adrien Maisonneuve, 1950.

Instant et Cause, Le discontinu dans la pensée philosophique del'Inde.
(*In English: "Instant and Cause, The discontinuous in the philosophical thought of India"*)
PhD thesis, December 1948, with Honours. Paris, Vrin, 1955; re-edited De Boccard, 1989.

Le Paramārthasāra de Abhinavagupta
(In English:"The Paramārthasāra of Abhinavagupta").
Complementary thesis to PhD, December 1948.
Paris, Ed. De Boccard, 1957 (Institute of Indian Civilization (I.C.I.) Publications, N°5), reprinted 1995.

Vātūlanāthasūtra, avec le commentaire d'Anantaśaktipāda.
(In English:"Vātūlanāthasūtra, with Anantaśaktipāda's commentary")
French translation and critical analysis of the original.
Paris, De Boccard, 1959 (I.C.I. Publications, N°8), reprinted1995.

Le Vijñāna Bhairava
(In English: "The Vijñāna Bhairava")
French translation of, with commentary on, the original.
Paris, De Boccard, 1961 (I.CI. Publications, N°15) reprint 1983 and 1999.

La Bhakti. Le Stavacintāmani de Bhattanārāyana
(In English: "The Bhakti. Le Stavacintāmani of Bhattanārāyana")
French translation of the original with commentaries.
Paris, De Boccard, 1964 (I.C.I. Publications, N°19), reprinted 1979.

La Mahārthamanjarī de Mahesvarānanda, avec des extraits du Parimal.
(In English: "The Mahārthamanjarī of Mahesvarānanda, with extracts from Parimala")
French translation of, and introduction to, the original.
Paris, De Boccard, 1968 (I.C.I. Publications, N°29), reprinted 1995.

Hymnes de Abhinavagupta
(In English: "Hymns of Abhinavagupta")
French translation with commentaries on the original.
Paris, De Boccard, 1970 (I.C.I. Publications, N°31), reprinted 1986.

Hymnes aux Kālī. La roue des énergies divines.
(In English: "Hymns to the Kālī. The wheel of divine energies")
French translation of, and introduction to, the original.
Paris, De Boccard (I.C.I. Publications, N°40), reprinted 1995.

Śivasūtra et Vimarsinī de Ksemarāja
(In English "Śivasūtra and Vimarsinī of Ksemarāj")
French translation of, and introduction to, the original.
Paris, De Boccard, 1980 (I.C.I. Publications, N°47).

La Kundalinī ou l'énergie des profondeurs
Paris, Les Deux Océans, 1983 reprinted 1996.
English translation: **Kundalini. The Energy of the Depths**
Albany, SUNY Press, 1988. Translation by Jacques Gontier.

Spandakārikā, Stances sur la vibration de Vasugupta. Gloses de Bhatta Kallata, Ksemarāja, Utpalācārya. Śivadrsti (chapitre I) de Somānanda.
(In English: "Spandakārika, Stanzas on the vibration of Vasugupta. Comments of Bhatta kallata, Ksemarāj, Utpalācārya. Śivadrsti (Chapter 1) of Somānanda").
Introduction to, and translation into French of, the original.
Paris, De Boccard, 1990 (I.C.I. Publications, N°58).

Abhinavagupta. La Lumière sur les Tantras. Chapitres 1 à 5 du Tantrāloka.
(In English: "Abhinavagupta. The light on the Tantras. Chapters 1to 5 of the Tantrāloka").
With André Padoux, an annotated presentation and translation into French of the first 5 chapters.
Paris, Collège de France, Distribution De Boccard, 1998 (I.C.I. Publications, N°66).

Review Articles or Contributions to Collective Works

Un Hymne à énigmes du Rig Veda
(In English: "A hymn to puzzles of Rig Veda")
Journal de Psychologie Normale et Pathologique, July 1949, pp. 274-286.

Sur la notion de brahman,
(In English: "On the notion of Brahman")
Journal asiatique, 1949, tome 237, pp. 7-46.
These two articles were further included in a posthumous collection of the work of L. Renou: *L'Inde Fondamentale, études d'indianisme,* edited and presented by Charles Malamoud. Herman, 1978 (pp. 58-65 and 83-116).

Nirukta and Anirukta in Vedism,
(Published in English) Dr Lakshman Sarup Memorial Volume. Hoshiarpur, 1954.

Contributions to: *l'Inde Classique: Manuel des études indiennes*
(In English: "Classical India: Manual of Indian studies")
under the direction of Louis Renou and Jean Filliozat, Tome 1, Paris, Payot, 1947 and Tome 2, Paris, Imprimerie Nationale and Ecole Française d'Extrême-Orient, Hanoi, 1953:

- *Le Shivaïsme du Kashmir*, *(In English: "Kashmir Shaivism"),* tome 1, §§ 1296-99

- *La philosophie du Pancarātra*, *(In English: "The philosophy of Pancarātra")* §§ 1319-29

- *Le matérialisme : Les Nāstika, Lokāyatika et Cārvāka,*

- *(In English: "Materialism: the Nāstika, Lokāyatika and Cārvāka"),* tome 2, §§ 1497-1507

Anne-Marie Esnoul, Dir ., *L'Hindouisme, textes et traditions sacrés,*
(In English: "Hinduism, texts and sacred traditions")
Paris, Fayard Denoël, 1972:
- *Yoga sūtra*, pp. 303-344 and ***Advayatāraka Upanisad***, pp. 344-354 (in collaboration with A-M Esnoul).
- *Le **Vijnanabhairava Tantra***, pp. 506-569 (simplified version of the article published in 1961 in the Publications of the Institute of Indian Civilization).

Grand Atlas des Religions. Encyclopaedia Universalis, Paris,1988:
- *L'expérience mystique dans le bouddhisme indien,*
(In English "The mystical experience in Indian buddhism")
pp. 352-353.

Directory of Collective Works

Le Bouddhisme, *(In English:" Buddhism ") Texts translated and presented under the direction of Lilian Silburn,*
Paris, Fayard, 1977 ("Le Trésor Spirituel de l'Humanité"). Reissued: *Aux sources du bouddhisme, (In English: "At the sources of Buddhism"),*
Fayard/Denoël, 1977.
Chapters written by Lilian Silburn :
- *Le Bouddhisme ancient*: Chap. 1 *(In English: "Ancient Buddhism")*
- *Intériorité et universalité dans le Mahāyāna*: Chap.3 (*In English: Interiority and universality in the Mahāyāna")*
- *Le Madhyamaka, ou Ecole de la voie du milieu* : Chap. 5 *(In English: "The Madhyamaka, or middle way school")*
- *Le Vijnānavāda ou Yogācara*: Chap. 6
- *Le Sahajiyā*: part of Chap. 8. Translation and analysis of the Dohākosa of Saraha and of Kānha.

Hermès: Recherches sur l'expérience spirituelle. Nouvelle série.
(In English: "Research on the spiritual experience. New series")
Ed. Les Deux Océans, Paris:
N°1. ***Les Voies de la mystique, ou l'accès au sans-accès***,
(In English:"The Ways of the Mystique, or access to the non-access")
1981, 1993.

Chapters written by Lilian Silburn :

- *Introduction: Accès au Sans-accès*, *(In English: "Introduction: Access to the non-access")* pp. 43-79

- *Les trois voies et la non-voie dans le shivaïsme non dualiste du Kashmir, (In English: "The three ways and the non-way in non-dualist Kashmir Shaivism"),* with a previously unpublished translation of the first 5 chapters of Tantrasāra d'Abhinavagupta, pp. 141-99.

- *Le domptage du buffle, (In English: "The taming of the water buffalo")* pp. 231-33.

N°2. **Le Vide, expérience spirituelle en Occident et en Orient**, (In English: "Emptiness, spiritual experience in the Occident and in the Orient"), 1981, 1989 (reprinting of N° 6 of the 1969 edition).
Chapters written by Lilian Silburn :

- *Le vide, Le Rien, L'Abîme,*
(In English "Emptiness, nothingness and the abyss"), pp. 15-62.

- *Les sept vacuités d'après le Shivaïsme du Kashmir,* (In English: "The seven vacuities according to Kashmir Shaivism"), pp. 213- 21.

N°3. **Le Maître spirituel selon les grandes traditions et d'aprèsdes témoinages contemporains**,
(In English: "The Spiritual Master according to the great traditions and contemporary testimonials")
1983 (reprinting of N°4 of the 1967 edition)
Chapters written by Lilian Silburn :

- *Techniques de la transmission mystique dans le shivaïsme du Kashmir, (In English: "Mystical transmission techniques in Kashmir Shaivism"),* pp. 122-38.

- *De l'imposture à l'incompétence. Bons et mauvais disciples,*
(In English: "From imposture to incompetence. Good and bad disciples"), pp. 252-67.

- *Autour d'un Sadguru de l'inde contemporaine,*
(in English: "Around a Sadguru in Contemporary India") pp. 275-91.

N°4. **Tch'an. Zen, racines et floraisons**, 1985
(In English: "Tch'an. Zen, roots and flowering")
Chapter written by Lilian Silburn :
- *Un fil d'Ariane*
(In English: "A thread of Ariane") pp. 70-72.

Glossary

Abhyās, abhyāsa : assiduous practice, exercise, study
Adhikāra: responsibility, privilege given to one who is fit
Āgama: collection of ritual texts from different Indian religions
Akarta: non-fabricated, non-artificial
Ākaśa: ether of the heart
Ānanda: felicity, joy
Anāhatacakra: chakra of the heart
Anupāya: non-way
Asuras: demi-gods
Baqā': permanent union with the absolute
Basant or Vasant: springtime festival
Bhandara: days devoted to the memory of past masters
Bhāva: emotion
Cakra: center of subtle energy of the human body
Camatkāra: cry of surprise, of wonder
Darśan: vision, divine apparition, presence of the divine
Deepavali: festival of lights
Dewanini: wife of governor
Dhyāna: meditation
Dīkṣā: spiritual initiation
Fanā': extinction, disappearance, annihilation
Guru: spiritual master
Hṛdguhā: cavern of the heart
Jnāna: knowledge, wisdom
Kṣana: moment
Kṣanti: patience
Manas: spirit, mind
Mela: big ritual festival
Mokṣa: liberation
Nirguna: lacking in qualities or attributes
Nirvikalpasamādhi: samadhi without dualist thought
Paramānanda: supreme joy

Prakāśa: the light of consciousness
Prānayāma: holding of breath
Rishis: primordial mythical wise men who saw the Vedas
Sadguru: perfect master who can guide a disciple on the spiritual path
Sādhana: spiritual practice
Sādhu: Indian ascetic
Sahaj-samādhi: samadhi which one attains naturally, effortlessly
Samādhi: total absorption in the contemplation, direct but temporary experience of the Self; tomb of a saint
Samāpatti: delight, bringing into unison
Samskāra: fabrication tendencies, unconscious energies
Sannyāsin: one who has renounced the world
Śānti: peace
Satsang: company, frequenting the masters or the wise men, being together
Satsangi: those in the presence of a master, who participate in satsang
Siddhi: supernatural powers
Śiṣya: disciple
Spanda: vibration
Suṣupti: deep sleep
Tawajjah: spiritual transmission
Turya: the fourth (state)
Turyātīta: beyond the fourth (state)
Vairāgya: detachment
Vidyā: science
Vikalpa: dualistic thought, conceptual bipartition
Vimarśa: awareness
Vismaya: wonderous awareness
Zikar: quivering, vibration

Footnotes

[1] Radha Mohan Lal Adhauliya, cf. Meeting with the guru.

[2] Village in the Pyrenees where Lilian was spending holidays. See chapter: Ayguatebia.

[3] Lilian's guest house in Auvergne. See chapter: Puech-Redon.

[4] See note on the 'holes' at the end of the chapter.

[5] See Publications.

[6] Research trips to India and Kashmir from 1949 to 1953, then in 1954, 1957, 1960, 1963.

[7] Sanskritist, close friend of Lilian.

[8] See chapter: Lilian and the Guru, year 1952, extracts from Lilian's diary.

[9] Renowned claivoyant at that time.

[10] The master of her Guru, Abdul Ghani Khan. See The Masters of the Lineage.

[11] "Instant and Cause," the discontinuous in the philosophical thought of India. PhD Thesis (with honors). Complementary thesis: "The Paramarthasara," by Abhinavagupta.

[12] See chapter: Overview of the stays in Kaśmīr.

[13] "Song of the Blessed One": central part of the *Mahabharata*, famous epic of Hinduism.

[14] Foreword, p. vii, "Śivasūtra" (see Publications).

[15] See: Note on "holes."

[16] See Chapter: Childhood and youth, Notes on the "holes."

[17] "Spiritual Master," page 268, Hermes n°3, new series.

[18] Baha-ud-din Naqshband Bukhari: 1318-1389.

[19] The "renovator, " Ahmad al-Faruqi al-Sirhindî (1564-1624).

[20] Mirza Mazhar Jan-i Janan (1699-1781).

[21] The Master of Lilian's Guru, Radha Mohan.

[22] Excerpt from *Autobiography of a Sufi* (p. 55-56), Ed. Dinaysh Kr Saxena.

[23] Term used by Lilian when referring to the master of her Guru, who she also calls "the great Sufi."

[24] Raghubar Dayal, the Guru's father.

[25] Another testimonial about Chachaji can be read in the article: "Around a Sadguru in contemporary India," published in the Hermes review, New Serie N°3, pp. 277-278.

[26] Abdul Ghani Khan, "the Sufi."

[27] Diploma of higher studies.

[28] For a description of the very special atmosphere around the Guru, one can refer to the testimonials (among which an anonymous one written by Lilian) published in the article "Around a Sadguru in contemporary India," in "Le Maître Spirituel," Hermes N°3, Ed. Les deux Océans.

[29] At an altitude of approximately 2000 meters [6,561 feet].

[30] See chapter: Meeting with the Guru, Bathing in the Ganges.

[31] In her diary Lilian wrote: *My guru wrote to me saying that the tingling sensation which I feel in my hands, arms, legs, face and lips is a good sign.*

[32] Lilian's diary: *Letter from my Guru. I am only on the "threshold" of mystical life. So what can be the wonders awaiting within the castle?*

[33] One of the systems of Kashmiri Shaivism, see Publications.

[34] Catholic priest, missionary in India (1895-1957).

[35] Dr. Thérèse Brosse, who specialized in using instruments to study yoga techniques (1902-1991).

[36] See chapter: Childhood and youth, Love Life.

[37] 1909-1975. Author, director of the collection of Spiritual Documents at Fayard, editor of the Hermes magazine.

[38] Indian philosopher, Sanskritist, specialized in the study of Kashmir Shivaism (1887-1976).

[39] In Hindi: elder brother (expression of respect).

[40] Lilian notes: "At his first glance, the Guru loves the disciple without his knowing. Then, it's the disciple's turn to love the Guru (he gradually discovers the Master's love), then, again, the Master loves him more and does more for him. Thereafter, the disciple loves infinitely, and, again, the Guru loves even

more." As the Guru says: "Table is turned when disciple is merged."

[41] See *Vijñāna Bhairava*.

[42] Pushpa, a charming Indian lady whom she met in 1951 at a wedding, had the advantage of living near the Guru's house. She offered Lilian hospitality sometime after they met, and hosted all the French friends who came to visit the Guru.

[43] When we can no longer distinguish exteriority and inner life, outside world and ecstasy are well balanced.

[44] On this matter, Lilian used to tell the following anecdote: The evening when my Guru passed on the wonderful thing to me, he had received a shock in the afternoon: his salary and the rest of his money for paying the expenses of the Bhandara (500 Rs. in total) were in a safe in which he thought he had put them; suddenly, the judge called him, and when he came back, the money was no longer there. At first, he was devastated. But then he bathed in that bliss of which I only had a faint echo that evening. God wants him poor, there is nothing to do about it! But what is worth noting down, is that during painful emotions, the divine grace also flows (Letter, 1952).

[45] In the Bulletin of the Transpersonnel, n°86, 2007.

[46] *As internal resistance builds up and intensifies, it becomes obstructive before melting under the influence of grace.* See Hermes, "The Emptiness." Also see here, Chapter 8, The mystical dimension, Necessity of the Guru.

[47] See Hermes N°6 for the 1969 edition, N°2 for the new edition.

[48] "Around a Sadguru in contemporary India", Hermes N°4, edition 1967.

[49] Hermès N°3 et N°2, new edition.

[50] Hermès N°1, 1981.

[51] Hermes N°4, 1985.

[52] See Publications.

[53] See article: "Access to the non-access" (pp. 43-79) in "Les Voies de la mystique," Hermes N°1.

[54] See also the article: "Which master for which disciple?" (pp. 9- 21), in "The Spiritual Master," Hermes N°3.

[55] See also: "From imposture to incompetence," Hermes, "The Spiritual Master" (pp. 252-267).

[56] See also the article: "La transmission directe" ("Direct transmission") in "Le maître spirituel" ("The Spiritual Master"), Hermes N°3 (pp.268-274).

About the Book

THIS BOOK PRESENTS THE LIFE AND WORK OF
LILIAN SILBURN (1908- 1993),
one of the greatest French Indianists, and a specialist in Kashmir Shaivism, Tantrism and Buddhism.

A philosopher by training, and director of research at the CNRS (French National Center for Scientific Research), Lilian Silburn turned to Oriental philosophies very early on.

She was one of the first to make known in the West the writings of the Kashmiri mystical philosophers.

She was also a disciple of a great Indian Sufi master, Radha Mohan Lal Adhauliya–"Bhai Sahib"– with whom she will make many and long stays until his death in 1966.

Composed of a large number of personal writings never published to date, this book presents us with the testimony of an exceptional spiritual and philosophical experience.

It also evokes the atmosphere of the life she led near Paris in Le Vésinet after the death of her master ... a simple, active life, devoted to her Work.

Surrounded by friends attracted by her personality and her spiritual "efficiency," Lilian Silburn endeavored to help others discover, within the silence and the most varied forms of ordinary life, the "non-way" which had been revealed to her by her master.

Illustrated with photographs, ***Lilian Silburn: A Mystical Life*** contains various testimonies which give a fuller view of this extraordinary personality– both a great scholar and a great mystic.

About the Author

JACQUELINE CHAMBRON, who was a professor of classical letters, met Lilian Silburn in 1965. She was one of her very close friends and assisted her among other things in materializing some of her work. It is to Jacqueline that Lilian Silburn entrusted the personal documents, diaries, correspondence, and various notes, which are the source material for this work.

Jacqueline was born in 1926 at the foot of the extinct volcanoes of Auvergne, France in Aurillac, her father's country. When she was six years old, her family moved to Agen on the banks of the Garonne, her mother's country. She lived there until the age of eighteen, even during the war. This city was spared the horrors of the bombings. However, a strong friendship with an Israelite high school classmate introduced her to the barbarity of anti-Semitic persecution.

At the age of fifteen she was initiated into the mysticism of Saint John of the Cross by a Discalced Carmelite monk, a discovery which will remain important, but which locked her into an ideal of renouncement little suited to the vitality of a fifteen-year-old girl.

At eighteen she left home to study, which led her to discover Paris in the intellectual ferment of the post-war years. She was fortunate enough to live in community houses where communist and catholic student couples lived together. It was a rich and eventful period.

After her marriage, two successive pregnancies made it difficult for her to complete her studies. Once she finally graduated, she experienced the joy of teaching, which had been her dream since childhood.

Her husband, having completed his medical studies, moved the family to Toulouse where the fourth child was born. There she heard about Lilian Silburn for the first time and, thanks to an appointment teaching in a local high school, she was able to move to Le Vésinet, and afterwards lived in Lilian's wake.

Motivated by Lilian, she wrote several articles published in the *Hermès* review:

- The three advents of Christ in the soul, according to Ruysbroeck the Admirable. (*Hermes* n ° 1)

- The three ways and the non-way in the light of Meister Eckhart. (*Hermes* n ° 1)
 - The void according to Saint John of the Cross. (*Hermes* n ° 2)
 - Nowadays, which master for which disciple? (*Hermes* n ° 3)
 - Direct transmission. (*Hermes* n ° 3)

Since Lilian Silburn's death, Jacqueline has continued living in Le Vésinet, surrounded by a few friends. Over the years, she has organized a series of trips with some of them: first to India, where they prayed, filled with gratitude, on the graves of the masters of the lineage of Radha Mohan. Later to Iran, in the footsteps of Bistami, Kharakhani, Ruzbehan, Omar Khayyam.... And finally to Uzbekistan where they venerated the tomb of Naqshband in Bukhara.

Jacqueline wrote and compiled this book, anxious to preserve the account of Lilian's experience as faithfully as possible, and also to describe the living effects of direct transmission through her.

ALSO BY PELICAN POND / BLUE DOLPHIN PUBLISHING

Living with the Eternal Truth
From the Lineage of Golden Sufis

ISBN: 978-0-942444-08-7, 130 pp., paperback, $16.00

The eternal question remains the same in all ages and before all seekers of the truth: "Who am I? and what is the purpose of this life?"

Living with the Eternal Truth, compiled by Ravindra, the son of Radha Mohan, explains in simple language the main principles of Sufism and the techniques of spiritual training as taught and modified by three great Sufi saints of the past century, who are highlighted in *Lilian Silburn, a mystical life*. Included is Radha Mohan's Basant Bhandara Speech of 1958.

The Naqshbandiya Sufis are called the Golden Sufis or the silent Sufis because they practice silent meditation. They do not use music or dancing or any definite practice. They are not limited to any country or civilization, but work according to the needs of the people at the time.

This path is also known as "Raja Yoga," in the sense of being kingly or royal, and is considered to be a direct road to Absolute Truth, capable of awakening someone to full perfection in this lifetime.

"One comes nearer to God if there is tranquility and serenity inside the heart. Absolute Truth can be realized only in silence. In this system, the universal Soul speaks to the soul of the individual.... One sheds the ego and purifies the heart, while leading an ordinary life in society."

Sufis in this lineage live in the world and enjoy material wealth and possessions without being attached to them. Their "way of being" is all-embracing, and can be accepted and incorporated into any religion.

These three profound and revered Masters have so preserved the teachings, explanations and wisdom of their predecessors that this book will long be a guide for anyone who truly yearns to become a realized being.

LILIAN SILBURN, A MYSTICAL LIFE / LETTERS, DOCUMENTS, TESTIMONIALS

Lightning Source UK Ltd.
Milton Keynes UK
UKHW012210041022
409924UK00004B/185